POSTCARD HISTORY SERIES

Altoona

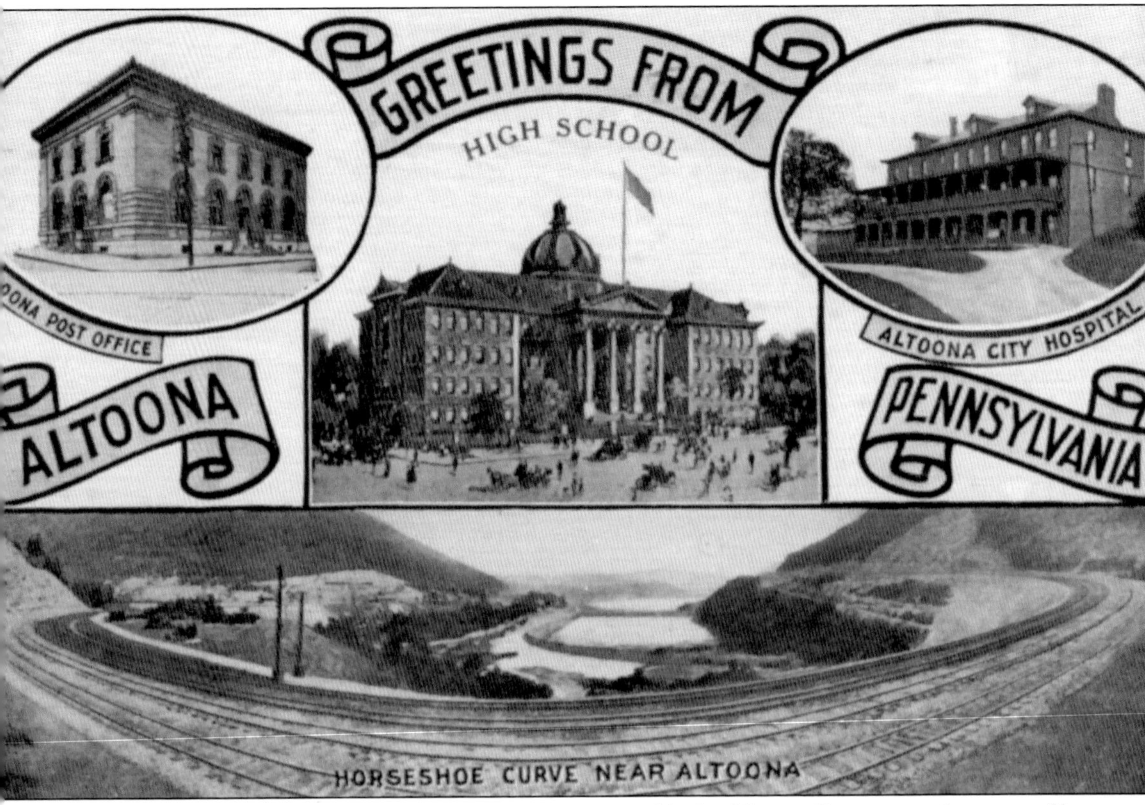

This image depicts vintage views of Altoona's notable buildings. Shown are the post office and federal courthouse, the Altoona High School, and the Altoona Hospital, which had its origins with the Pennsylvania Railroad (PRR). Also shown is Altoona's best-known landmark, Horseshoe Curve on the mainline of the PRR, 5 miles west of the city.

On the Front Cover: This 1930s view from the Gospel Hill promontory shows the city of Altoona and the Pennsylvania Railroad's prominent Altoona Works. Altoona was founded by the PRR in 1849; railroading remained its principal industry for a century. Within 75 years, its farmland had been converted into a city of 75,000. (Author's collection.)

On the Back Cover: Altoona, founded by the PRR, was noted worldwide for its railroad shops, vast classification yards, and test department, which established standards in the industry. This partial view of the westbound classification yard in the vicinity of "WJ" and "WH" classification towers (named for telegraph signal designations) represents just a small view of the vast operations here. (Author's collection.)

POSTCARD HISTORY SERIES

Altoona

David W. Seidel

ARCADIA
PUBLISHING

ISBN 978-0-7385-7261-1

Published by Arcadia Publishing
Charleston, South Carolina

Printed in the United States of America

Library of Congress Control Number: 2009936318

For all general information contact Arcadia Publishing at:
Telephone 843-853-2070
Fax 843-853-0044
E-mail sales@arcadiapublishing.com
For customer service and orders:
Toll-Free 1-888-313-2665

Visit us on the Internet at www.arcadiapublishing.com

Dedicated to the members of the Blair County Historical Society, living and deceased.

And to the Bishop Guilfoyle High School Class of 1956 (formerly Altoona Catholic High School), living and deceased.

Contents

Acknowledgments

The assistance of Michael Albanese, Elaine Conrad, Dorothy Rouzer, Virginia Seidel, Leonard E. Alwine, John Conlon, Tom Sharp, David J. Kirsch, H. Wayne Burket, Joseph Stevens III, Guido Santella, Railroader's Memorial Museum, Jean Lohr, Dale Delozier, Jeannine Treese, and Marlene Stone of the Blair County Historical Society; Blair County Genealogical Society, is appreciated. The postcards are from the collection of the author, unless otherwise noted.

Introduction

Fifteen years prior to the Civil War, Altoona did not exist. On April 13, 1846, a corporation was chartered forming the Pennsylvania Railroad (PRR), which intended to create an all-rail route from Philadelphia to Pittsburgh, allowing much easier travel and shipping between Pennsylvania's two largest cities. Before the railroad, travelers labored along the Main Line of the Public Works, a system of canals and portages over the Allegheny Mountains, as well as horse and wagon.

Primarily following a water-level routing, the new railroad advanced westward from the mighty Susquehanna, along the Juniata River valley, and on to the base of the Allegheny Mountain range. The land it traversed was primitive by most standards, save for the David Robeson farm on the valley floor of what later became Altoona.

Having arrived at this point, the engineering/survey teams of the PRR, led by J. Edgar Thomson, advanced westward into the Allegheny Mountains to try to devise the all-rail route over this rugged terrain. The valley floor became a staging location of supplies and equipment for this effort. Thomson and his team approached a type of cul-de-sac valley on the mountain, which seemed impossible to navigate until they devised a slight detour in their route, creating the world-famous Horseshoe Curve, which enabled the railroad to climb the mountain while continually gaining elevation. No engineering principle devised such a method previously. The route finally culminated at Gallitzin with a tunnel to achieve the crossing of the summit (and the Eastern Continental Divide) by rail, at an acceptable grade.

The PRR founded the town of Altoona in 1849 by purchasing the David Robeson farm, and soon people began arriving to work for the railroad. The railroad was constructed over the mountain from 1850 to 1854 by 450 Irish laborers, many of whom left Ireland during the potato famine. The staging area in the little town of Altoona later developed into a repair and maintenance facility for that early railroad because the mountain route was hard on locomotives and cars. The first shop buildings were constructed in 1850 and expanded as the single-track railroad gradually became two, three, and finally four tracks. The locomotives and cars grew larger, requiring skilled labor, which migrated to Altoona from many European countries. By 1855, the shops of the PRR employed over 1,000 men. By 1866, they not only maintained locomotives and cars, but also began to build them as well.

Altoona grew from a sleepy village to a major manufacturing center with the PRR as its primary employer and benefactor. The community was not, however, a traditional company town. The stores in Altoona were not owned by the railroad, nor were most of the residences. Independent, private home ownership and commercial enterprise enabled Altoona to grow and prosper, evolving to a town of 75,000 people in 75 years.

Altoona became world famous for its railroad engineering and technology, railroad industry-testing principles, and yes, the Horseshoe Curve 5 miles west of the city. The design of this curve enabled railroads everywhere to conquer mountainous terrain following the same principle. After 150-plus years, the principle is still valid, and the first example, near Altoona, survives into the 21st century as a vital link in the transcontinental route.

The coming of the railroad firmly established Altoona's place in history and the railroad continues to play an important role in the town today. Four railroads have now owned the route and facilities, and the Juniata Locomotive Shops of Norfolk Southern Railroad continue to be a prominent employer in the greater Altoona area.

Legend states that *Altoona* comes from a Cherokee Indian word meaning "highland of great worth," reportedly borrowed from Allatoona Pass in Georgia, where J. Edgar Thomson had some prior railroad experience.

The success of completing the all-rail route over the Allegheny Mountains west of Altoona, connecting Philadelphia and Pittsburgh, further complemented the westward expansion efforts. In these days prior to the advent of Pullman Palace cars and overnight travel, railroads constructed hotels for the comfort of their passengers, and Altoona was home to one such lodging. The Logan House Hotel, constructed in 1854 adjacent to the passenger station, was the center of social life in young Altoona, elegant in contrast to the early industrial town around it. The opening of the railroad west via Horseshoe Curve on February 15, 1854, came a mere seven years prior to the start of the Civil War. Altoona played an important role by hosting the Loyal War Governor conference, which met at the Logan House. There, Northern governors affirmed their allegiance and support to the Union on September 24 and 25, 1862. Although Lincoln did not attend, the conclave, organized by Pennsylvania governor Andrew Gregg Curtin, was a much-needed show of support for Lincoln during the dark early days of the war.

As the PRR Company grew and prospered, so did Altoona. Significant expansion of facilities took place in the late 19th century and into the 20th century. Altoona was a city of immigrants (primarily German, Irish, Polish, and Italian), with other minority groups in smaller numbers. Each ethnic group had its own bank, enabling workers to send money back to relatives in the "old" country or to purchase their own homes in Altoona, resulting in ethnic neighborhood designations for many years. Times were hard during World War I, the Great Depression years, and then World War II, not unlike in many industrial towns. The zenith of the steam era was during World War II, but things began to change in the 1950s with the advent of the diesel-electric locomotive, which resulted in major layoffs in all the steam-era railroad crafts. Altoona began to diversify its industrial and manufacturing base out of necessity, resulting in a major socio-economic adjustment for the city. An industrial development campaign, "Jobs for Joes," helped bring new industry to town.

Progressing into the 21st century, the railroad has seen four major changes of ownership and restructuring. The PRR, Altoona's founder, ceased to exist on February 1, 1968, when it became the Penn Central Railroad. In a few short years, the Penn Central Railroad's bankruptcy sent shock waves through the community and the states it served. This resulted in the formation of Conrail, a combination of several bankrupt eastern railroads, but Altoona continued to maintain its role as a locomotive and car repair facility (1976–1999). On June 1, 1999, Norfolk Southern became the fourth railroad to own and operate the system and the Altoona shop complex. The Conrail and Norfolk Southern Railroad periods brought stability to local employment despite the closure of the nearby Hollidaysburg Car Shop. Today the local economy has stabilized and the railroad's new owner has revolutionized all facets of the industry with emerging technologies. Today, an alliance between Railroader's Memorial Museum and Penn State Altoona is expected to develop a college level railroad curriculum to train future rail industry managers and specialists.

Altoona is not *just* a railroad town, but the railroad industry has inarguably had a huge role in the founding and growth of the city. Many other manufacturers and employers are part of the town's economy, including support and service industries, but the railroad is the one common denominator tied to the founding of Altoona and its subsequent development.

One

Altoona, the City

Despite Altoona's humble beginnings, the construction of PRR shops and facilities brought principal managers and subsequently their families to the burgeoning town. As immigrants also flocked to Altoona for employment, the challenge was to provide the diverse first generation of Altoonans with the amenities found in cities such as Philadelphia. The growing railroad economy contributed to the rapid development of the new town, powering rapid growth in the second half of the 19th century. The PRR's Logan House Hotel (1854–1931) was a focal point of town life for many years, catering not only to weary travelers, but also to the social needs of the community. Numerous ethnic and fraternal societies and associations formed, expanding the fabric of social life outside of the workplace.

Gradually, the dirt streets gave way to pavement and other refinements. The Industrial Revolution brought municipal gas and water (1859), the opening of the first telephone exchange (1880), an electric company (1886), and a new passenger station (1887). Cultural developments included the construction of the Mountain City Theatre and the addition of the Eleventh Avenue Opera House (1888), gradually weaving together a fabric of civilization in an otherwise rustic frontier region.

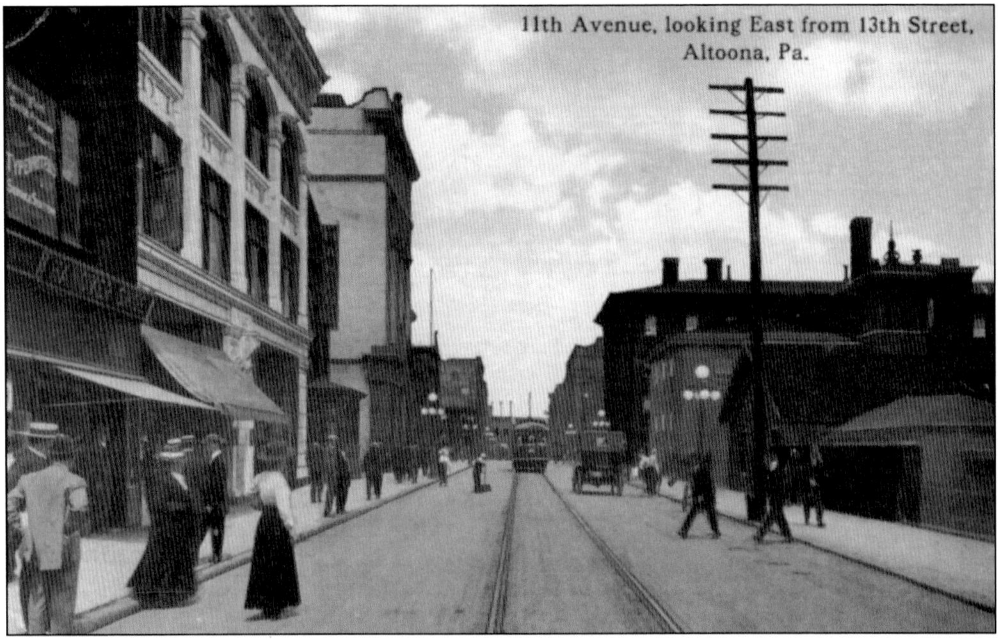

This easterly view of Altoona's main business thoroughfare, Eleventh Avenue (formerly Virginia Avenue), from Thirteenth Street, shows the PRR property along the right side, including the famed four-story Logan House Hotel. Commercial businesses line the left side of the street in this postcard from around the second decade of the 20th century, while a trolley of the Altoona and Logan Valley Electric Railway approaches. This card was cancelled at Bellwood, Pennsylvania, on October 14, 1919.

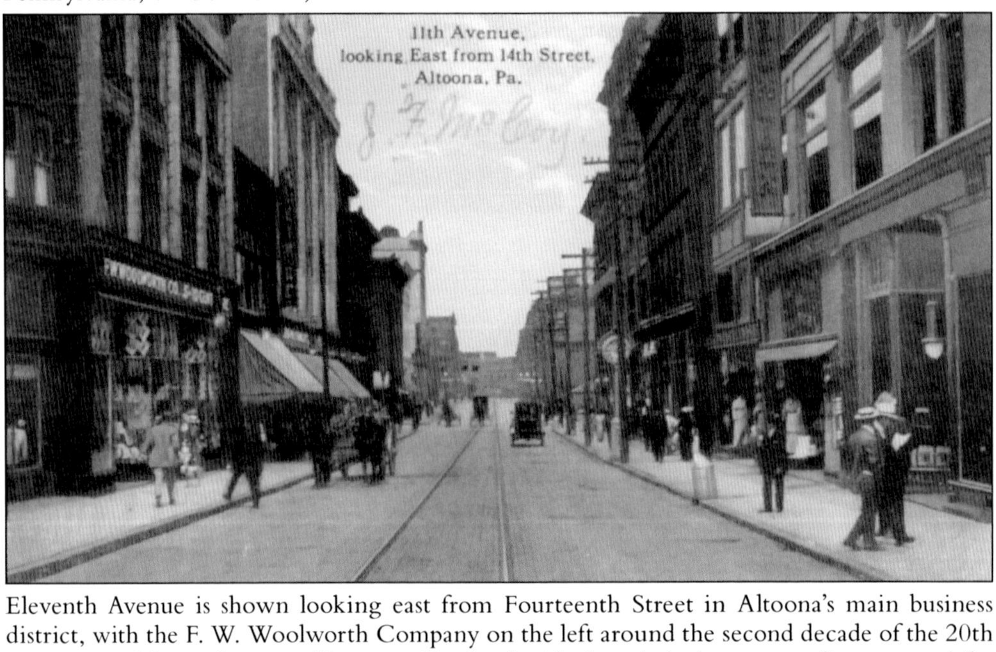

Eleventh Avenue is shown looking east from Fourteenth Street in Altoona's main business district, with the F. W. Woolworth Company on the left around the second decade of the 20th century. In this era, horse and buggy still mixed with the relatively new gasoline automobile. Although no electric lines are visible, the trolley system was electrified on July 4, 1891. This card was postmarked Altoona on November 23, 1913.

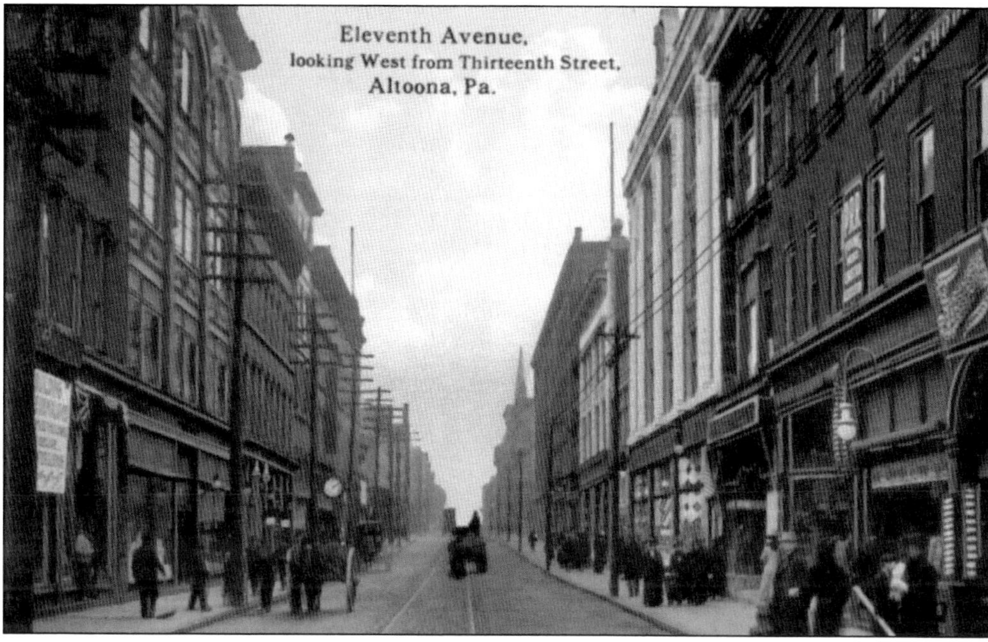

This view shows Eleventh Avenue, looking west from Thirteenth Street in the main business district in the early 20th century. On the right is the Zeth School, a business school that later became known as the Altoona School of Commerce. This view shows the steeple of First Baptist Church in the distance. The postmark is June 22, 1914, but the post office is not identified.

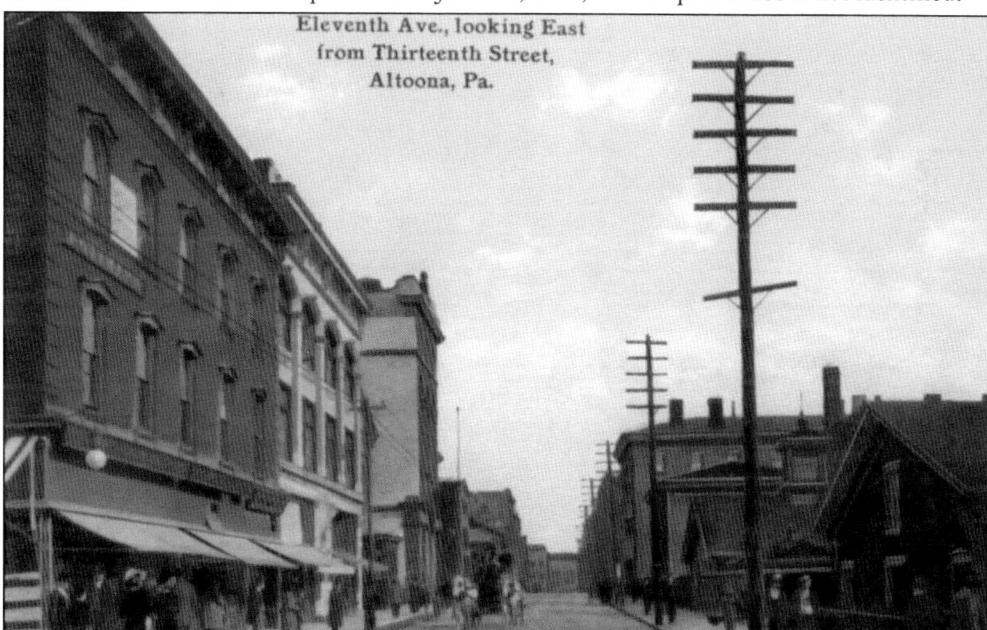

In this postcard dated October 17, 1914, an easterly view of businesses along Eleventh Avenue shows some of the town's early commercial properties, notably the Bollman Building on the immediate left. This card carries a Railway Post Office cancellation aboard train 451, The Altoona and Henrietta branch line of the PRR, which also served Hollidaysburg, Roaring Spring, and Martinsburg in southern Blair County.

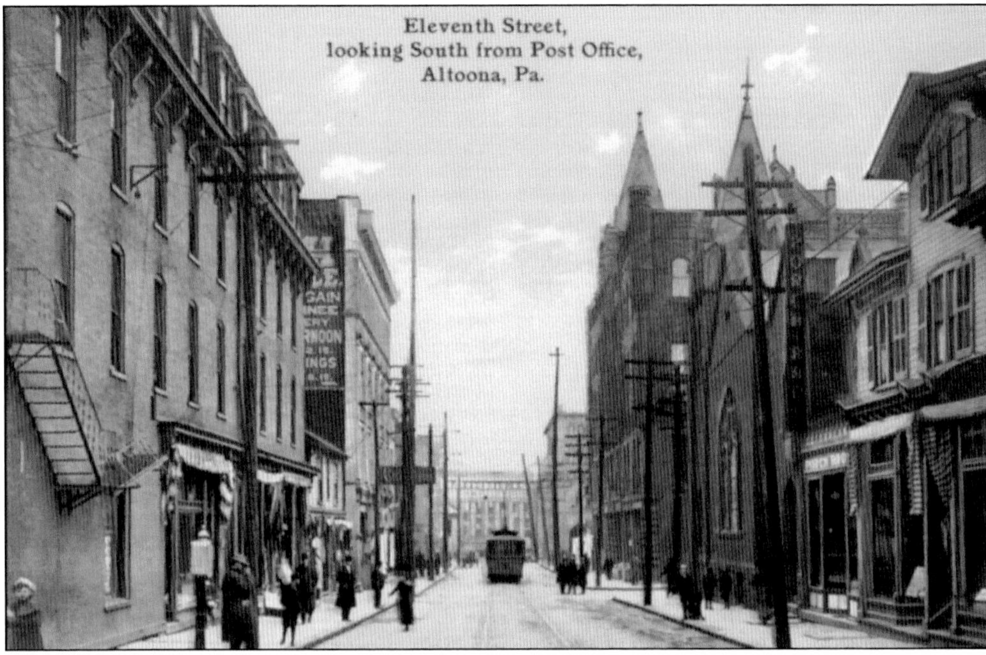

This is a view of Eleventh Street, looking south from the post office (and federal courthouse), from Chestnut Avenue toward Tenth Avenue. This was a busy commercial street that contained the four-story Masonic lodge on the right and the Orpheum Theatre on the left, with the shops of the PRR at the end of the street along the mainline.

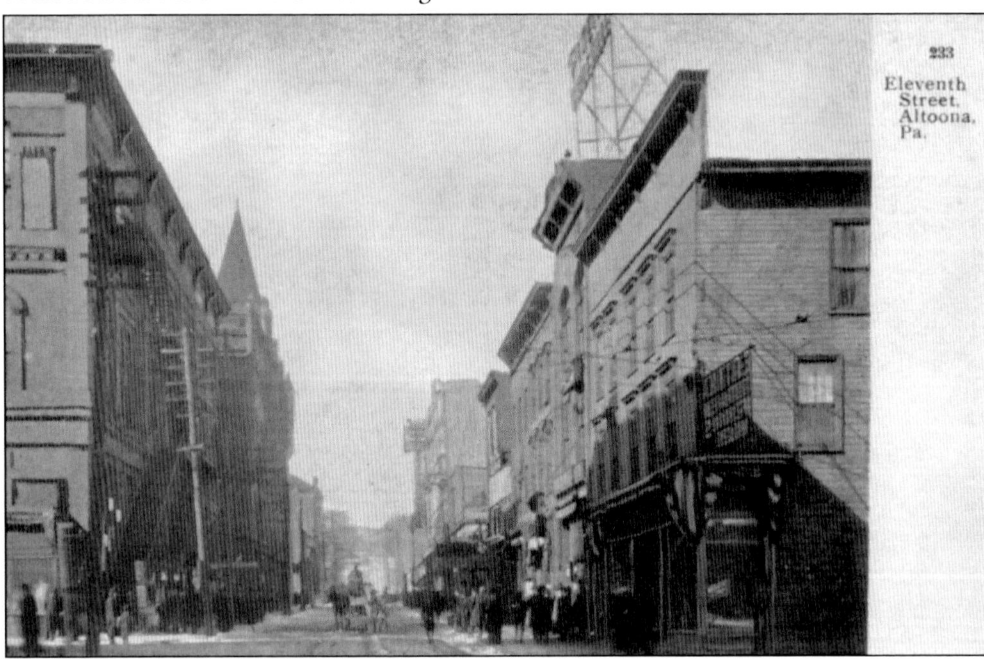

Seen here is a view of Eleventh Street, looking north from Eleventh Avenue. On the immediate left is the corner of the Eleventh Avenue Opera House, which burned down on June 14, 1907. The Opera House was on the second and third floors, a practice later deemed contrary to fire code. The Baltzell department store occupied the ground floor.

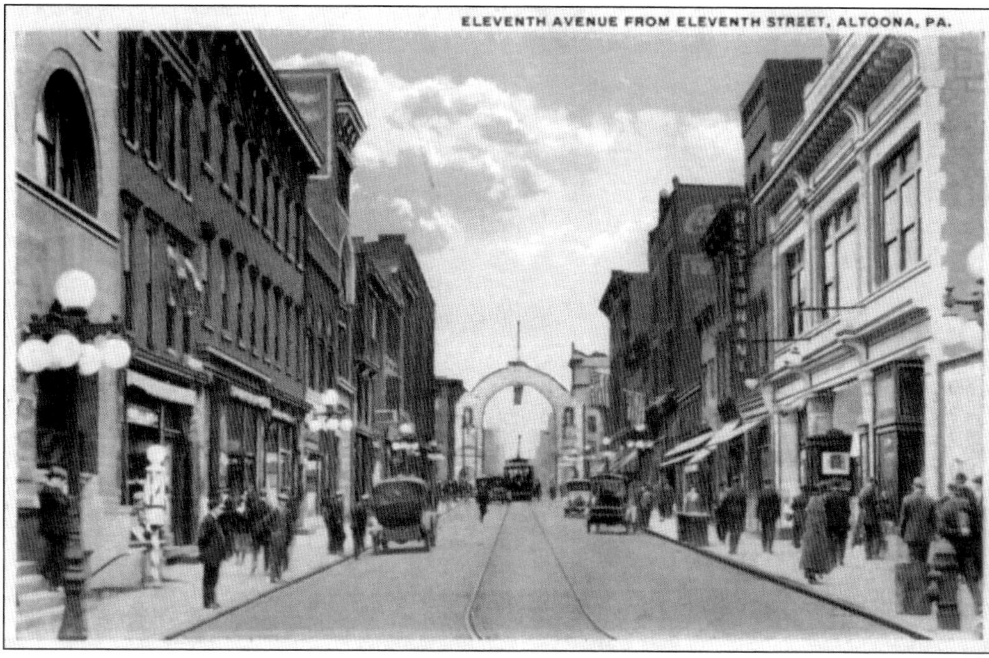

This is a *c.* 1919 westerly view of Eleventh Avenue from Eleventh Street. On the right is the Olympic Theatre, built by Alexander Notopoulos in 1915 on part of the site where the Eleventh Avenue Opera House stood until the fire of June 14, 1907. The Victory Arch in the distance was erected in the 1200 block of Eleventh Avenue to commemorate the armistice of World War I.

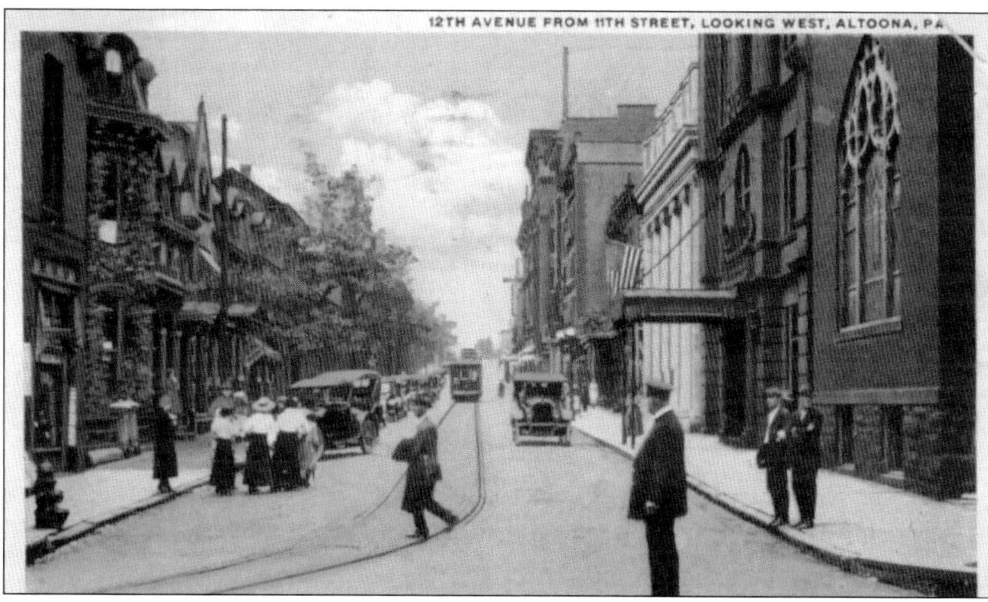

This postcard of Twelfth Avenue looks west from Eleventh Street and shows a parallel main business district street around the second decade of the 20th century: a mixture of prominent residences with commercial enterprises and churches. On the right are Grace Lutheran Church, the Fraternal Order of Eagles, and the Lincoln Deposit and Trust Company. The Eagles building, vacant several years, was razed in November 2009. This postcard is postmarked Altoona, Pennsylvania, April 22, 1921.

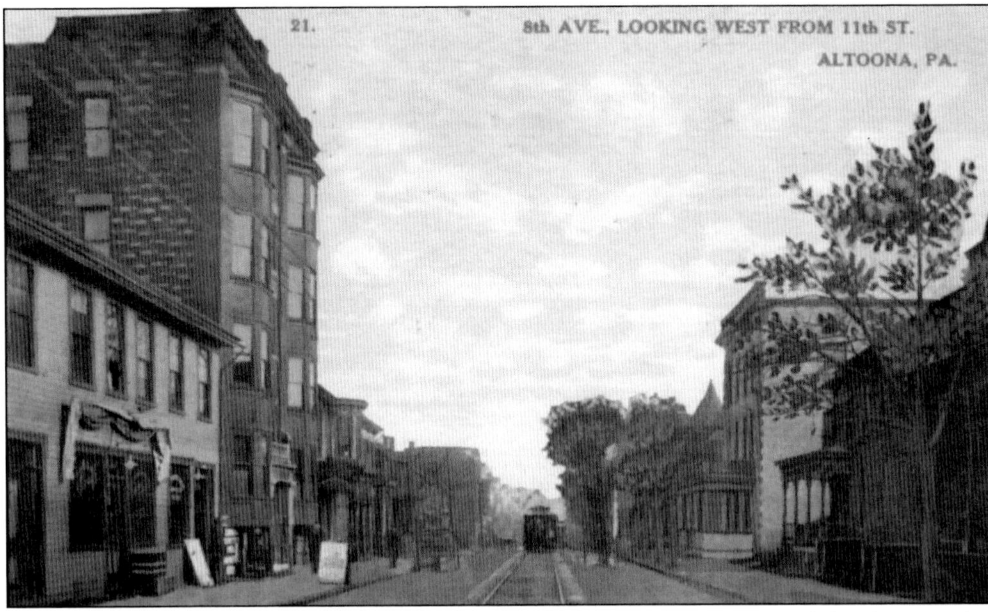

Eighth Avenue is pictured looking west from Eleventh Street on this postcard dated September 16, 1908. On this corner, the Catholic parish of Our Lady of Mount Carmel was established in 1905 to serve the needs of the Italian American community, a parish that would be staffed by the Franciscans Third Order Regular (TOR) for over 100 years. This parish is still a vibrant church today.

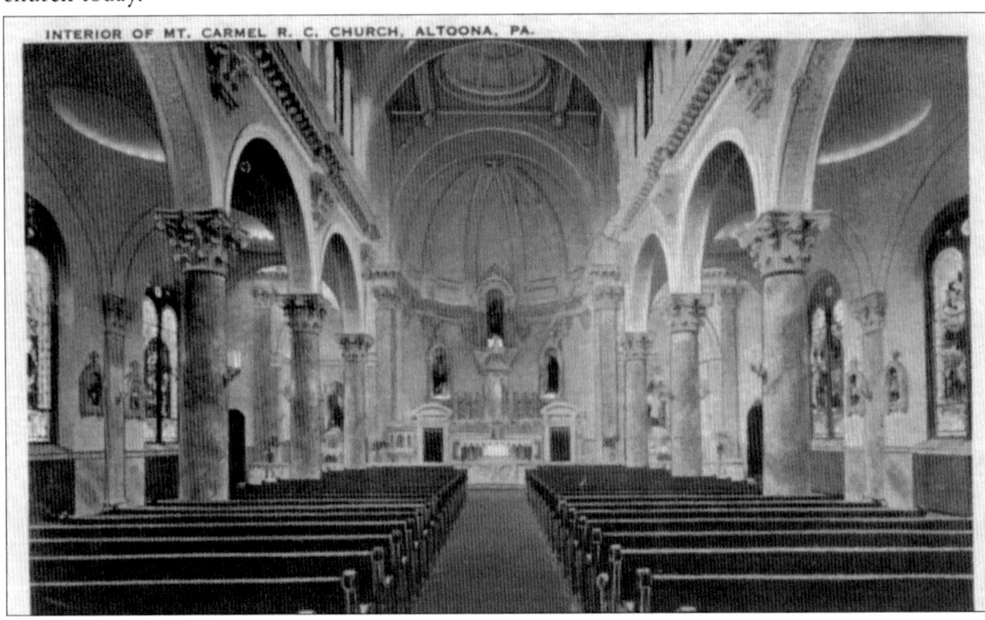

This is an interior view of Our Lady of Mount Carmel Catholic Church. Constructed of Hummelstown Brownstone on the exterior, it was dedicated in 1912, but the interior was not completed until 1923. The Romanesque interior remained unpainted until its first restoration in 1953. The parish remains staffed by the Franciscans TOR today, and the building has seen two subsequent restorations by John Rita, a member of the parish. The parish centenary was celebrated in 1995; the church remains a focal point for the Italian American community.

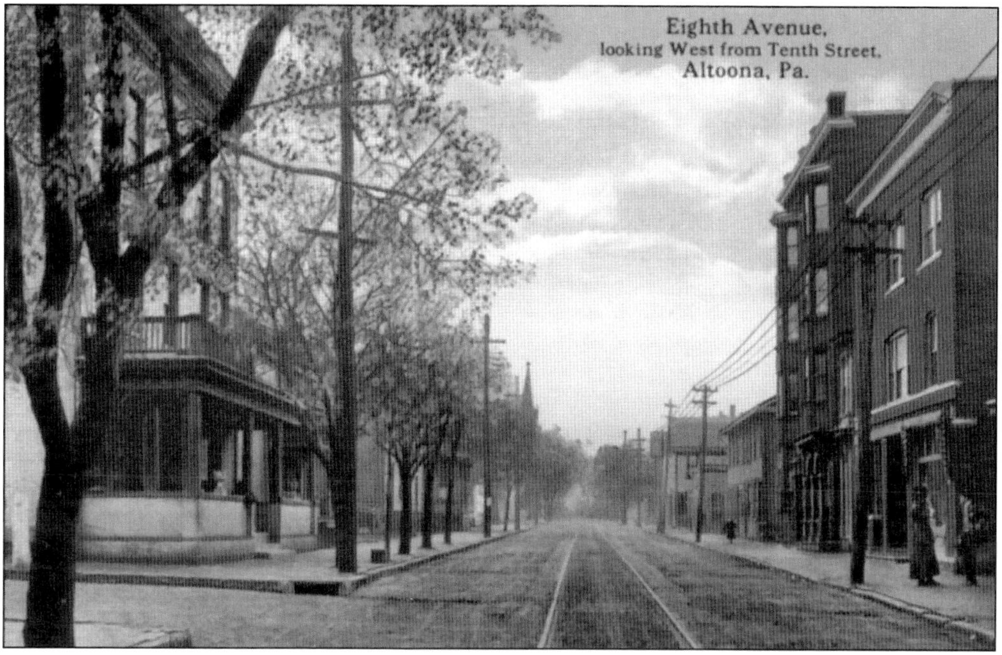

This view shows Eighth Avenue looking west from Tenth Street. In the early 20th century, Eighth Avenue was in close proximity to the Altoona Works of the PRR and home to much of the Italian American and Irish community that found employment with the railroad. The tracks of the Altoona and Logan Valley Electric Railway served the needs of the avenue's residents.

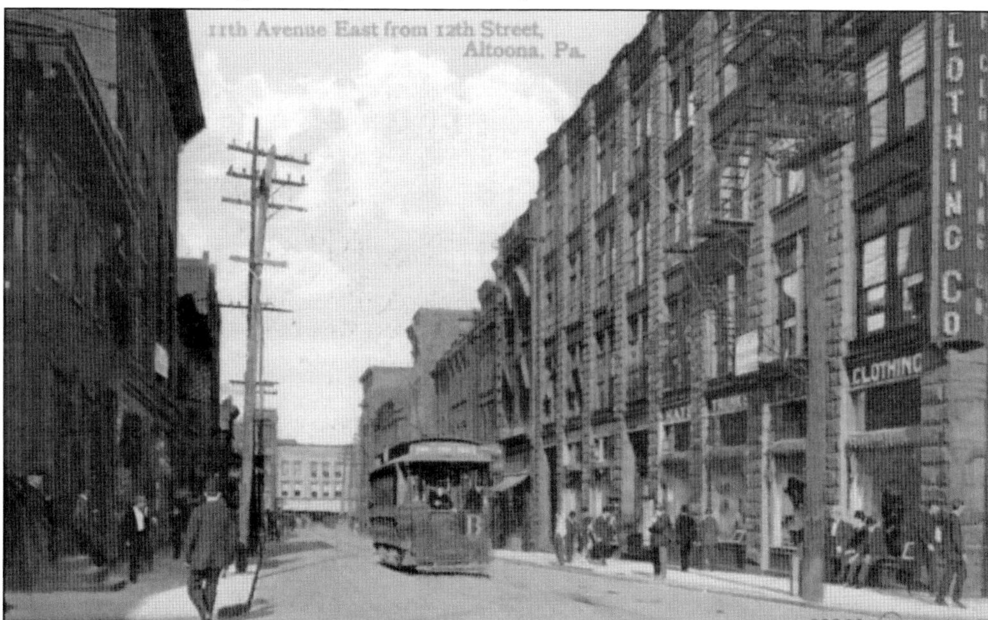

This postcard shows Eleventh Avenue looking east from Twelfth Street. This view from around 1908 shows an open car of the Altoona and Logan Valley Railway westbound in the business district. This entire block was razed during the 1970s for Altoona's redevelopment program and the restructuring of the entire business district. The former Goldschmidt Building is on the right.

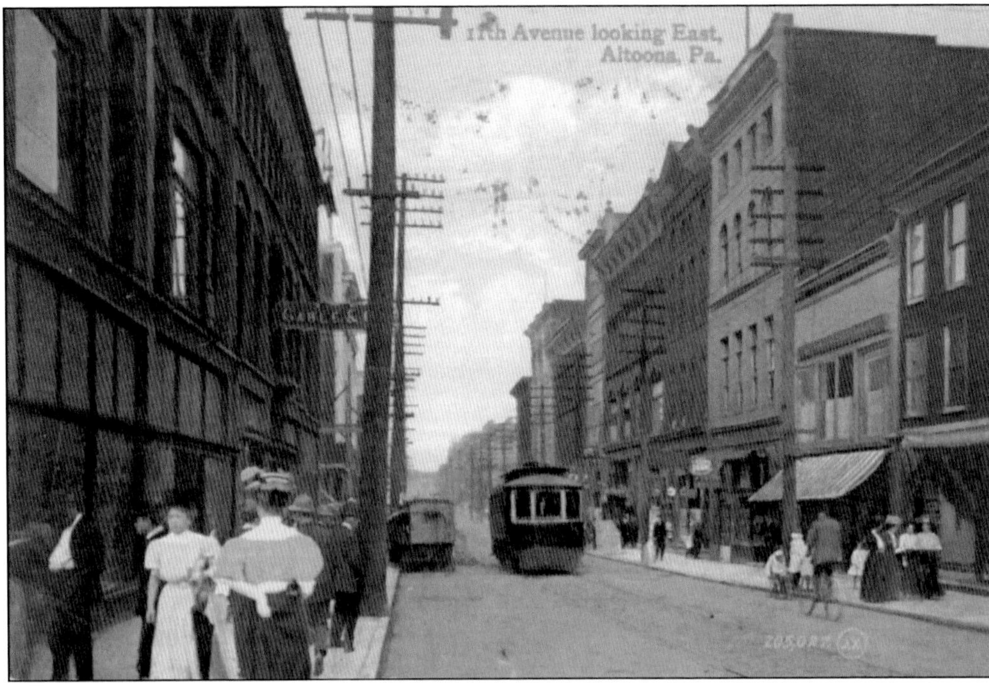

On the left of this easterly view of Eleventh Avenue from Fourteenth Street is the Gable and Company department store, which evolved into the leading department store in downtown Altoona until the summer of 1980, when it was forced to close. An early trolley of the Altoona and Logan Valley Electric Railway glides through the business district in this scene postmarked September 6, 1909.

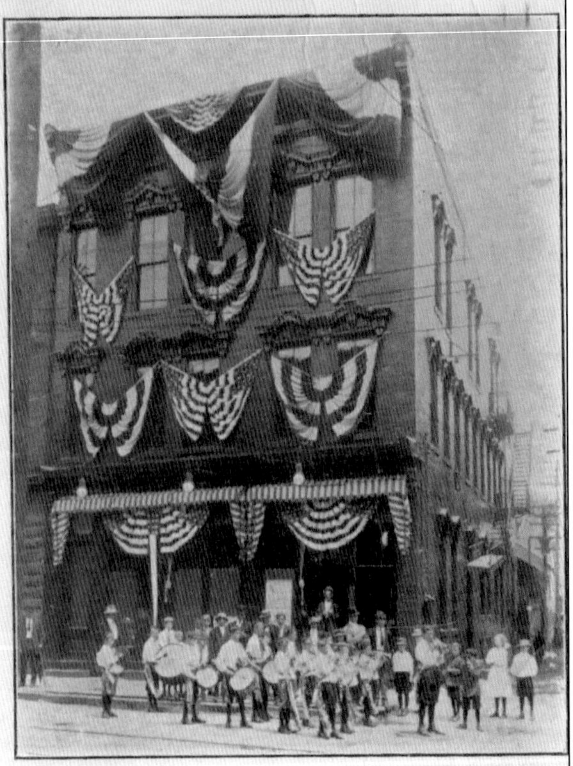

Home of THE TRIBUNE
Altoona's Oldest and Most Reliable Home Newspaper

This is the "Home of The Tribune, Altoona's Oldest and Most Reliable Home Newspaper," as this postcard indicates. The Tribune building is festooned with patriotic bunting indicating a popular holiday such as Independence Day or, possibly, September 1912, when three days of parades marked the 50th anniversary of the Loyal (Civil) War Governor's Conference. The card is postmarked November 30, 1914.

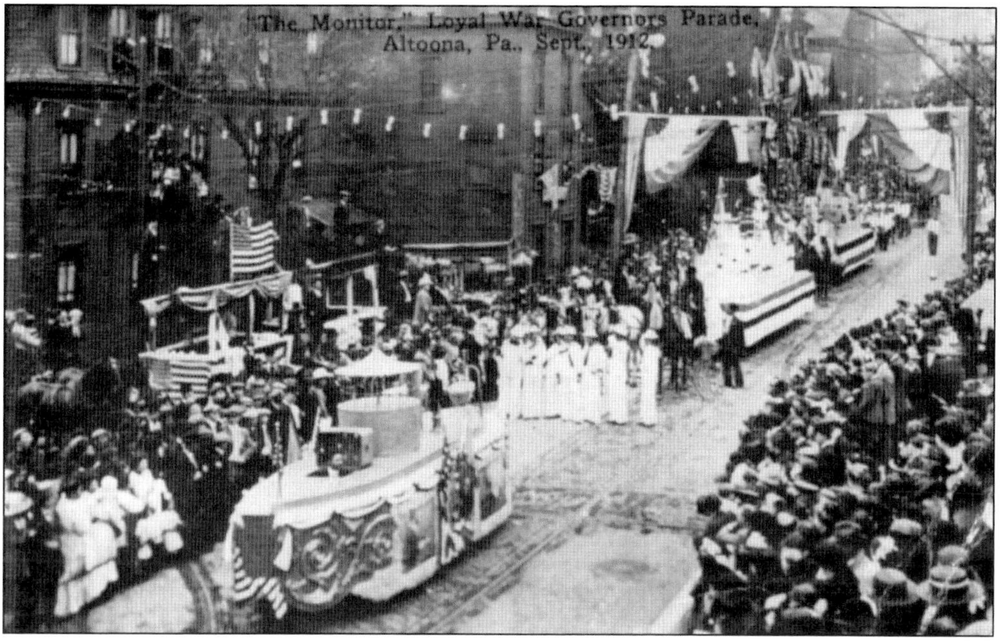

The parade float Monitor is pictured in the Loyal War Governor's Parade in September 1912, marking the 50th anniversary of a meeting of northern governors at Altoona in 1862. The card is postmarked January 13, 1913.

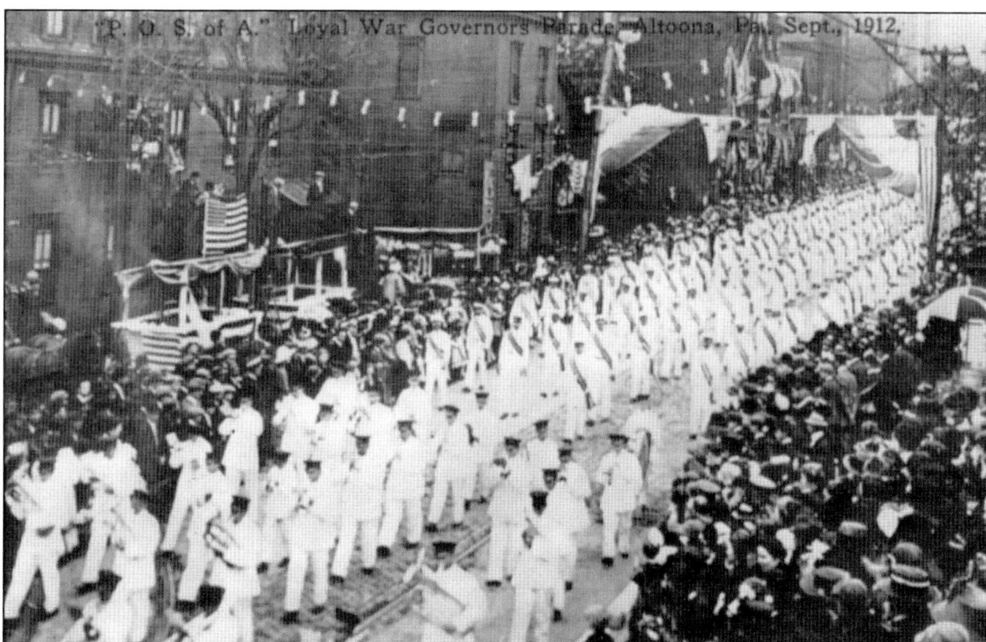

This parade marked the 50th anniversary of the Loyal War Governors Conference in September 1912. Here, the Patriotic Sons of America march down Eleventh Avenue near the PRR's Logan House Hotel, which hosted the Loyal (northern) Governors in 1862, affirming support and allegiance to President Lincoln.

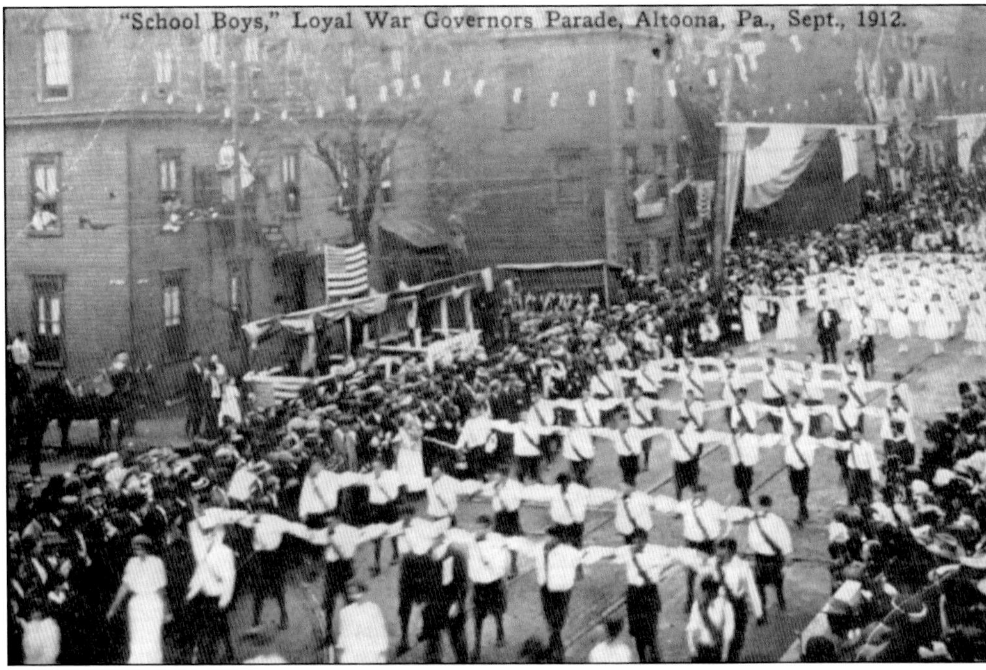

School boys marching in the Loyal War Governor's Parade in September 1912 pass the PRR's Logan House Hotel, which hosted the conference of Loyal (northern) Governors, under the leadership of Pennsylvania governor Andrew Curtin, in 1862.

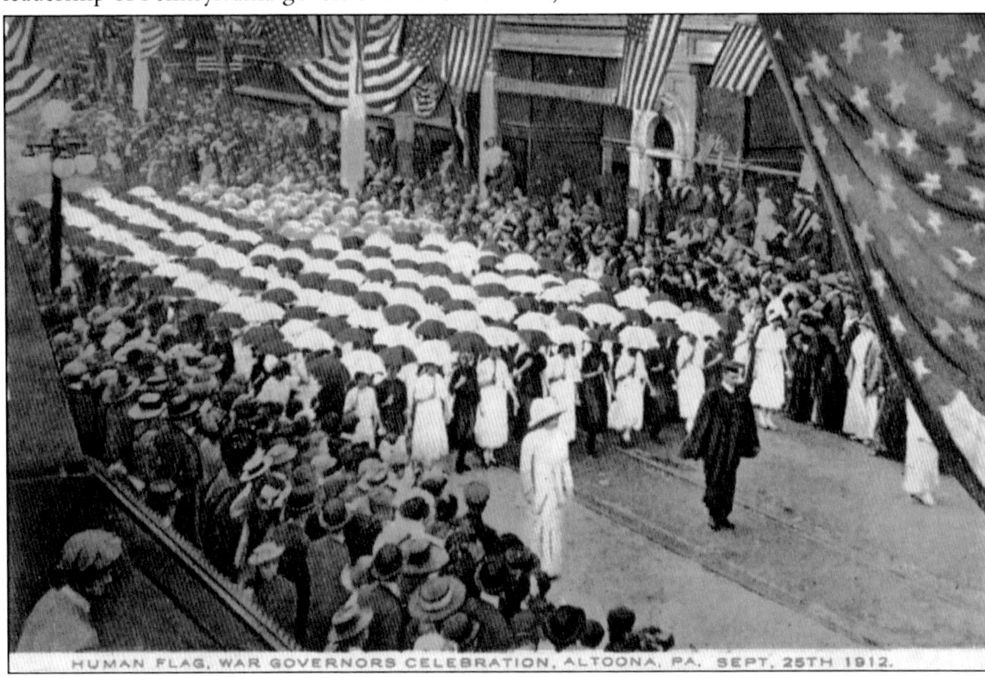

Women carrying red or white or blue/white umbrellas created a human U.S. flag for the War Governor's Parade on September 25, 1912. In 1862, under the leadership of Pennsylvania governor Andrew Curtin, governors of northern states met in Altoona at the new PRR Logan House Hotel to affirm their states' loyalty to the Union.

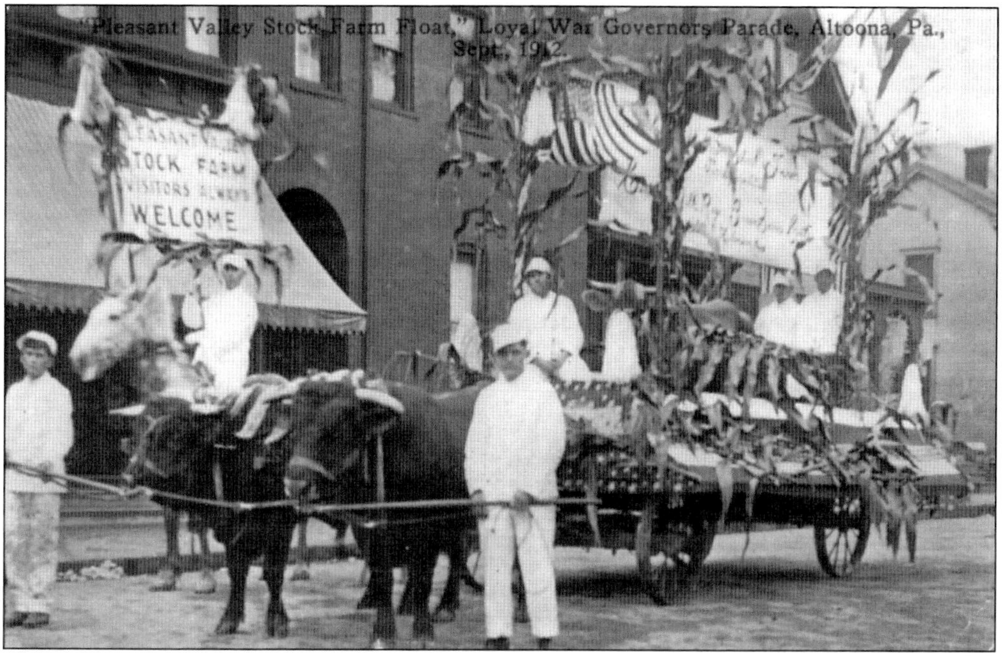

The Pleasant Valley Stock Farm float is pictured in the Loyal War Governor's (50th anniversary) Parade in September 1912. The float was led by Blair Hileman, owner of the farm. The event was comprised of three days of parades that were attended by Pres. William Howard Taft, who was in his last six months of office. This postcard was postmarked December 29, 1913.

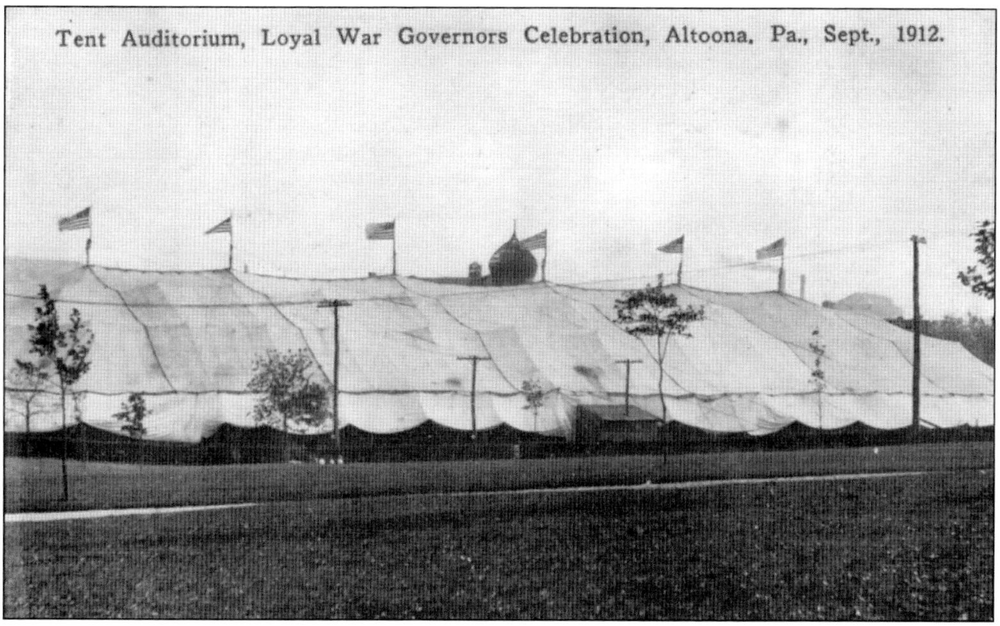

A tent auditorium for the Loyal War Governors Celebration in September 1912 was erected at the PRR's Cricket Field athletic grounds. The tent hosted celebratory events during three days of festivities, including the appearance of President Taft. The cricket field was located opposite the PRR's passenger car shops at Chestnut Avenue and Seventh Street, as well as the Altoona Hospital along Howard Avenue to the north.

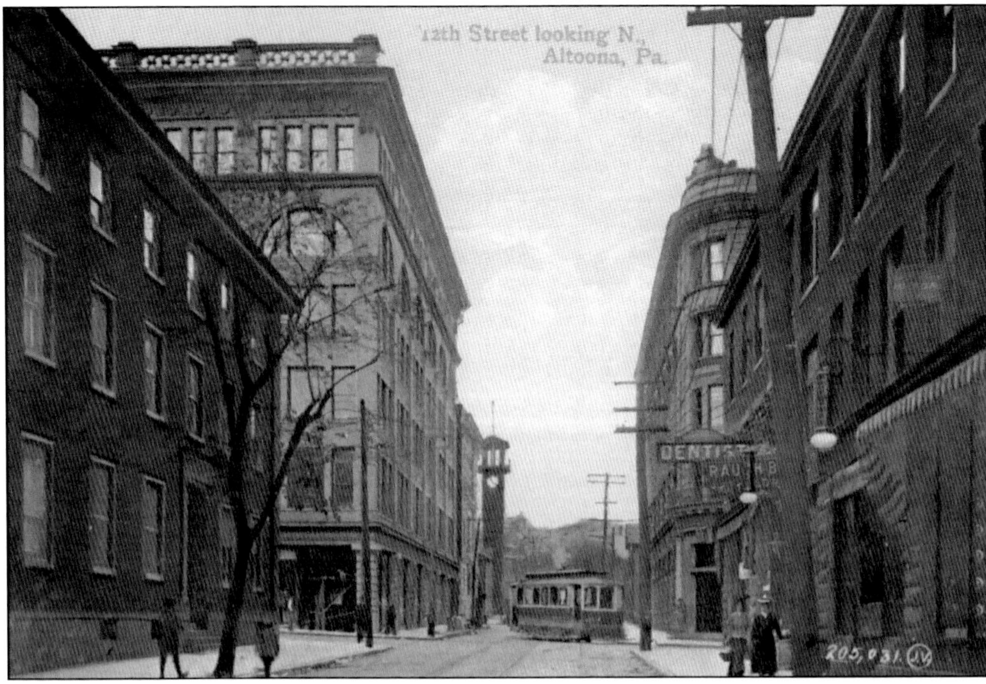

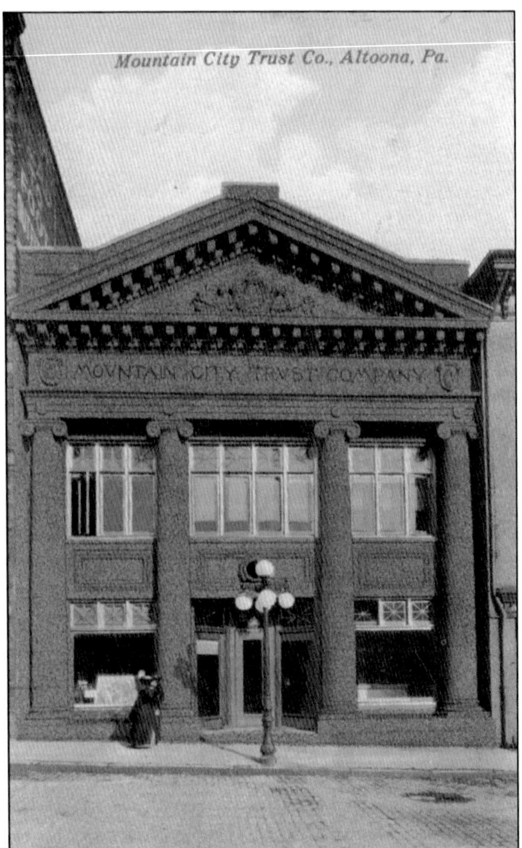

This view of Twelfth Street looks north from Eleventh Avenue to Twelfth Avenue. The six-story building on the left is the Rothert Department Store that previously burned down on October 19, 1906 (and was rebuilt), along with the Mishler Theatre (adjacent and out of view), and the BPOE Elks Lodge to the rear. A short four-wheel trolley of the Altoona and Logan Valley Electric Railway rounds the corner on the Fairview line.

The Mountain City Trust Company, shown here, was formerly located in the 1000 block of Twelfth Street opposite the lawn of the PRR Logan House Hotel. This was one of the banks that failed with the stock market crash of October 1929. In later years, the site accommodated Simmonds Ladies Apparel and the second floor housed the offices of the Jubelirer Law Firm. This card was postmarked at Fort Wayne, Indiana, on July 4, 1919.

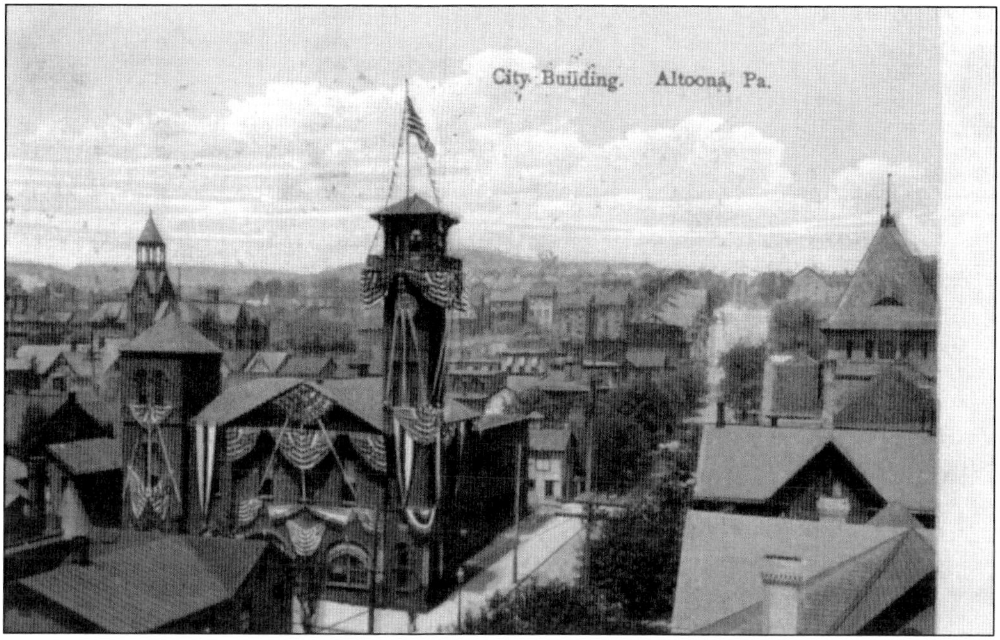

The building seen here housed city offices as well as the Vigilant Volunteer Fire Department (1870–1923). The flags and bunting on the building in summertime suggest an Independence Day celebration. The tower at the distant left is Wright Elementary School, and the peak at the right is First Presbyterian Church. The Altoona postmark is July 16, 1910.

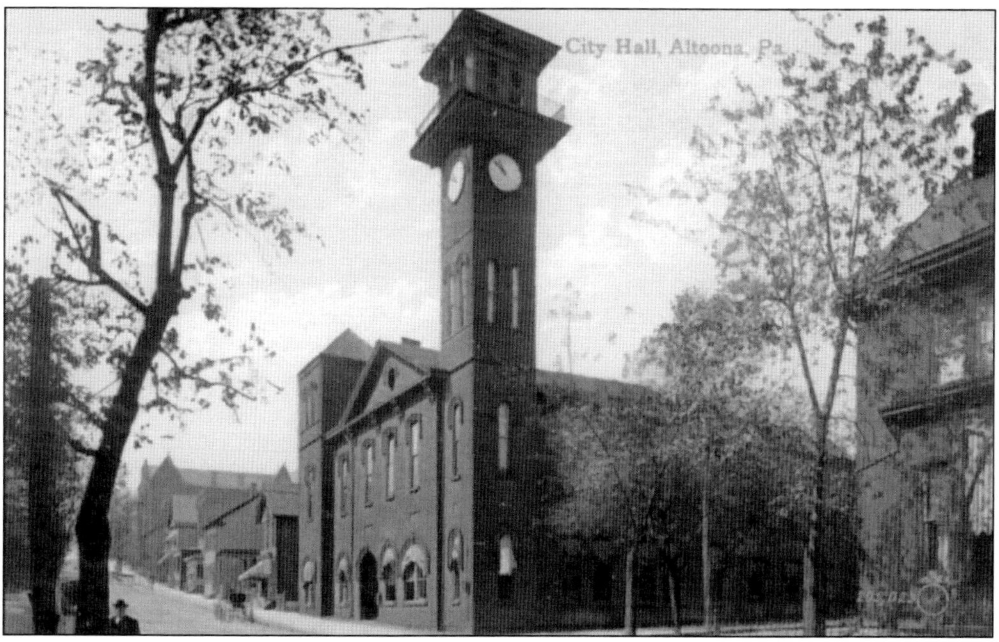

Here is another view of the prominent Altoona City Hall and Vigilant Volunteer Fire Department headquarters. This view is westerly on Thirteenth Avenue, with St. John's Catholic Elementary school near the top of the hill. The residence at the right was later demolished for construction of Altoona's premier Penn-Alto Hotel, which was the center of Altoona society for many years. The card is postmarked Altoona, August 25, 1914.

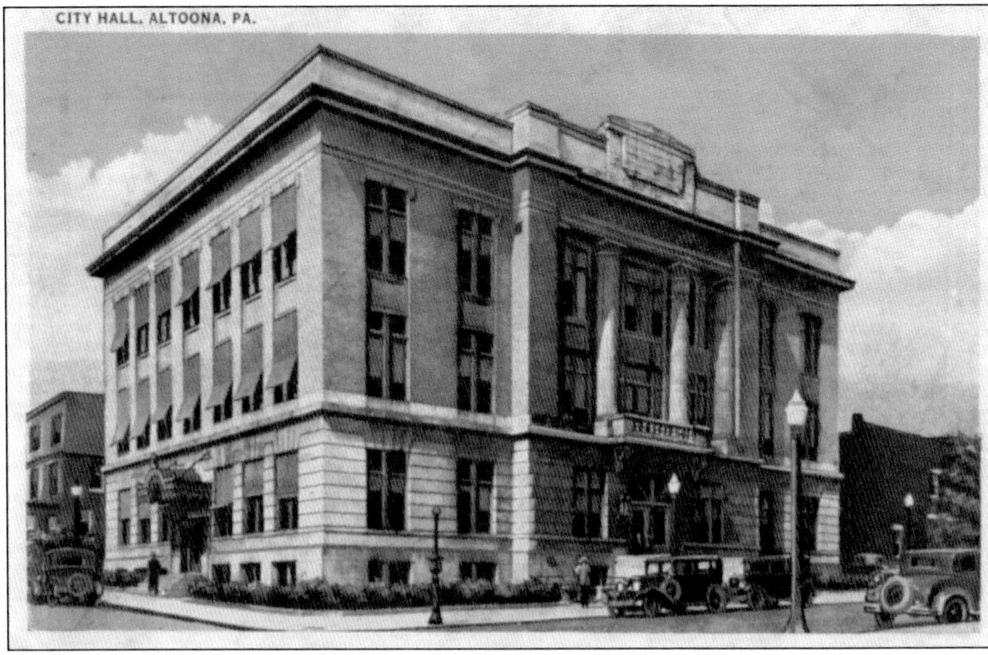

Altoona City Hall replaced the former City Hall and Vigilant Volunteer Fire Company on the same location at Thirteenth Avenue and Twelfth Street. This building still houses the principal city offices through the 21st century. The card was postmarked Altoona, June 25, 1936, just three months after disastrous floods affected the entire state of Pennsylvania on March 17.

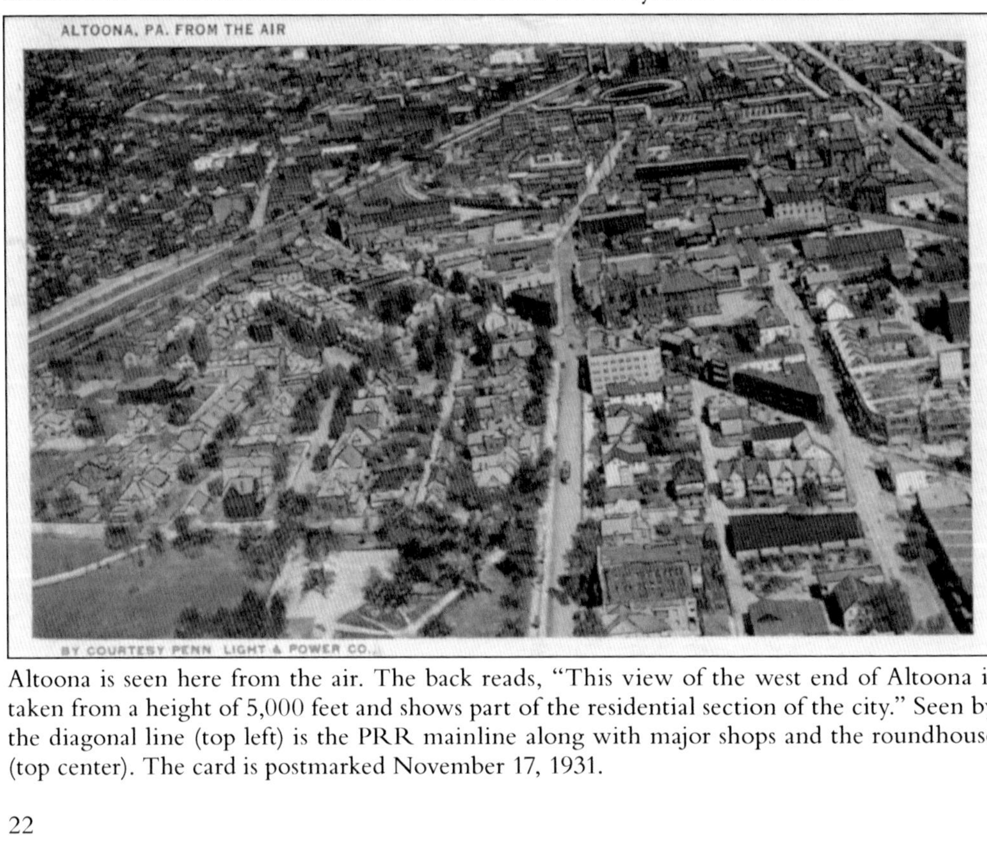

Altoona is seen here from the air. The back reads, "This view of the west end of Altoona is taken from a height of 5,000 feet and shows part of the residential section of the city." Seen by the diagonal line (top left) is the PRR mainline along with major shops and the roundhouse (top center). The card is postmarked November 17, 1931.

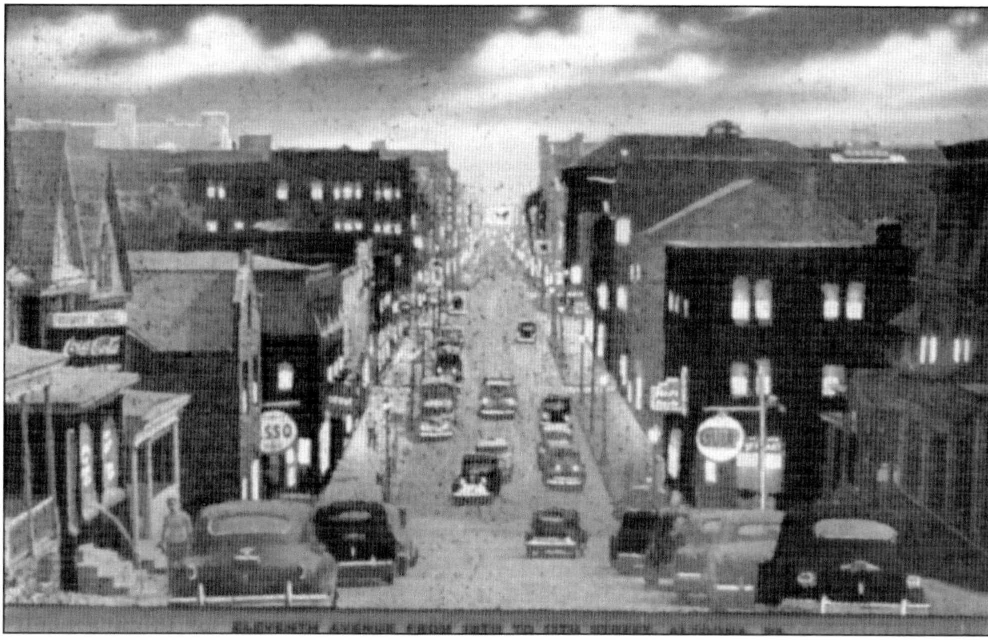

This *c.* 1940s view of Eleventh Avenue from Eighteenth Street looks east toward Eleventh Street. The hillside marked the departure from the central business district but offered a commanding view of downtown, especially as the lights came on in the commercial district. Eighteenth Street marked Route 36 north and south through the city, as well as a primary access to downtown for the Altoona and Logan Valley Electric Railway.

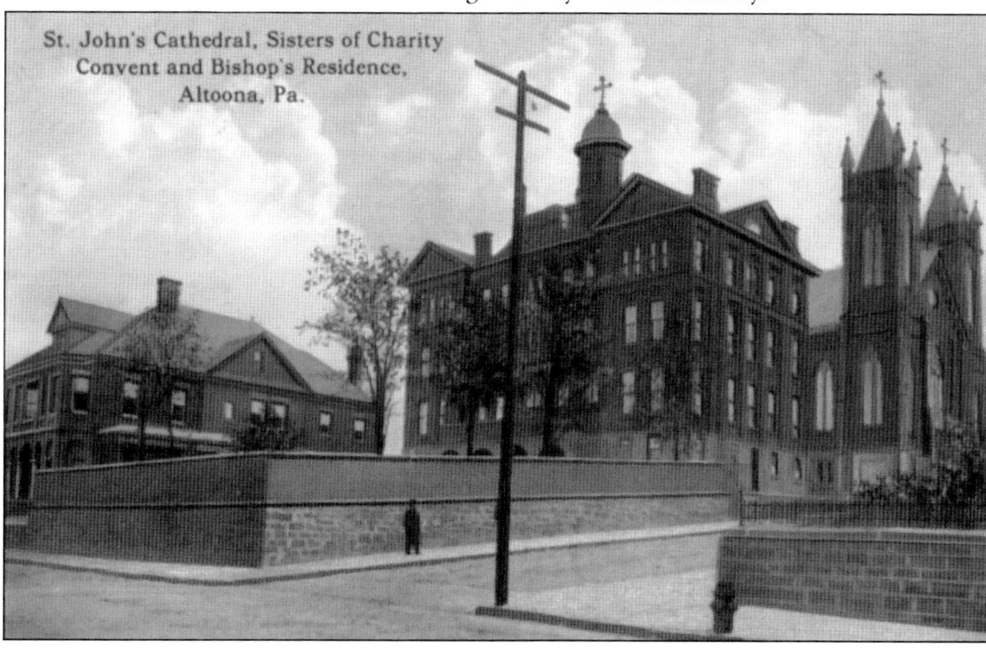

The old St. John's Convent and Church at the corner of Thirteenth Avenue and Thirteenth Street was the seat of the Altoona-Johnstown Diocese. The convent and church were demolished around 1927 for construction of the new Cathedral of the Blessed Sacrament, seen on the following pages. The Bishop's residence (left) remained until the 1960s.

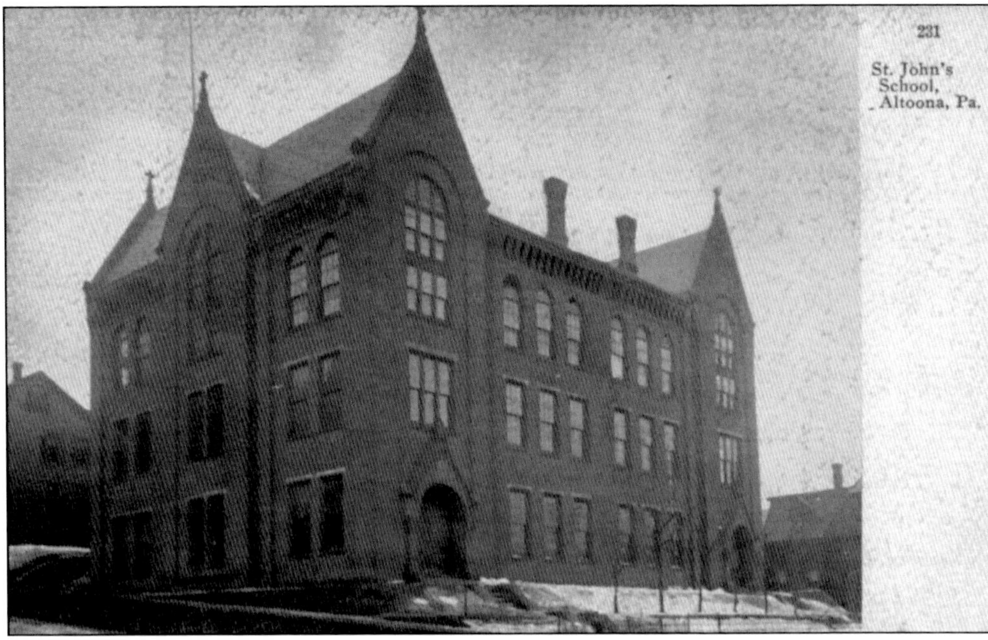

St. John's Elementary School, located opposite St. John the Evangelist Catholic Church (preceding page), was the seat of Catholic education for families of the parish. This structure, modernized on the interior over these many years, still survives into the 21st century, although it is no longer a parish elementary school.

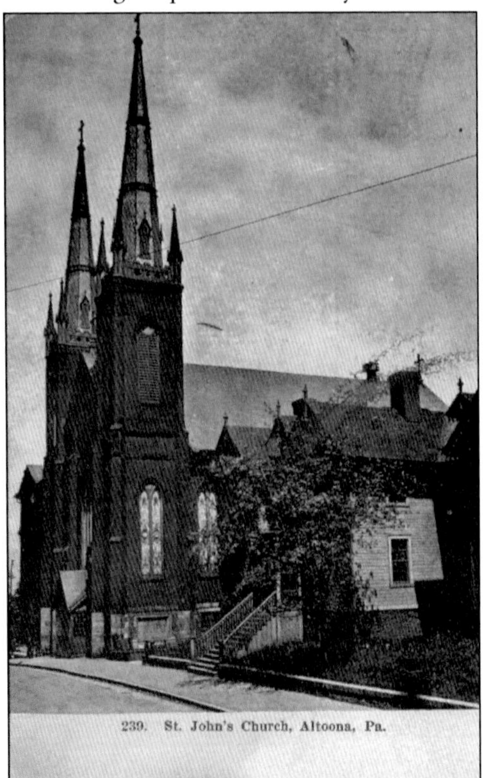

Here is another view of St. John the Evangelist Catholic Church from the west. Although a beautiful twin-steeple Gothic style edifice, the change in status to a cathedral for the new diocese between Harrisburg and Pittsburgh in June 1901, with Altoona as its Episcopal See, would bring many changes. The Right Reverend Eugene A. Garvey, D.D., was named first bishop of Altoona. The card is postmarked August 21, 1908.

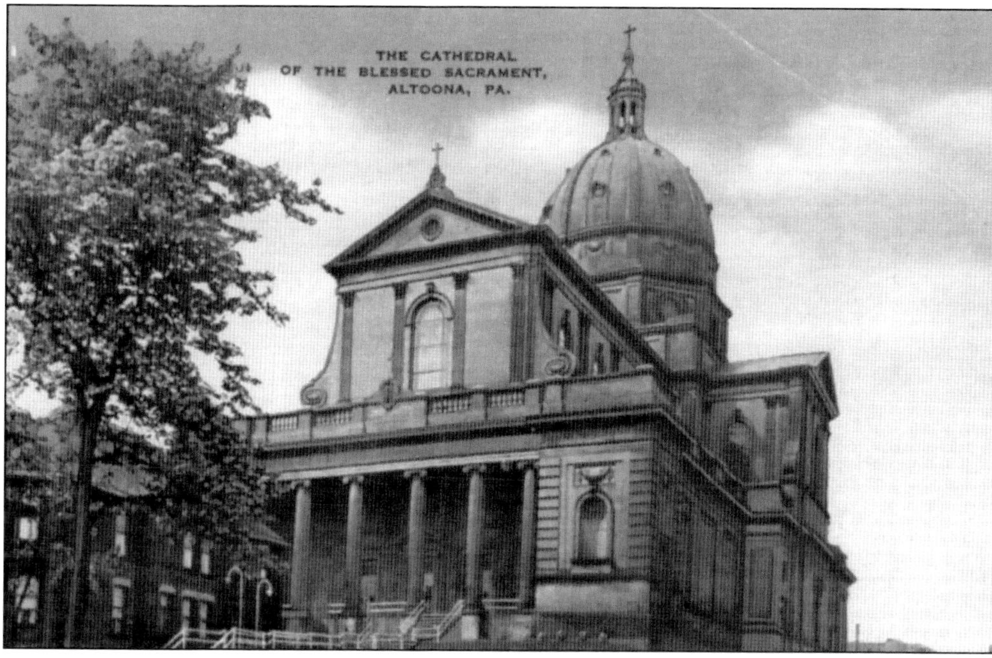

Early Renaissance architecture influenced the design of the new Cathedral of the Blessed Sacrament, which replaced St. John's Cathedral in the preceding images. The bold vision of Bishop John McCort, the second bishop of the diocese, it was completed on the exterior in 1933 but remained unfinished on the interior until the early 1960s. In this early view the Bishop's residence is still in place at the left front corner. Major structural steel was donated by Charles M. Schwab of Bethlehem Steel Corporation, whose summer estate, Immergrun, was near Altoona at Loretto.

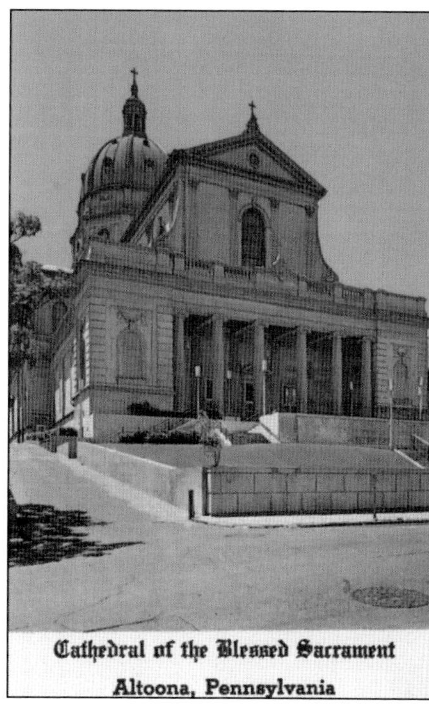

The Cathedral of the Blessed Sacrament is shown completed in the early 1960s. Gone is the bishop's residence on the front left corner, replaced by new steps and terraces. In later years, the front niches were adorned with bronze statues of St. Elizabeth Ann Seton, founder of the Sisters of Charity, which served the parish (right); and St. John Neuman, Bishop of Philadelphia (left).

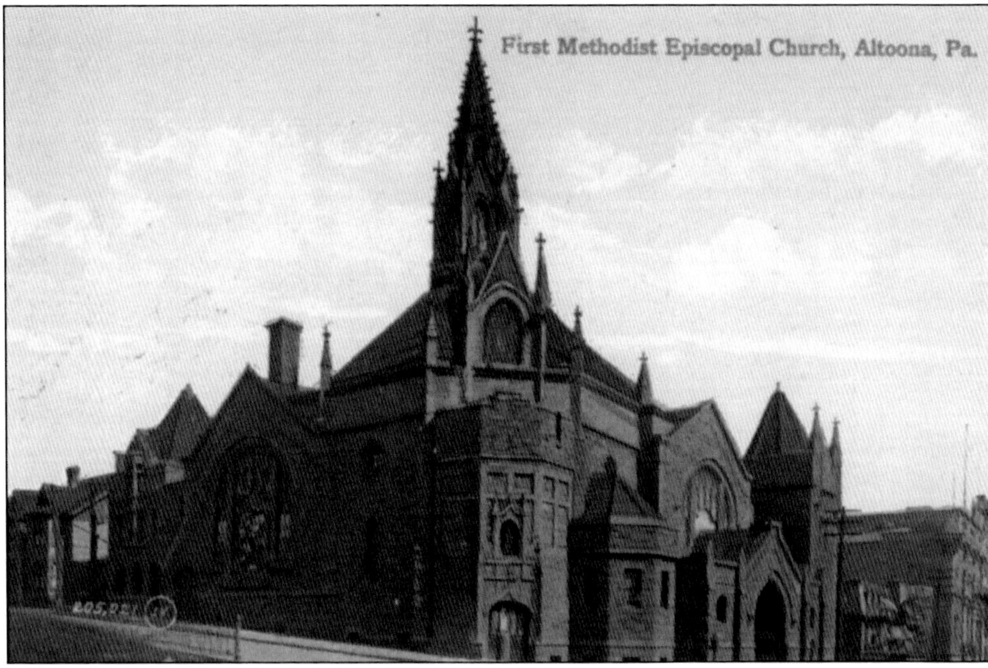

The First Methodist Episcopal Church is located a half block from the Cathedral of the Blessed Sacrament on the preceding page. This church is constructed of Hummelstown Brownstone with ornate pinnacles and a central spire. However, the spire was removed in later years following a lightning strike. At the extreme right is Altoona's historic Mishler Theatre.

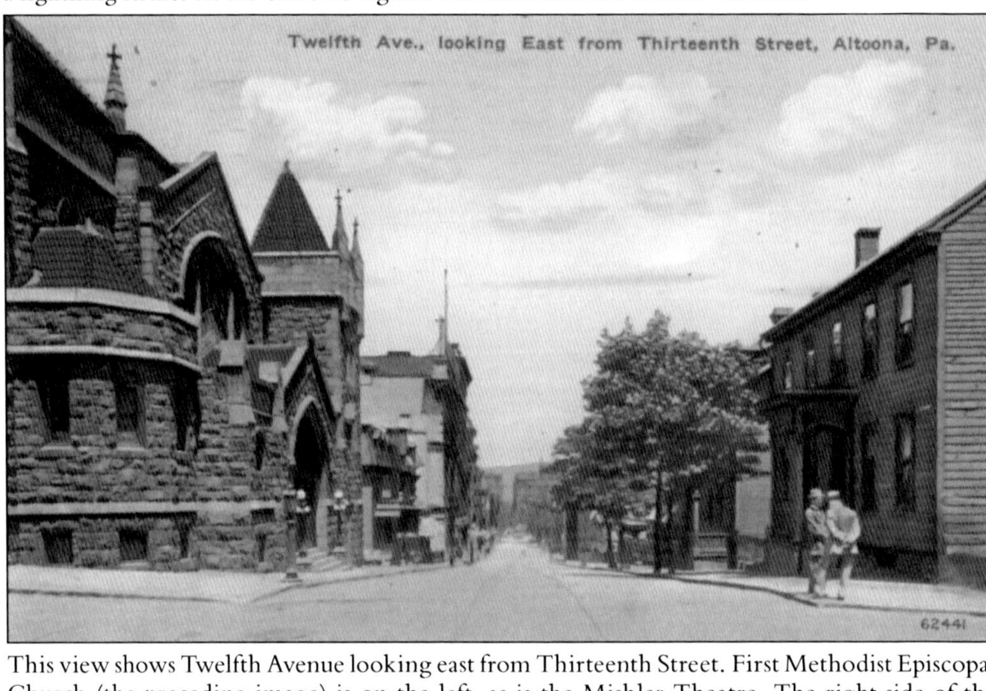

This view shows Twelfth Avenue looking east from Thirteenth Street. First Methodist Episcopal Church (the preceding image) is on the left, as is the Mishler Theatre. The right side of the street had residences, some belonging to civic leaders, but the commercial district was starting to encroach on these homes. The card is postmarked August 8, 1913.

The University Club was adjacent to First Methodist Episcopal Church (preceding page) in the 1200 block of Twelfth Avenue. This structure was originally the Baltzell mansion (owned by the family of a prominent local merchant) and was razed in later years to construct an educational facility for First Methodist Episcopal Church. At one time, Twelfth Avenue hosted a number of prominent residences, but they were gradually displaced by Altoona's growing commercial district.

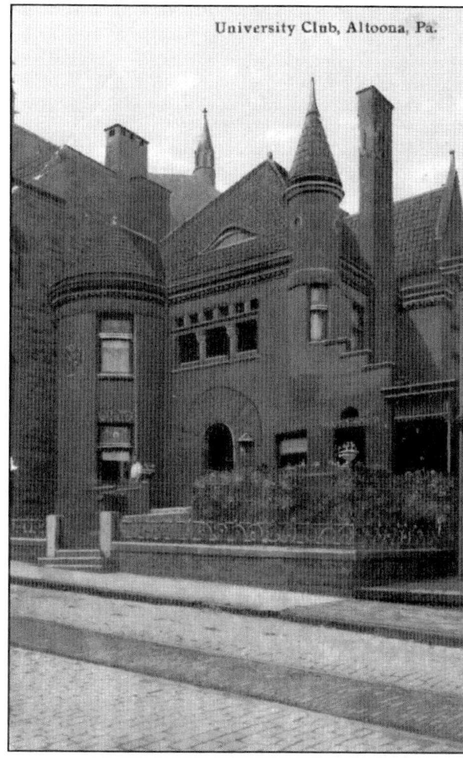

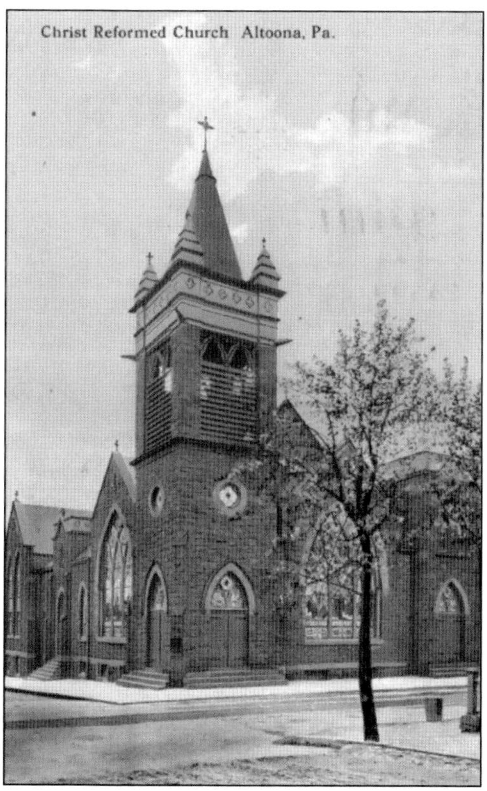

Christ Reformed Church is seen at Twelfth Avenue and Fifteenth Street. Religious life in Altoona evolved from its earliest days as immigrants came to the city. It seemed every city block had a church. This Protestant congregation disbanded in the 1990s, but the structure still stands at the end of the first decade of the 21st century. The card was postmarked April 1, 1915.

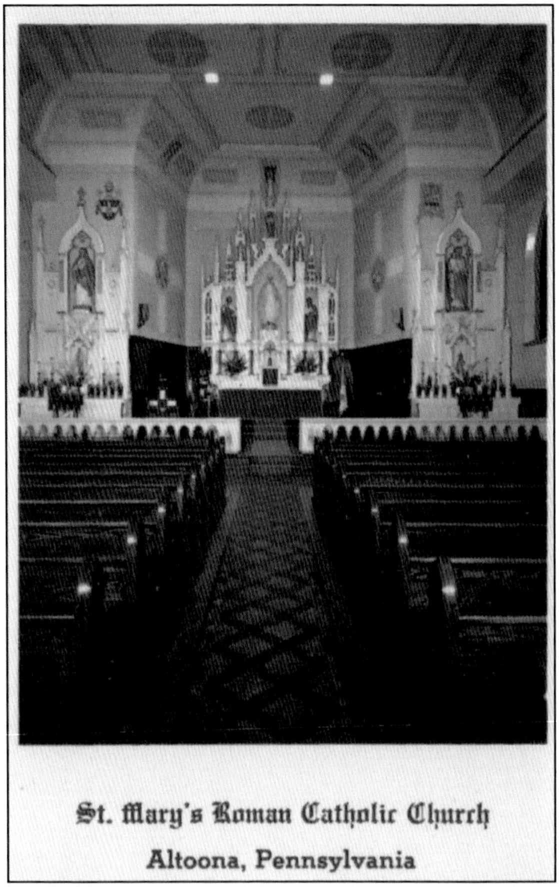

This is an interior view of the very ornate altar of Immaculate Conception (St. Mary's) Catholic Church. Founded for immigrant German Catholics, it is Altoona's second oldest church, predating the Civil War by one year, just 11 years following the founding of Altoona by the PRR. Sadly this artistic altar was removed after Vatican II and the interior modernized.

St. Mark's Catholic Church and School at Sixth Avenue and Fourth Street served a diverse population of predominantly PRR families. Just one block away was the west end of the vast PRR classification yards. For years, St. Mark's used a bell that called railroad workers at shift changes. This bell is still used by the parish today, although the ornate bell tower, housing a clock and the original church bell, is long gone because of deterioration. The card is postmarked December 15, 1911.

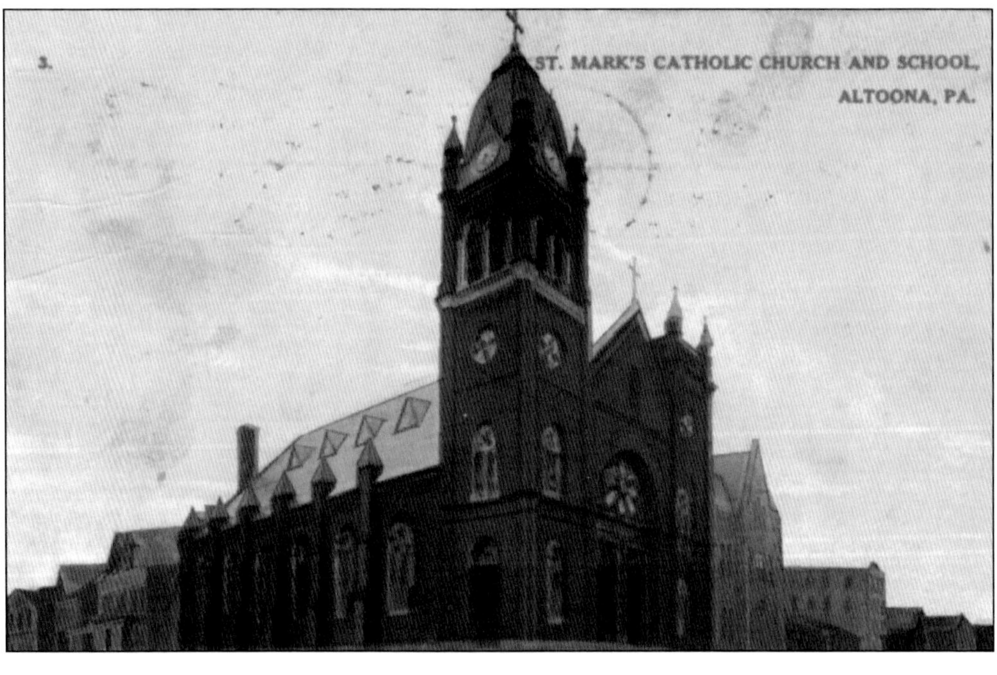

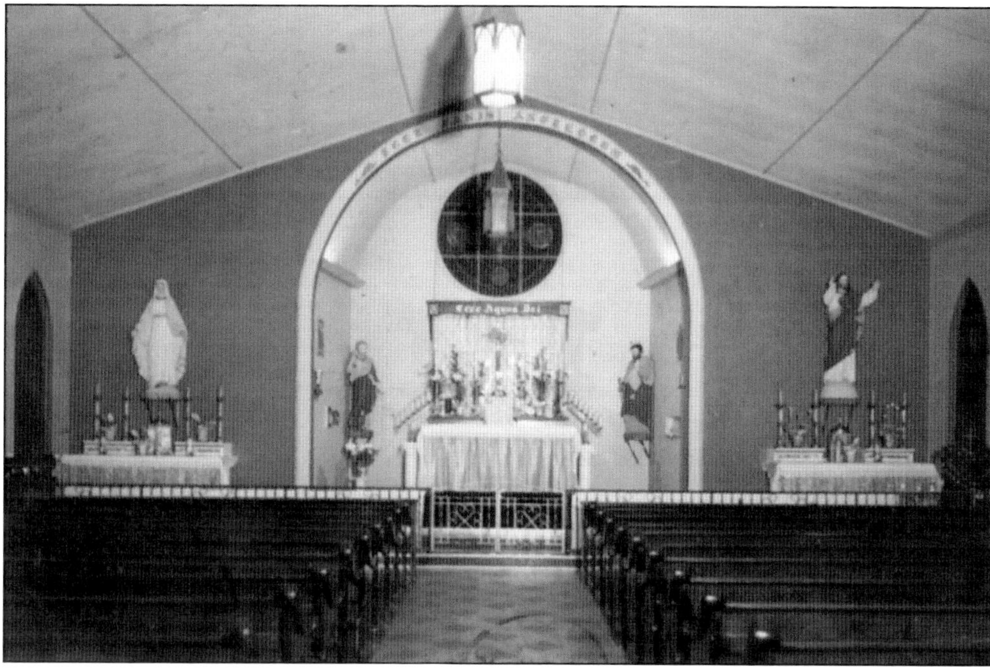

This view shows the interior of Sts. Peter and Paul Roman Catholic Church at 1906 Nineteenth Street. Many Catholic churches served the needs of their ethnic populations, and Sts. Peter and Paul met the needs of the Polish community, utilizing their native language up through the 1950s. Dwindling population and parish mergers have relegated this facility to a chapel for sister parish Our Lady of Fatima. The card is postmarked June 23, 1960.

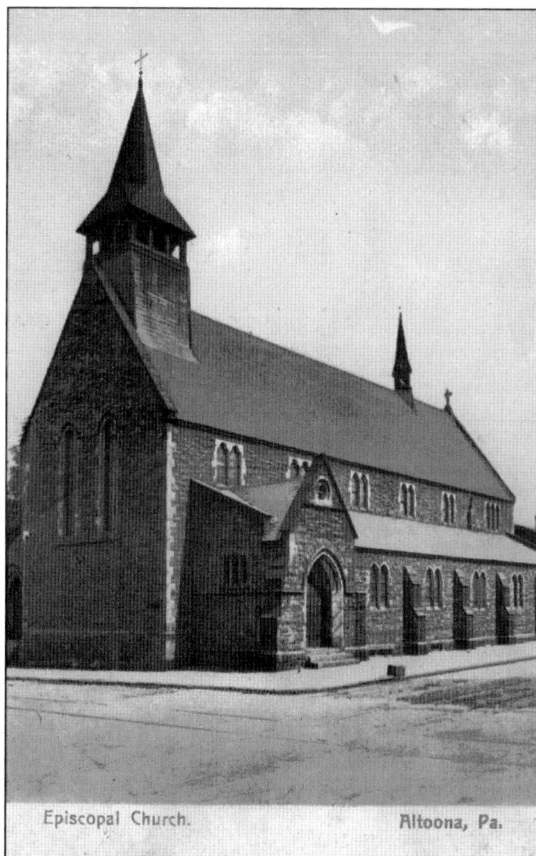

St. Luke's Episcopal Church, located at Eighth Avenue and Thirteenth Street, is just one block from the PRR's Altoona Works. Early steam railroading technology originated in Great Britain. Thus many early railroad officials had a British-Anglican background, and were Anglicans served by the Episcopal Church in America. St. Luke's was founded in 1849, along with Altoona, and is the city's oldest church community, still active into the 21st century. The structure boasts a genuine Tiffany stained-glass window. The card is postmarked June 21, 1911.

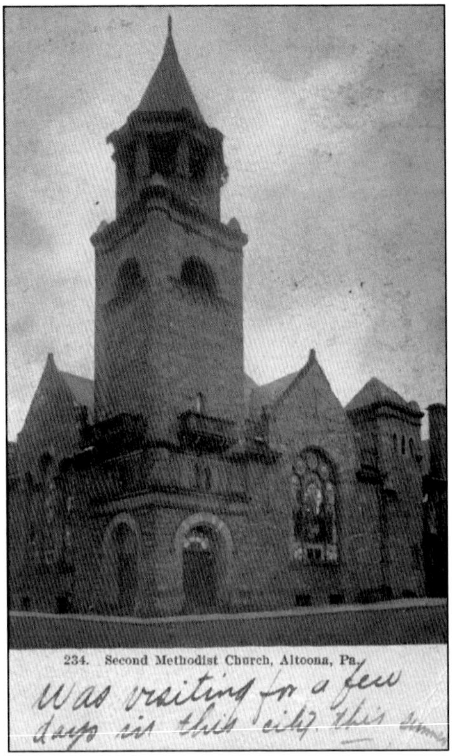

Second Methodist Church is located at Eighth Avenue and Twelfth Street, which was once a corner representing the second busiest commercial district in Altoona's center city because of its close proximity to the PRR's Altoona Works. Surrounded by ethnic neighborhoods at one time, change has eroded much of the commercial aspects. This edifice still survives into the 21st century but is no longer Methodist-affiliated. The card is postmarked October 5, 1912.

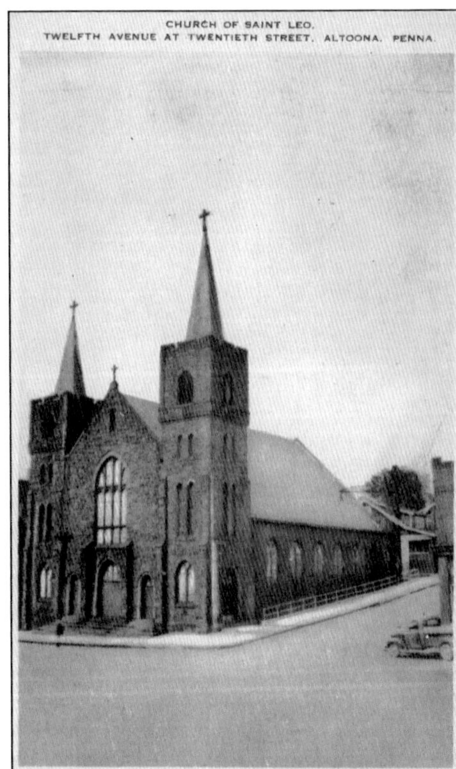

Church of St. Leo the Great is located at Twelfth Avenue and Twentieth Street. Perched on a hill west of the business district, the twin spires are visible from many parts of the city. A large bell was installed in the 1950s in memory of a parish member killed in the Korean War. A parish merger in the 1990s with Sts. Peter and Paul changed the name to Our Lady of Fatima.

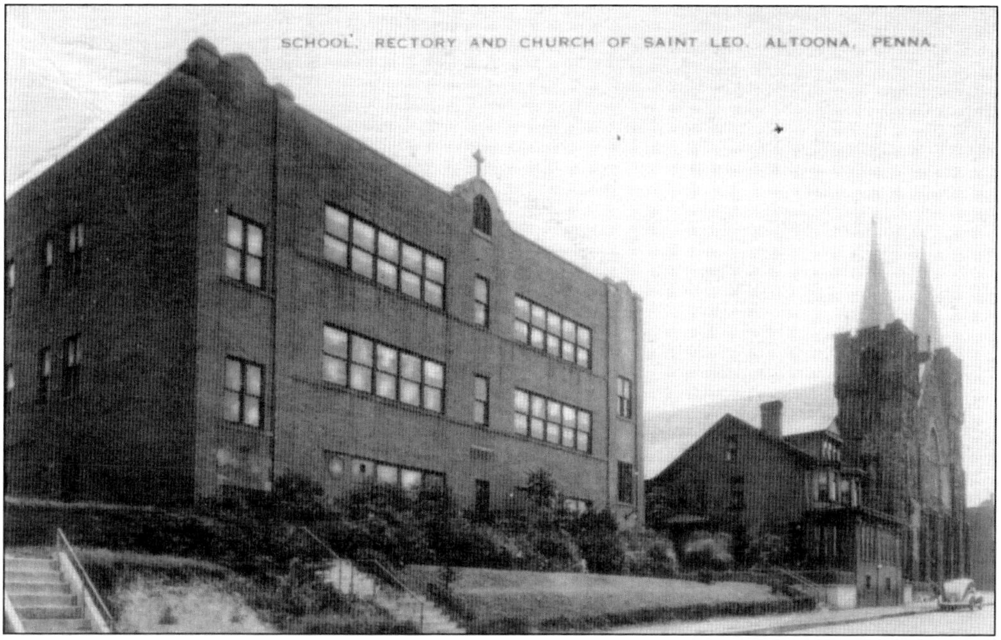

The school, rectory, and church of St. Leo (The Great) is pictured at Twelfth Avenue and Twentieth Street. With the consolidation of all city Catholic elementary schools post-1980, parish schools were under-used in subsequent years. Although used for religious classes, and home for a short period to the Blair County Genealogical Society, St. Leo Parish School was razed in the first decade of the 21st century.

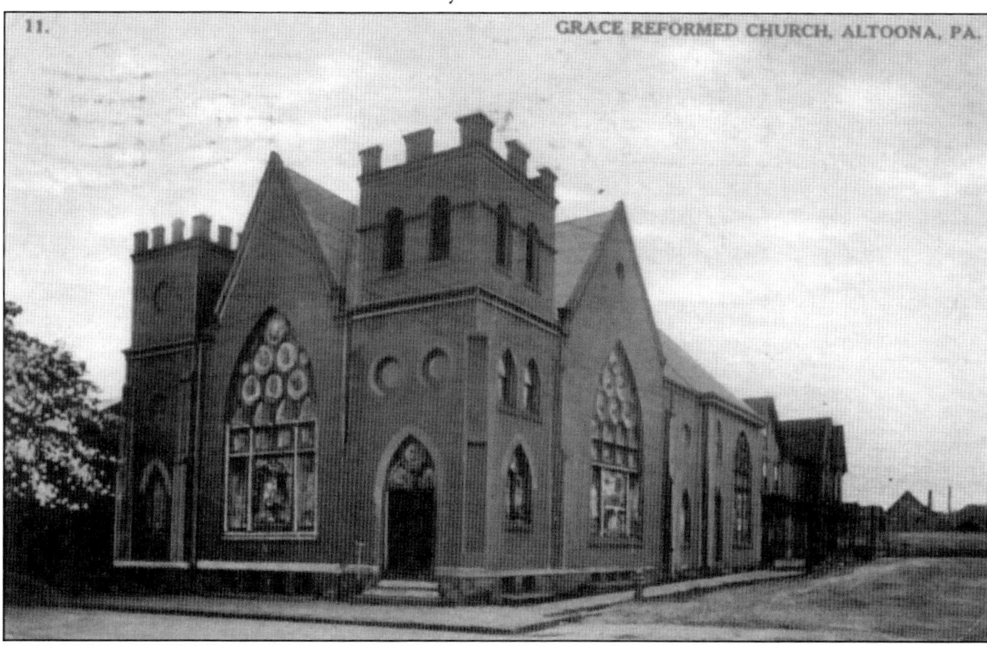

Grace Reformed Church is located at Eighth Avenue and Twenty-third Street. The church community is also active into the 21st century. Located in center city, it is one block from the branch line of the PRR leading to Hollidaysburg, the county seat. This card is postmarked April 17, 1910.

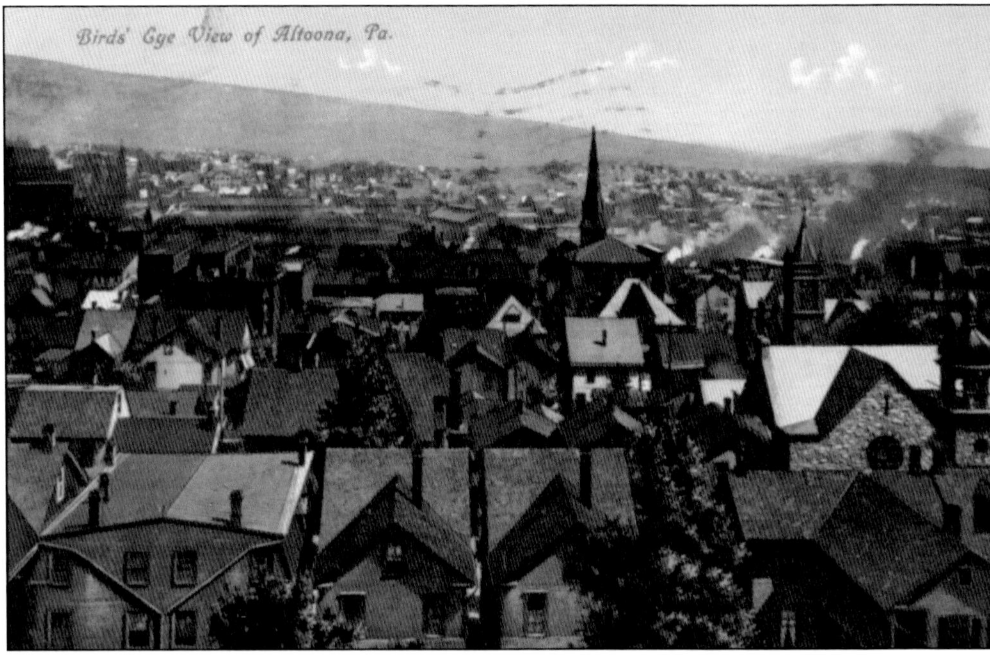

Shown is another bird's-eye view of Altoona's center from the promontory of Gospel Hill in a view from the north toward the south side of town. The church spire at Eleventh Avenue and Fifteenth Street belongs to First Baptist Church, which would be destroyed by fire on February 4, 1912. The card is postmarked August 4, 1908.

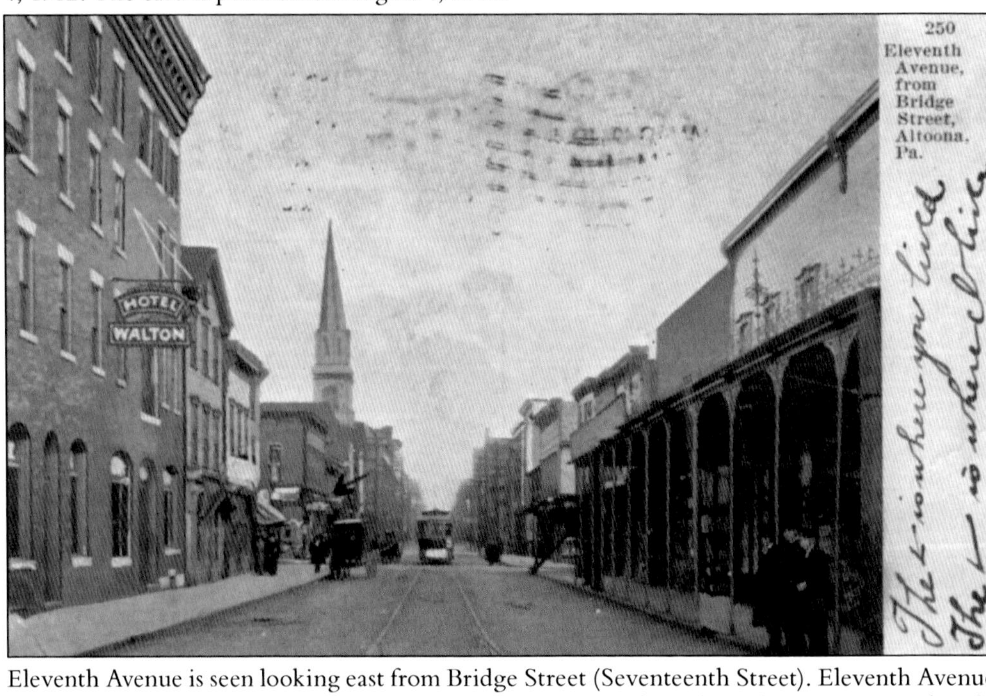

Eleventh Avenue is seen looking east from Bridge Street (Seventeenth Street). Eleventh Avenue is the principal business street, and the visible church steeple is that of First Baptist Church, at Fifteenth Street. The church was destroyed by fire on February 4, 1912. This postcard was postmarked 1909.

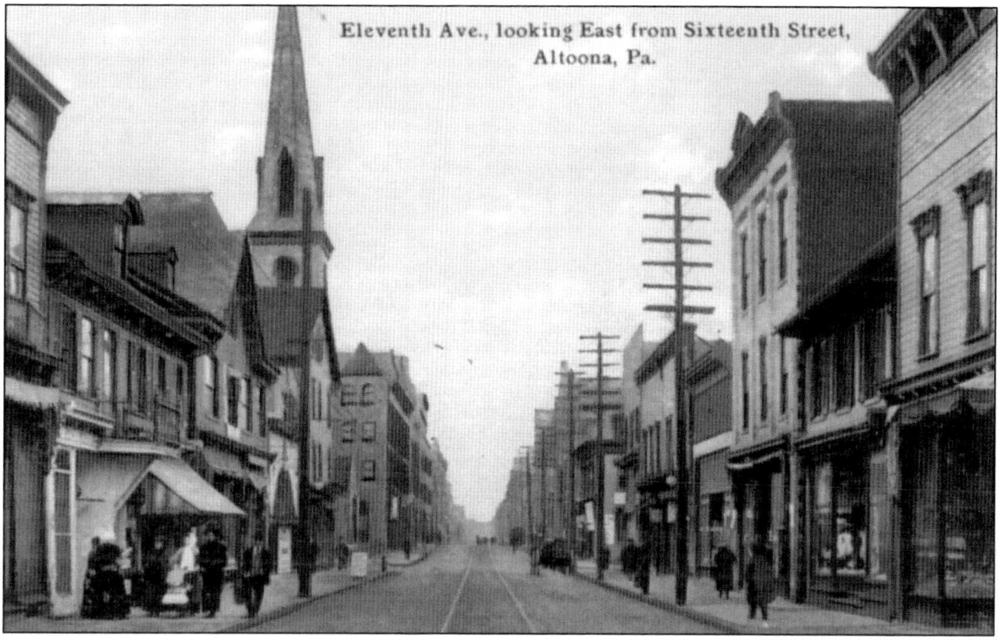

This view of Eleventh Avenue looks east from Sixteenth Street, showing the steeple of First Baptist Church at Fifteenth Street. The church was destroyed by fire on February 4, 1912, two months before the steamship *Titanic* sank. The tracks of the Altoona and Logan Valley Electric Railway traverse the center of this central business district for Altoona.

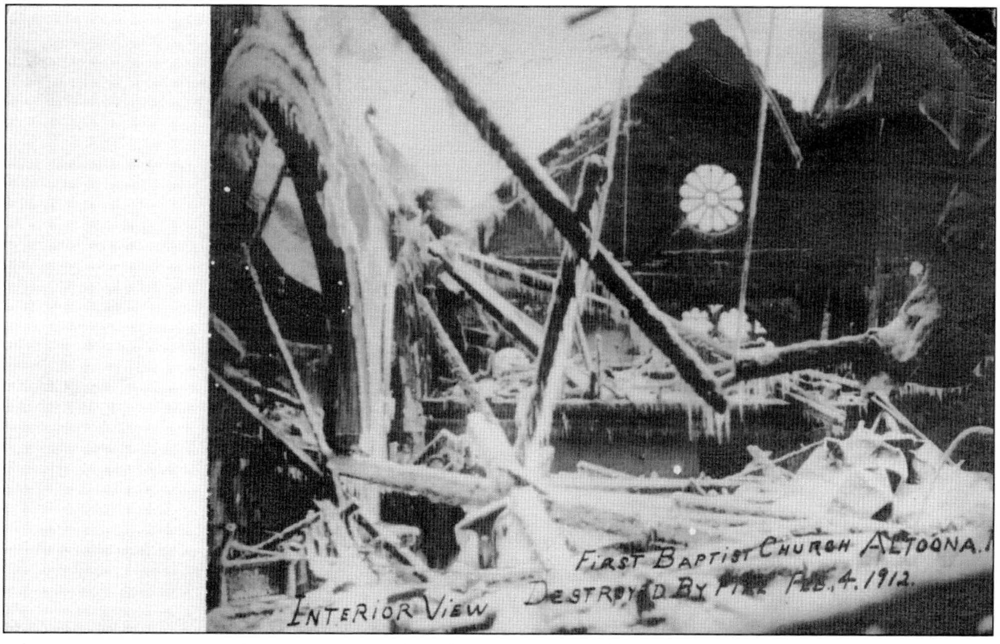

This interior view is of First Baptist Church, located on Eleventh Avenue and Fifteenth Street. The edifice, constructed in 1895, was destroyed by fire on February 4, 1912, seven months prior to the 50th anniversary of the Loyal War Governor's Conference held at the PRR's Logan House Hotel in 1862. The card was postmarked February 24, 1912.

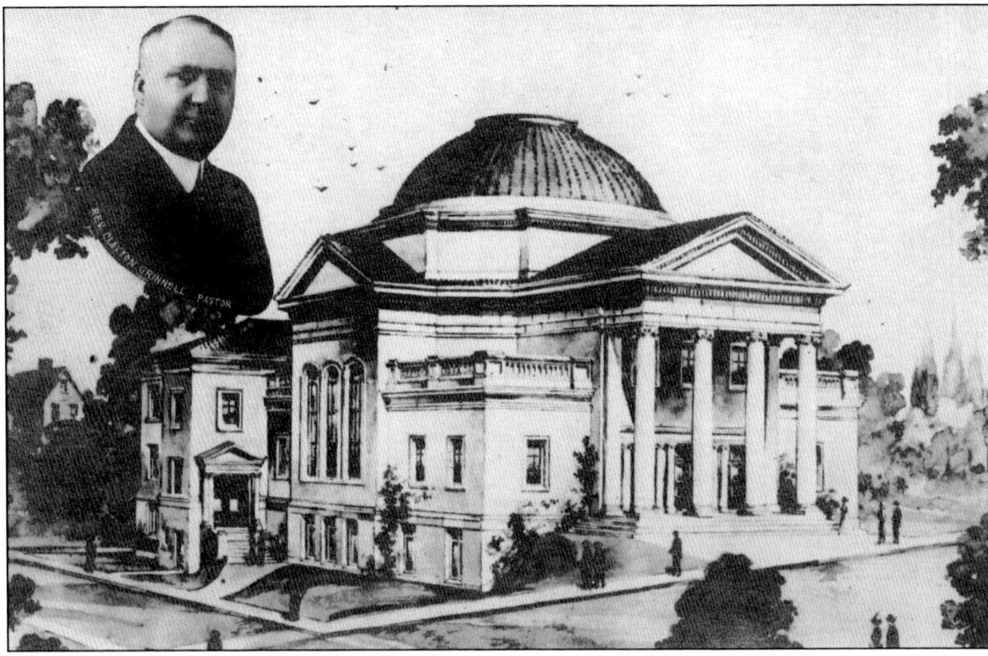

First Baptist Church is shown as designed and constructed following the fire of February 4, 1912, in the preceding image. The Rev. Clayton Grinell was pastor at this time. This magnificent edifice was constructed several blocks distant at Twelfth Avenue and Seventeenth Street and still serves the church community in the first decade of the 21st century, almost 100 years later.

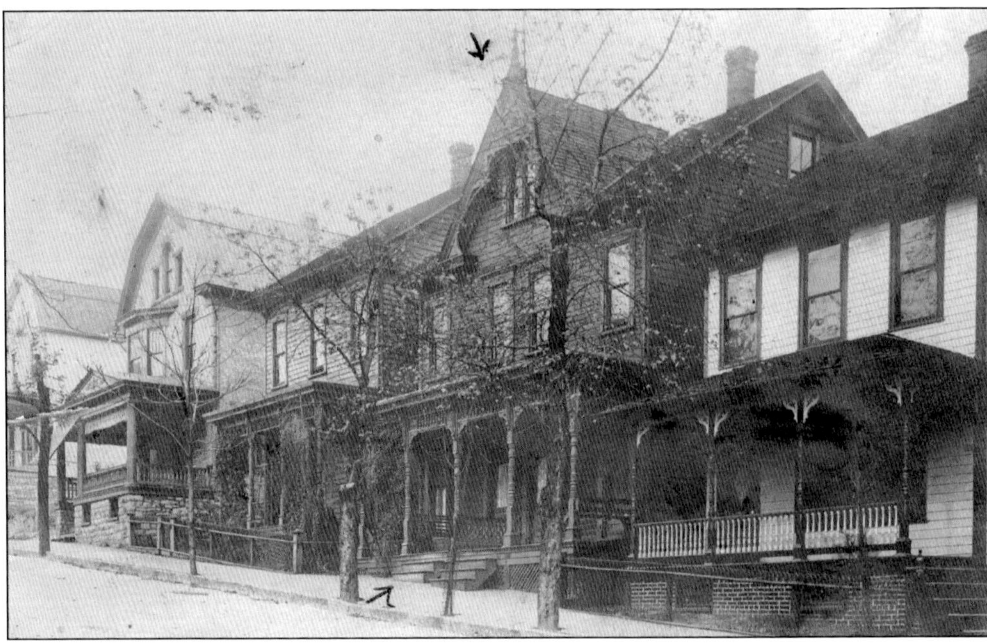

This is a view of the 1200 block of Seventeenth Street, directly opposite the image of First Baptist Church in the preceding view. Many Altoona homes in center city were built on 25-foot front lots with little space between buildings, as seen in this view. Some of these homes no longer exist.

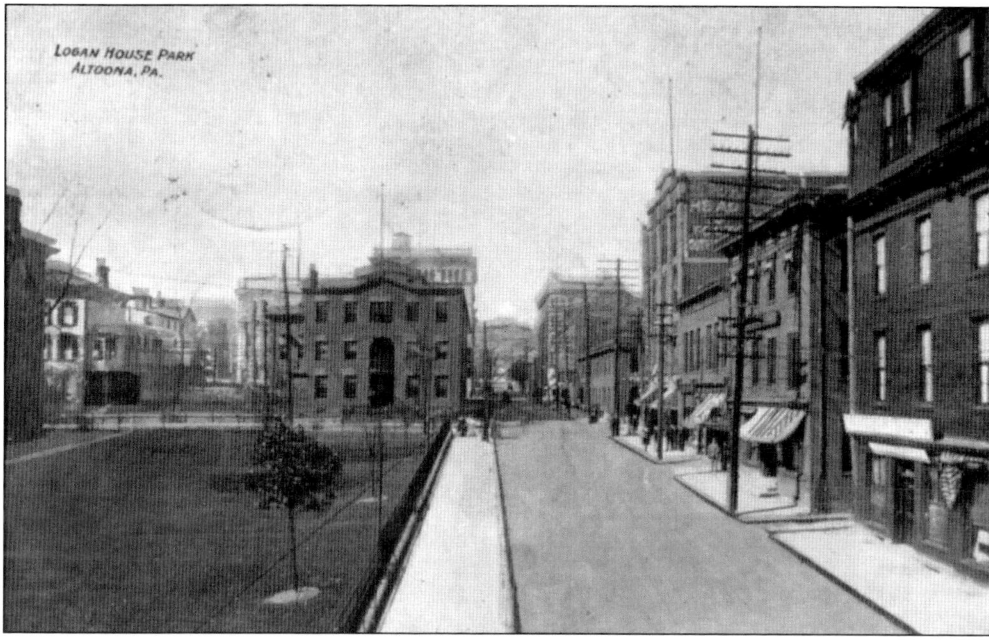

Pictured is a *c.* 1908 northerly view of Twelfth Street from the PRR mainline. The lawn at the left is on the grounds of the PRR's Logan House Hotel, adjacent to the passenger station one block west. The PRR office building faces the lawn and the residence of the PRR superintendent seen on the left. This postcard was published for the Union News Company and dated May 30, 1908.

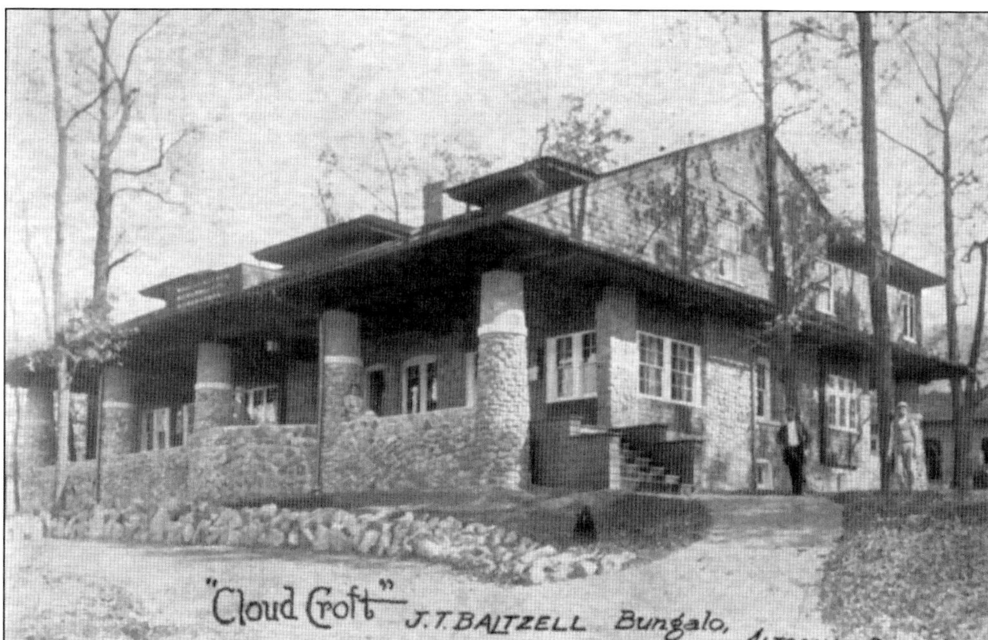

This is a view of Cloud Croft, the J. T. Baltzell bungalow. This residence with architectural elements constructed of smooth brook stone was located on Brush Mountain near Kettle Road, with commanding views of the city, above Rose Hill Cemetery.

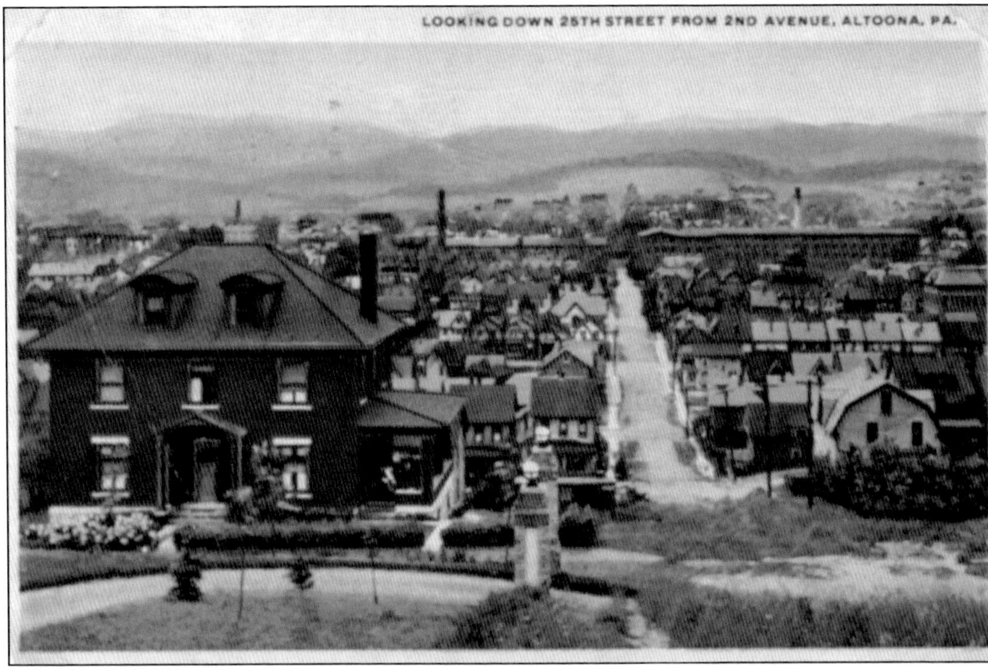

Pictured is an elevated view of the city from Second Avenue down Twenty-fifth Street. The factory in the distant right was the Altoona Silk Mill, which later became Puritan Sportswear and subsequently, Warnaco Sportswear. The factory is no longer a manufacturer, but it is still used for other purposes. This card was postmarked in Pittsburgh on July 23, 1920.

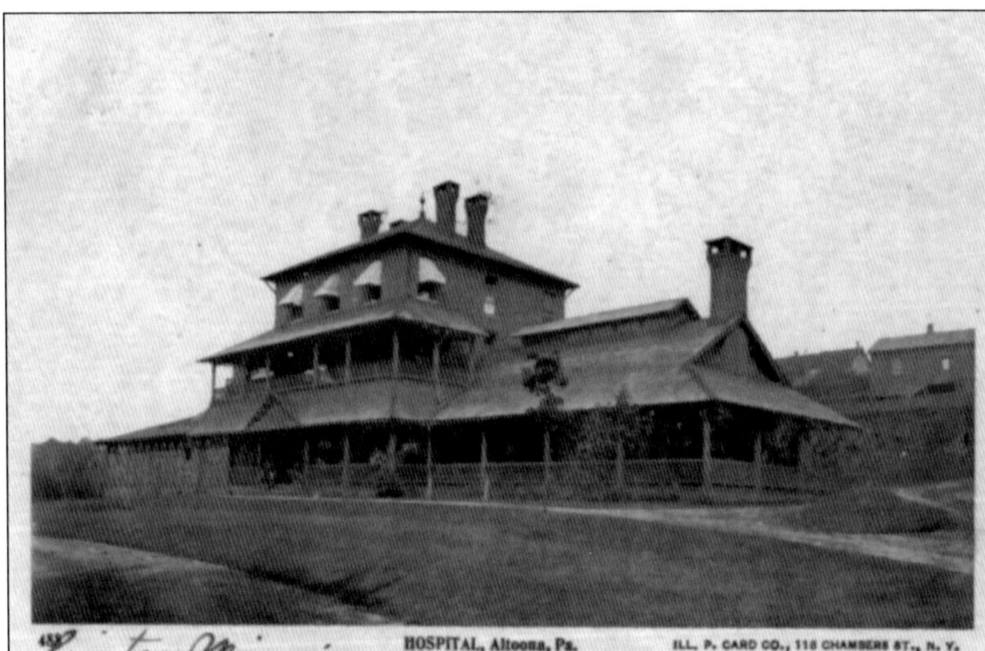

Altoona Hospital started under the auspices of the PRR. From these humble beginnings, this facility has blossomed into a major trauma center. This view is postmarked May 19, 1898.

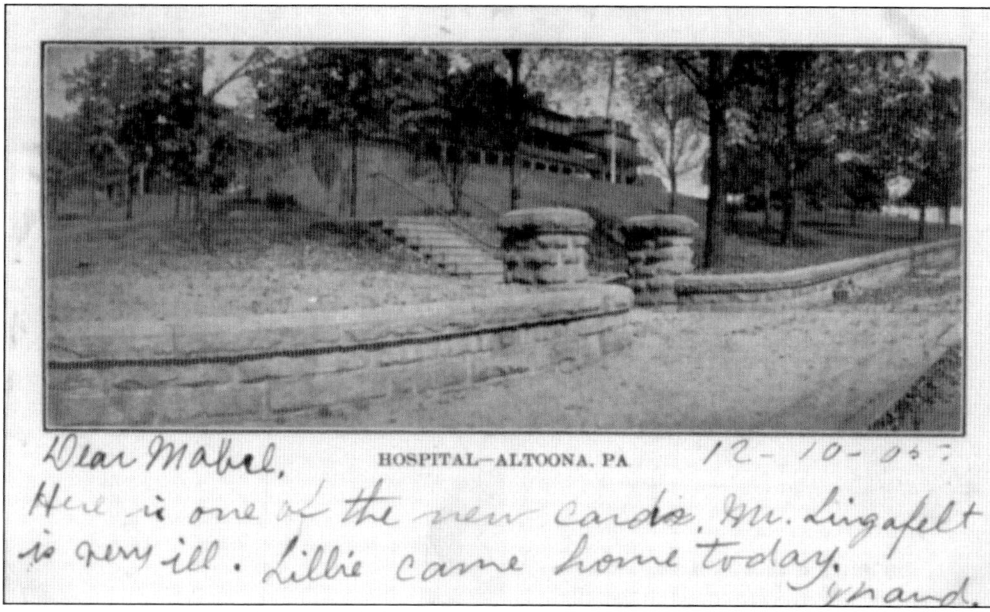

Seen here is a street-side view of the Altoona Hospital from Howard Avenue near Seventh Street. This hospital was across the street from the PRR's sports stadium, Cricket Field, where competitive sports between shops and divisions were held through the end of the steam era in the 1950s. The stone wall seen here is the only element from the original hospital that still survives. The card is postmarked December 12, 1905.

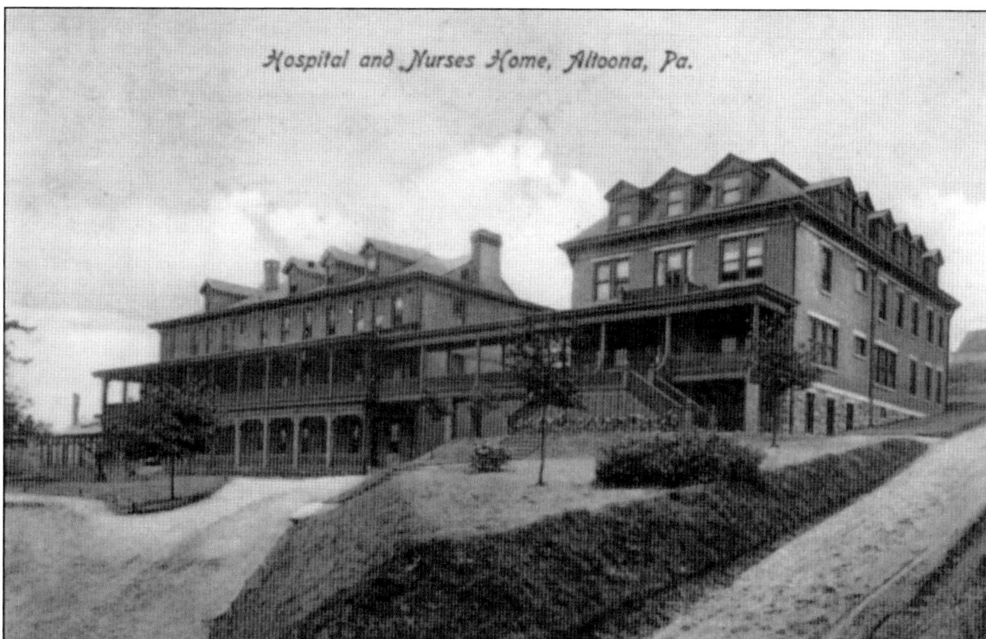

The Altoona Hospital (left) and Nurses' Home addition (right) are pictured in this postcard from July 5, 1908. Located on a hillside, the facility overlooked the Cricket Field Stadium of the PRR, as well as the passenger car shop at Chestnut Avenue and Seventh Street. The railroad power plants supplied steam heating to the hospital.

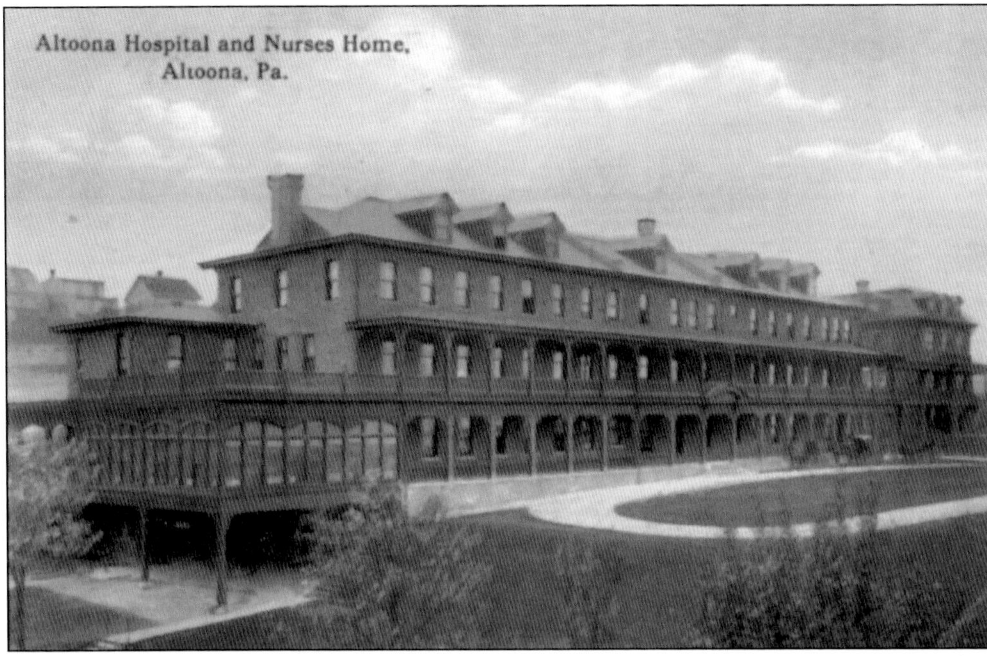

An expanded and enlarged Altoona Hospital and Nurses' Home is pictured in this card postmarked September 15, 1915. The hospital was characterized by long verandas. Ward accommodations were more common in this era to serve the needs of the shop workers and community.

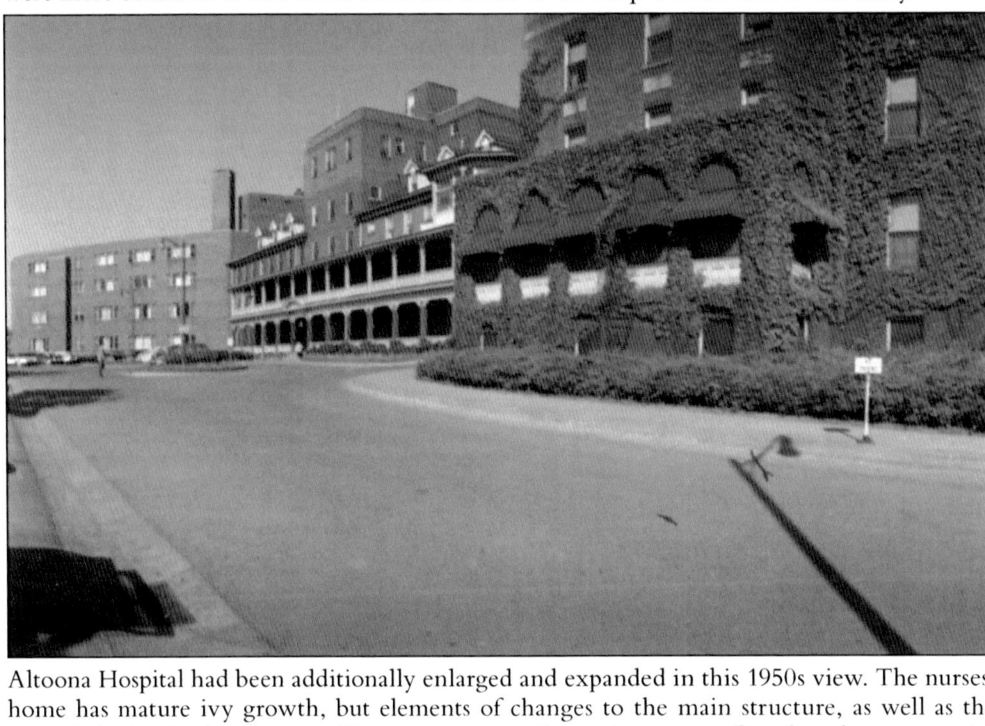

Altoona Hospital had been additionally enlarged and expanded in this 1950s view. The nurses' home has mature ivy growth, but elements of changes to the main structure, as well as the extended wing in the distance, illustrate progress. Expansions were often done by community support and payroll deduction. All but the nurses' home were replaced in the 1980s, creating a regional trauma center with major surgical-specialty disciplines.

In this *c.* 1940s view, Mercy Hospital, a Catholic facility operated by the Sisters of Nazareth, sustained many expansions over the years and ultimate replacement of the main campus. However, the competitive climate and health care changes mandated a merger with Altoona Hospital in later years in an attempt to avoid duplication of services.

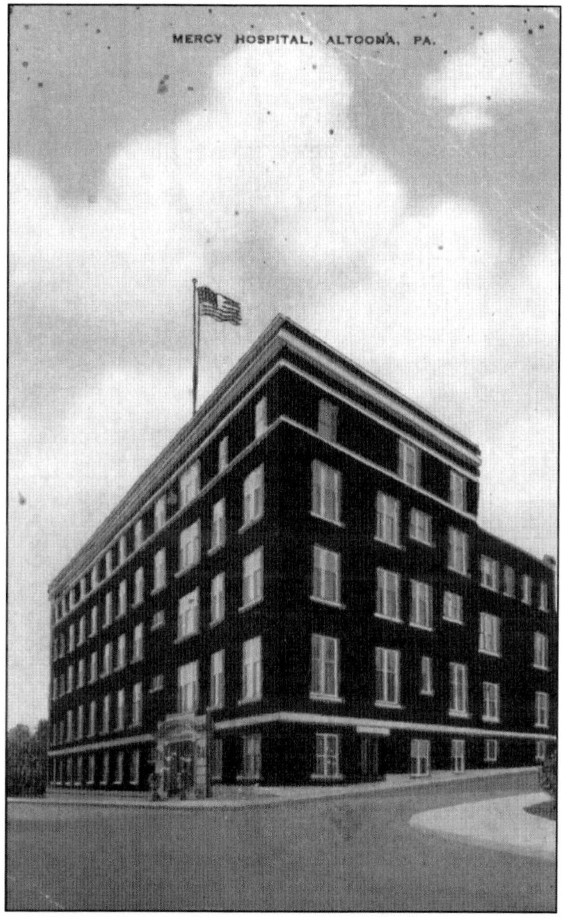

Patriotism preceding the second half of the 20th century was more visually stimulating than seems evident today. In this Armistice Day parade of November 11, 1920, just two years following the end of World War I, the participation by local residents and visitors is noteworthy. This view is on Twelfth Avenue at Eleventh Street, the principal corner where passengers changed trolley and bus lines.

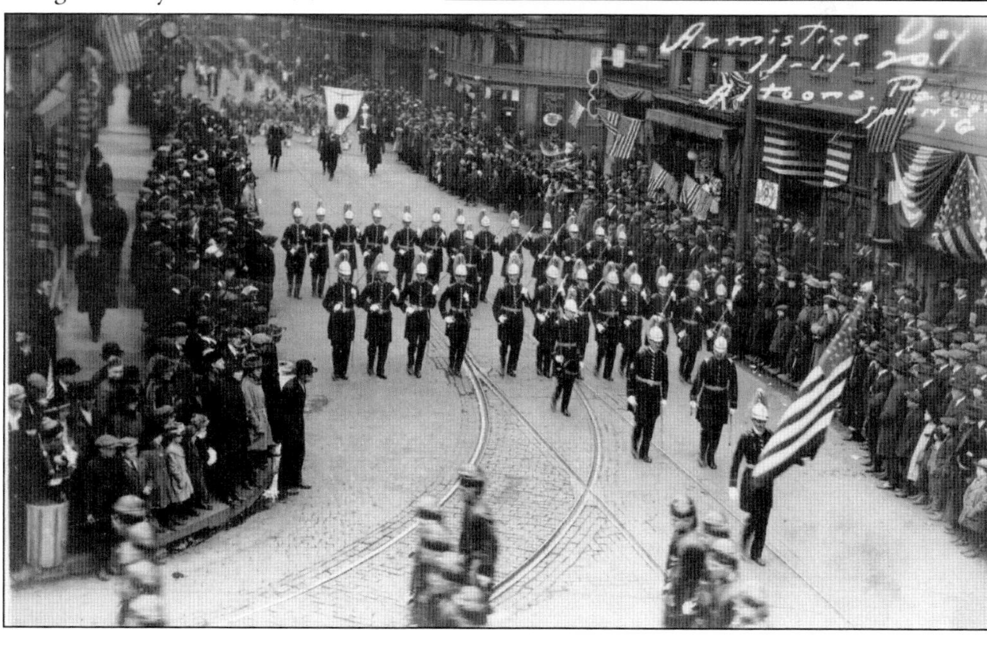

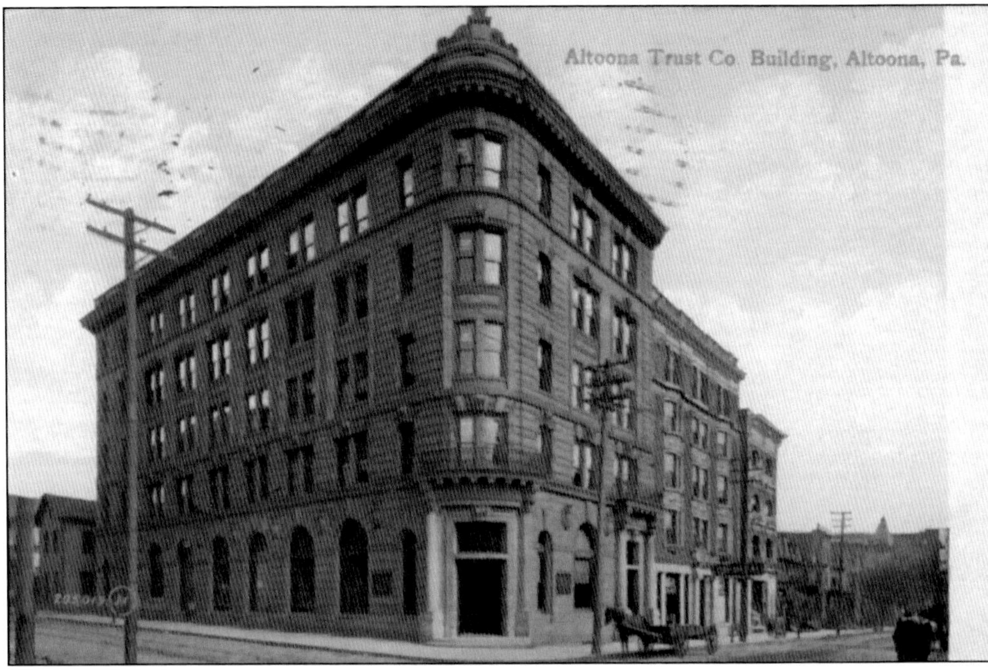

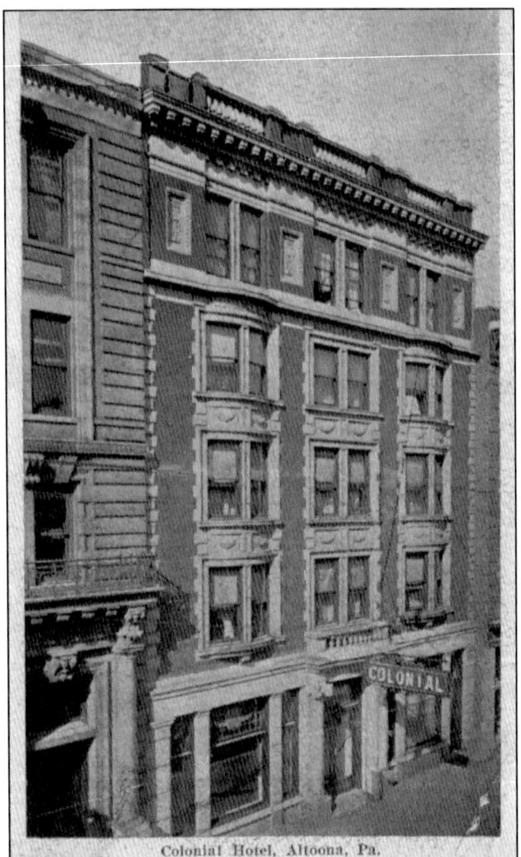

Altoona Trust Company, built 1901–1902 in the neo-classical style, is located at Twelfth Avenue and Twelfth Street in the heart of the business district, and it was the first building to have an electric elevator. Many mergers with other banking institutions occurred in succeeding years, but by the 1990s the building no longer housed any banking operations. Well maintained, this classic architecture is a staple of downtown Altoona and houses Pennsylvania's Office of Vocational Rehabilitation in 2009. Adjacent was the Colonial Hotel facing Twelfth Avenue. This postcard was postmarked January 20, 1909.

This postcard features the facade of the Colonial Hotel on Twelfth Avenue. This was a smaller but well-appointed hotel for business people, including in-hotel dining. This structure was razed in later years to provide a parking lot for Altoona Trust Company customers and its successor banking institutions, an architectural loss for the city of Altoona. The card is dated December 10, 1910.

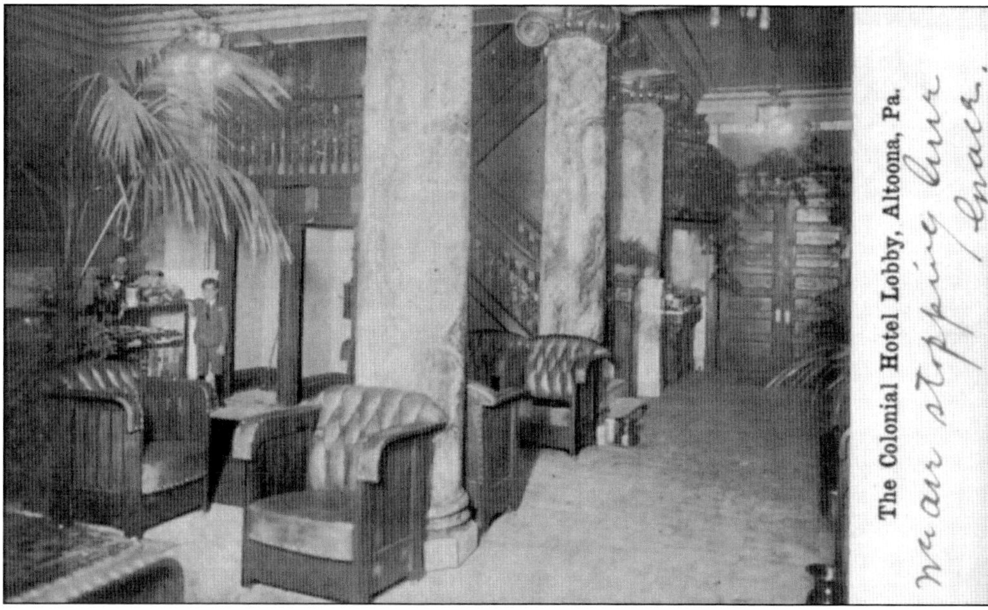

The Colonial Hotel lobby on Twelfth Avenue is shown here. A smaller hotel than the elegant Penn-Alto Hotel one block away, the Colonial nonetheless had architectural appointments and amenities that catered to the business traveler. The Corinthian style columns suggest, perhaps, Italian scagliola artificial marble. The postcard was postmarked July 16, 1909.

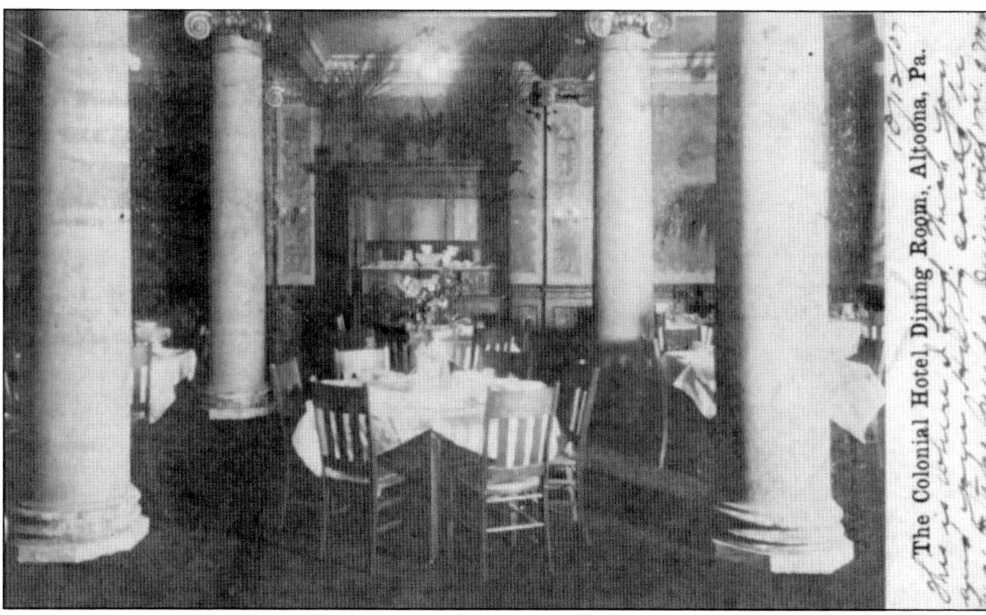

The Colonial Hotel dining room conveys elegance, intimacy, and fine-dining appointments that beckon the traveler or the restaurant patron. The architectural detail is striking, representing another lost treasure to the city in the 1950s when the adjacent bank needed the ground for additional parking and before historic preservation was much in vogue. The image is postmarked October 12, 1907.

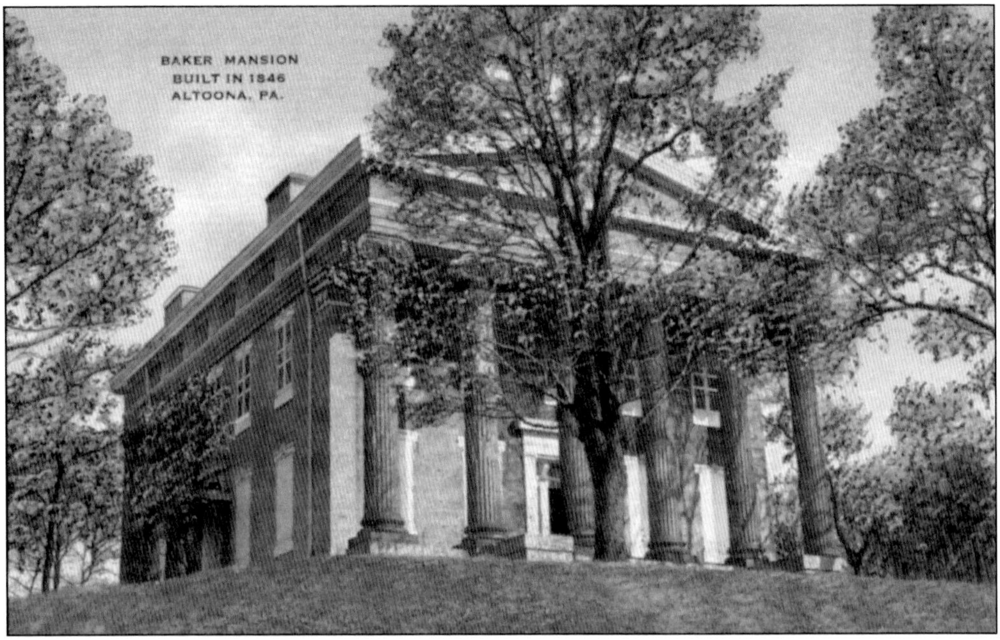

The Baker Mansion was built in 1846 (three years prior to Altoona's founding by the PRR) and is said to be one of the finest types of Greek Revival architecture in the United States. Originally the home of Ironmaster Elias Baker and his family, it now houses the Blair County Historical Society.

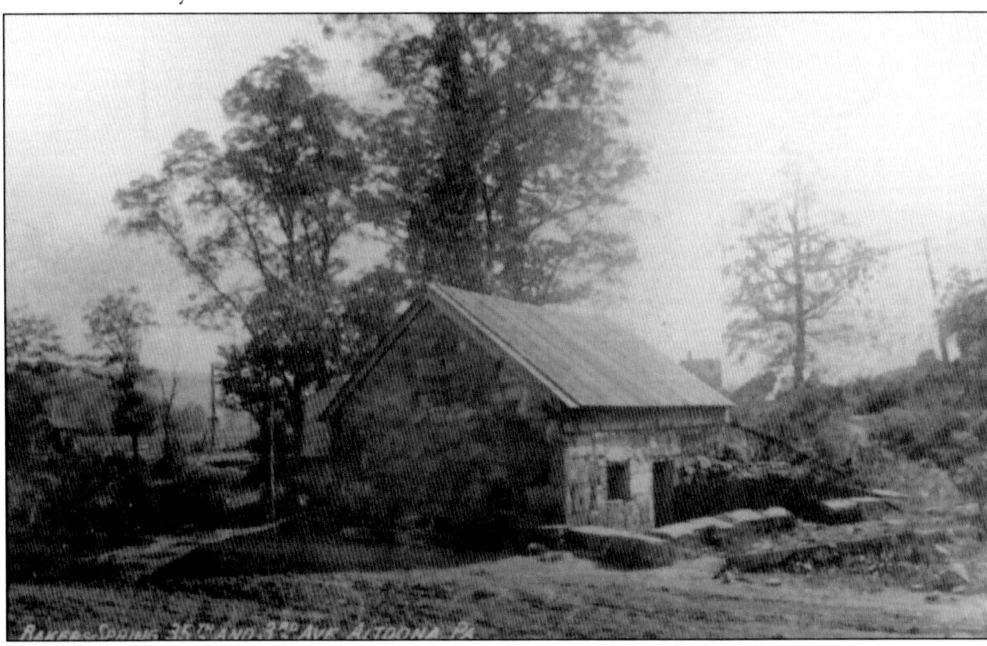

Baker Spring, pictured around the 1880s, is located at Thirty-fifth Street and Third Avenue. Part of Ironmaster Elias Baker's estate prior to the founding of Altoona by the PRR, it represents a significant portion of Altoona's history. Remaining today are elements of his Allegheny Furnace and Foreman's residence, now used by the Altoona Women's Club at Union Avenue and Crescent Road.

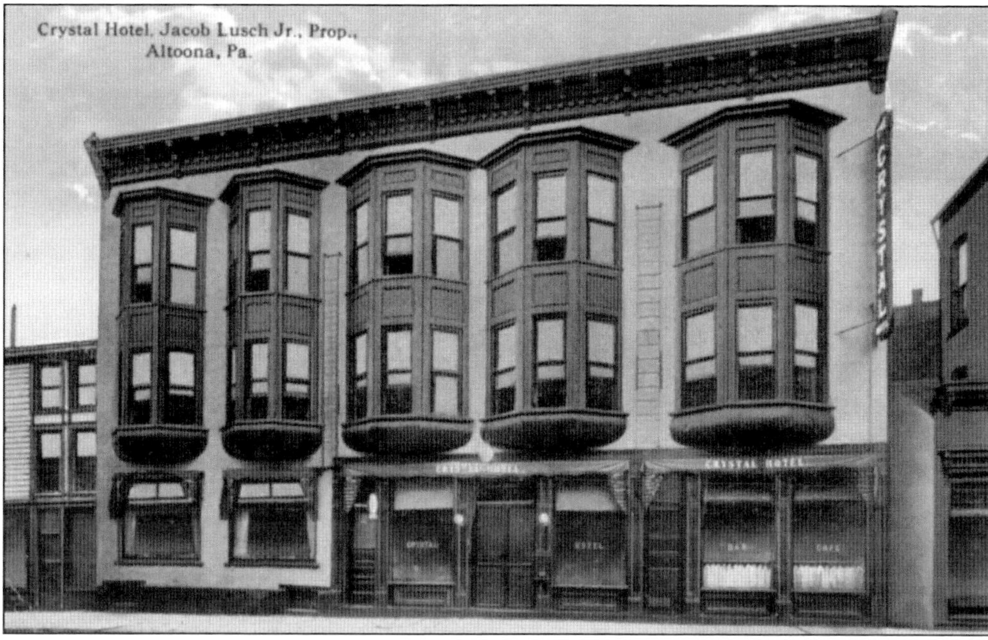

The Crystal Hotel at 1023 Green Avenue was representative of many smaller hotels throughout the city. In later years, many were converted to residential hotels with commercial businesses on the ground floor. In this view there was a bar and café, but during the 1950s, there was a cigar store and billiards hall.

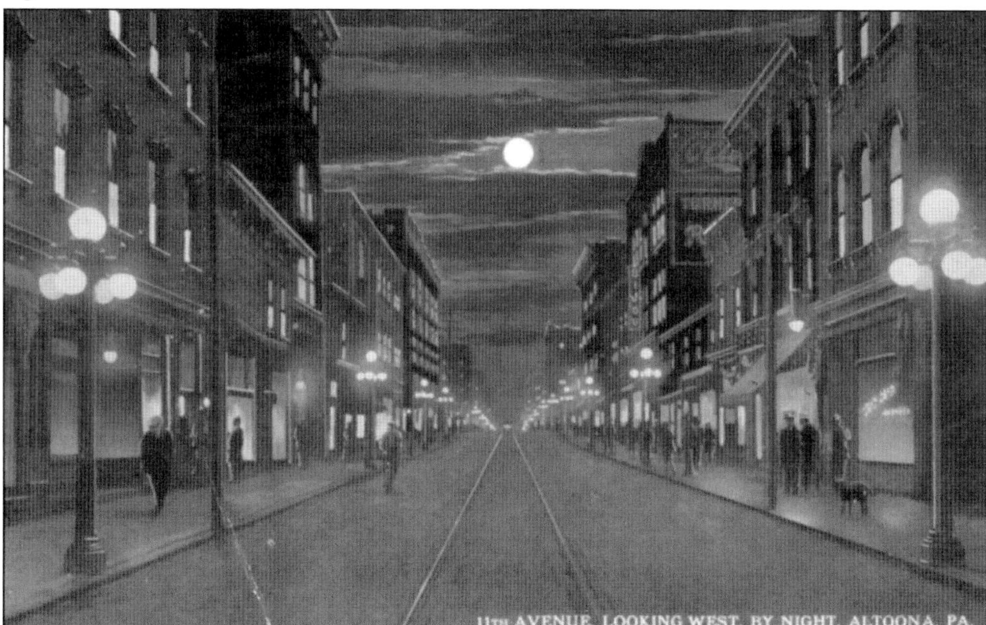

Seen here is Eleventh Avenue (the main business district street) looking west by night. Altoona's prosperity was directly tied to the PRR. With shops working three shifts and transportation crews variously in a 24-hour period, downtown Altoona was busy for most of those hours as well. Trolleys ran all night, and entertainment venues and stores and restaurants were similarly busy. This card is postmarked January 14, 1916.

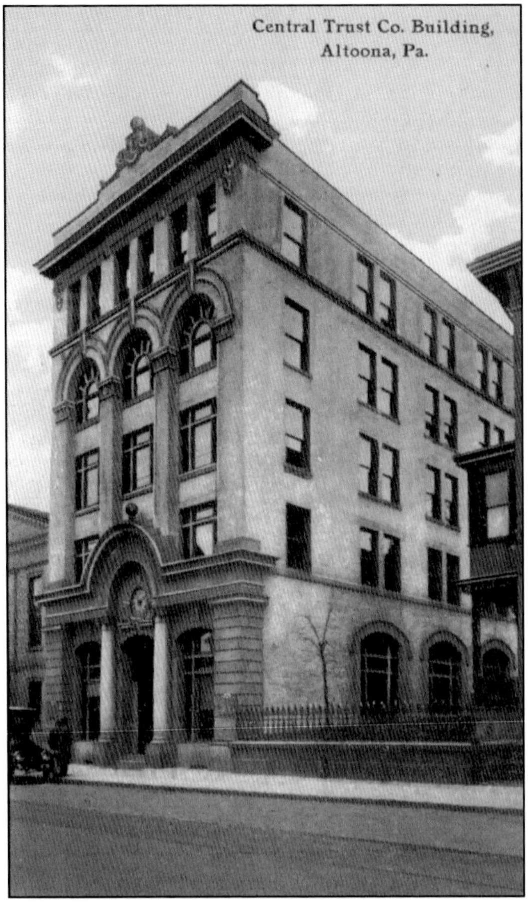

The Central Trust Company, built in 1905 and 1906, is shown at 1218 Eleventh Avenue. For many years the banking competitor of Altoona Trust Company, the two were merged after the 1950s. Almost visible to the right is the residence of the PRR general superintendent. To the left would be the Mechanic's Library and Reading Room around the second decade of the 20th century. Opposite would be the Logan House Hotel. The Central Trust building survives into the 21st century as offices and apartments.

Second Street in Juniata near Eighth Avenue is pictured here. Founded as a borough in 1893, Juniata was later annexed by Altoona but had identically numbered streets. Always referred to as "Juniata," street addresses are now formally recorded with an N (north) prefix for postal designations. Home to the Juniata Locomotive Shops (PRR, Penn Central Railroad, Conrail, and Norfolk Southern Railroad successively), Juniata was also a terminus for the Altoona Northern (Wopsononock) Railroad, a local scenic short-line. The card is postmarked April 30, 1913.

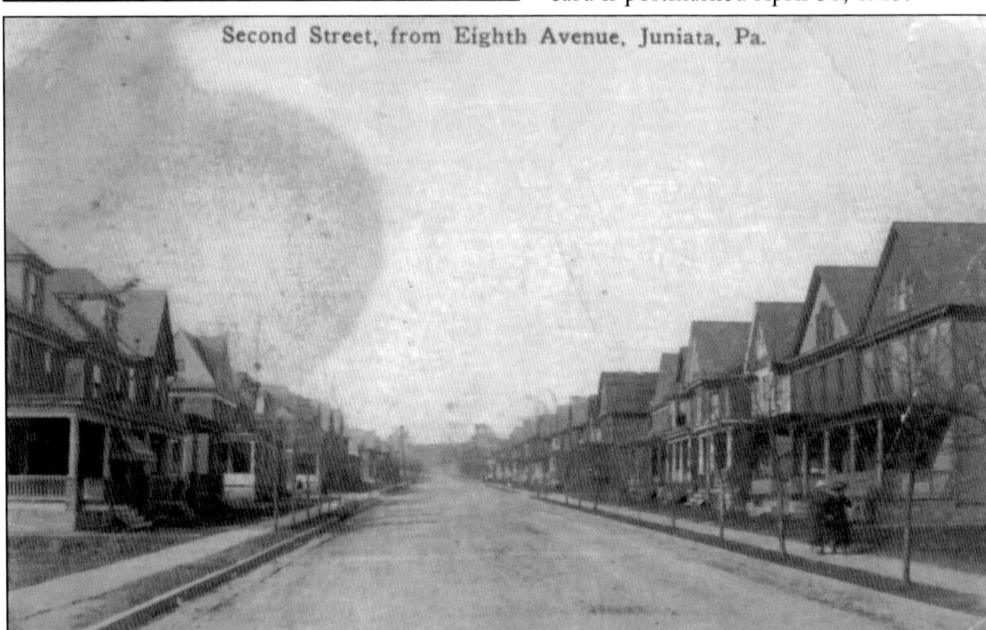

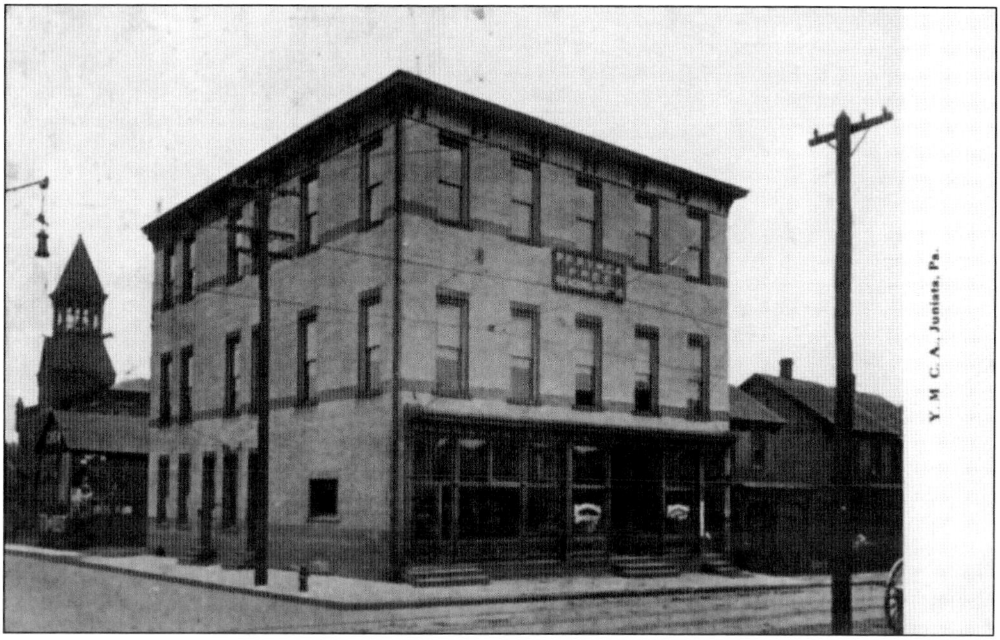

The YMCA in Juniata actually was the PRR YMCA for train crews with free reading rooms, according to the sign. Located at Fourth Avenue and Sixth Street, Juniata, the building is now used by Park Furniture Company. To the rear on the side street is a small barn advertising Mail Pouch Tobacco and the Juniata Elementary School. Juniata was later annexed into Altoona. This card is postmarked Juniata, May 24, 1909.

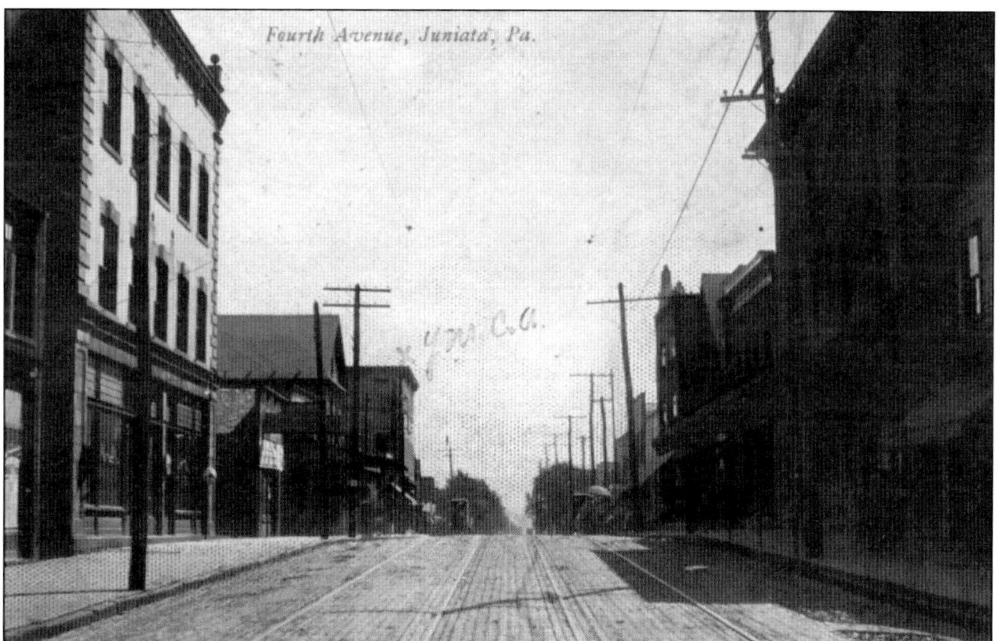

This view of Fourth Avenue in Juniata, the business district, looks west and shows the tracks of the Altoona and Logan Valley Electric Railway. The building in the distant left is the PRR YMCA that can be seen in the preceding image. The card is postmarked Juniata, March 10, 1913.

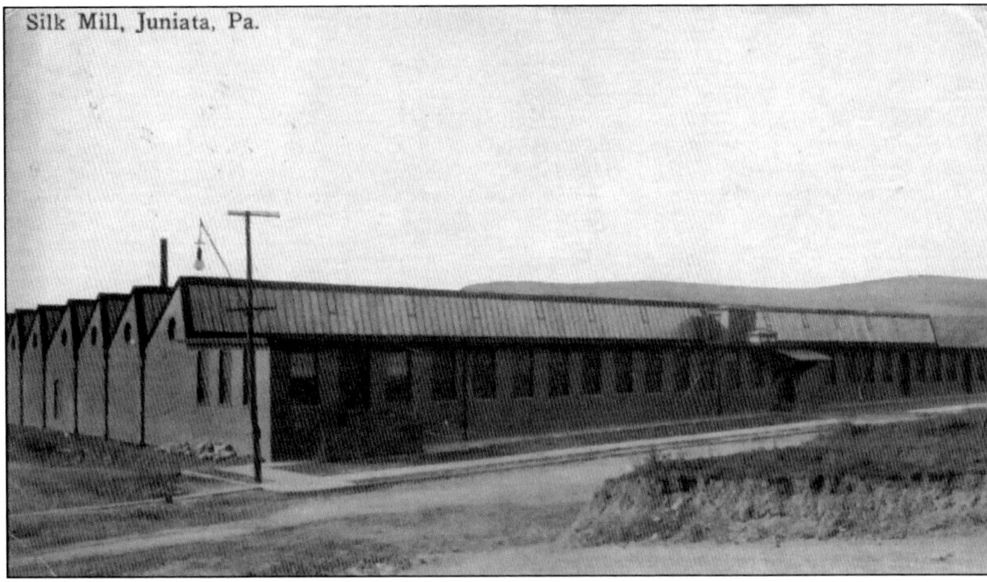

The Silk Mill in Juniata is shown here. This manufacturer started in Juniata in 1910–1911 and has changed owners over the years, but it was more familiarly known as the Schwartzenbach-Huber Company and manufactured various textile products for many years. The company is still in business as Juniata Fabrics Inc. The card is postmarked Juniata, February 20, 1917.

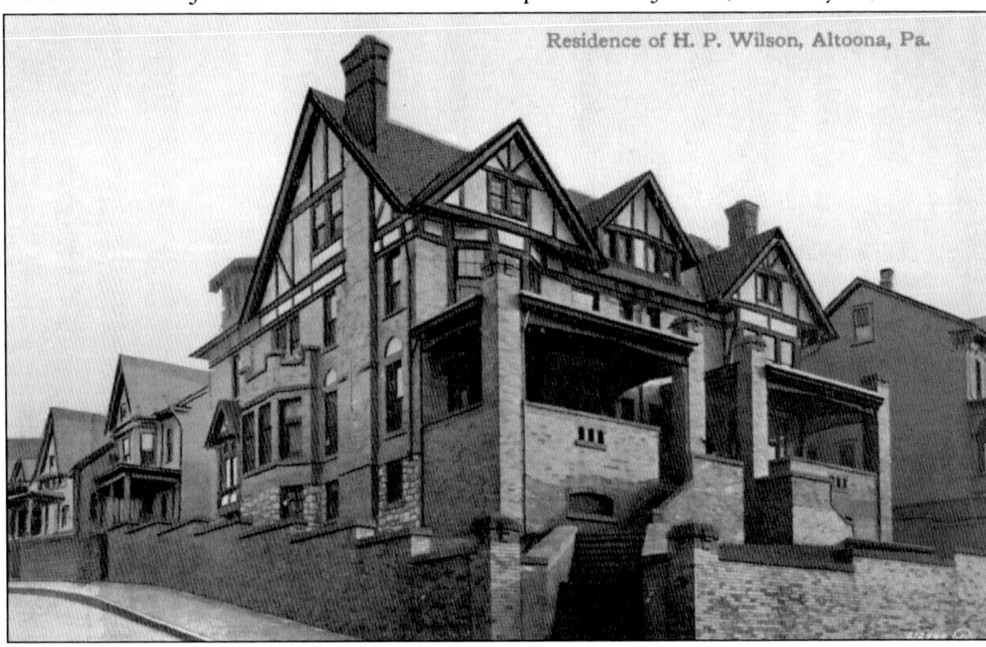

The stately residence of Hambledon P. Wilson, Altoona postmaster around 1896, was located at Fifteenth Avenue and Twelfth Street at the top of a steep hill overlooking city hall and downtown Altoona. Wilson was honored to break ground for the "new" post office and federal building when it opened in 1933 following the razing of the Logan House Hotel. This residence has been subdivided into apartments today but has most of the exterior architectural features of the 1930s. Originally a prominent duplex occupied by Wilson and Jake Sitnek, a local pharmacist, it now has eight units.

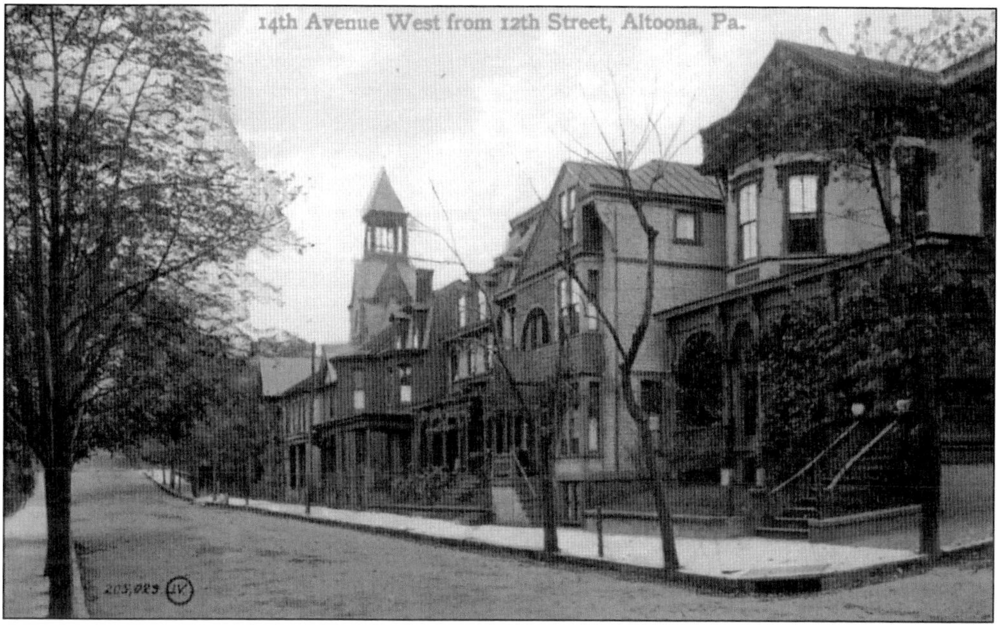

This Fourteenth Avenue view looks west from Twelfth Street. Once a fashionable street with homes belonging to city leaders, the avenue is host to rental properties today. The tower is that of Wright Elementary School, located on the corner of Thirteenth Street. This card is postmarked East Freedom, September 2, 1909.

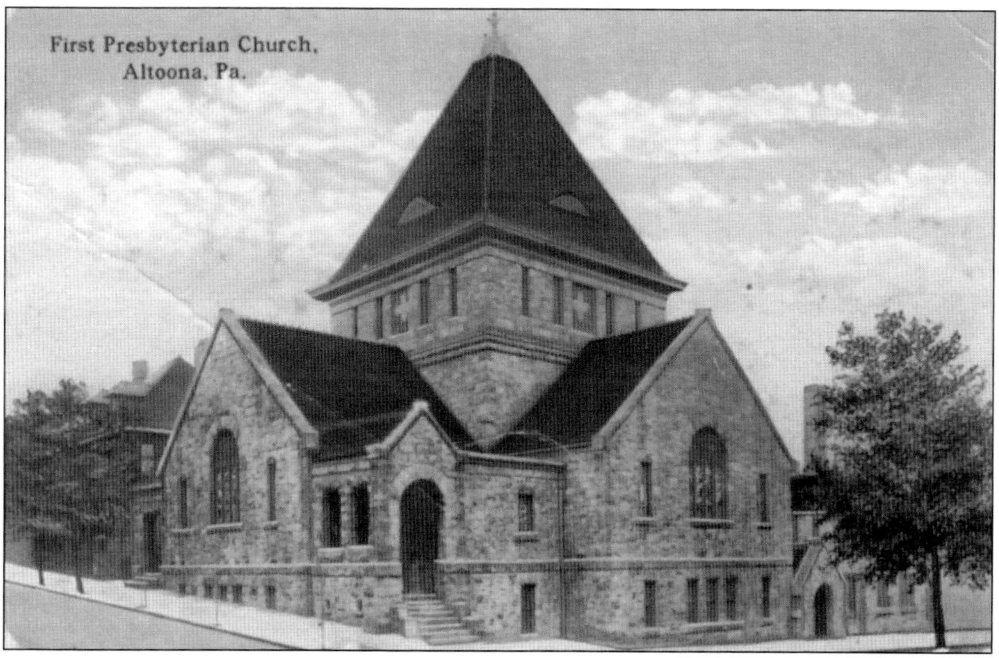

First Presbyterian Church, located at Fourteenth Avenue and Twelfth Street, was photographed from the opposite corner as seen in the preceding image (above). Forced to merge with another Presbyterian church in the first decade of the 21st century, the original architecture is still as constructed with Spanish tile roof and meticulous stonework; it is a landmark in downtown Altoona opposite city hall.

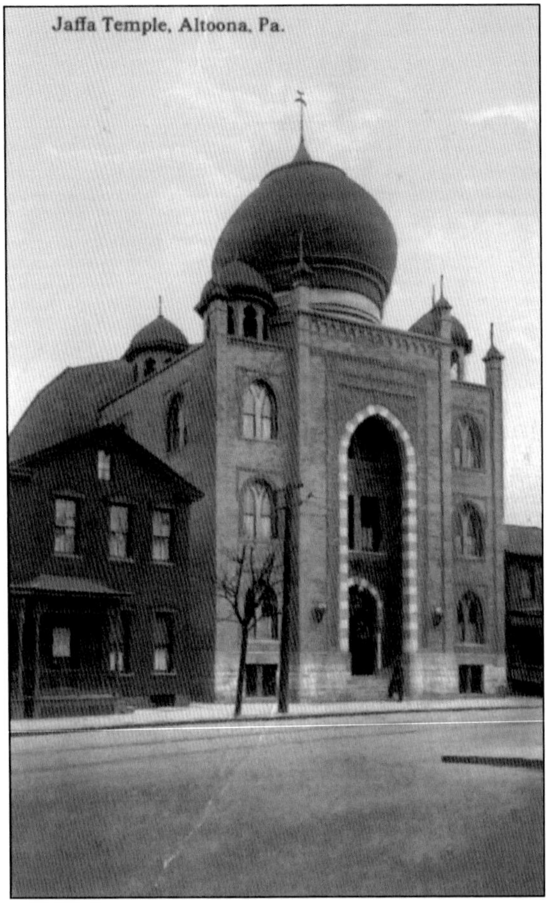

Jaffa Temple was located at Chestnut Avenue and Seventh Street in the first half of the 20th century. The Masonic temple was relocated to a new facility seen in the image next, around 1927. The image is postmarked East Freedom, August 10, 1913.

The new Jaffa Temple was erected around 1927 on Broad Avenue occupying an entire city block between Twenty-second and Twenty-third Streets, formerly home to the stately John Lloyd Mansion and Lloyd Park. Jaffa Temple is noted for its large auditorium and exhibit floor, which is a focus for many community events, including an annual circus. Many activities benefit Shriners' Children's Hospitals.

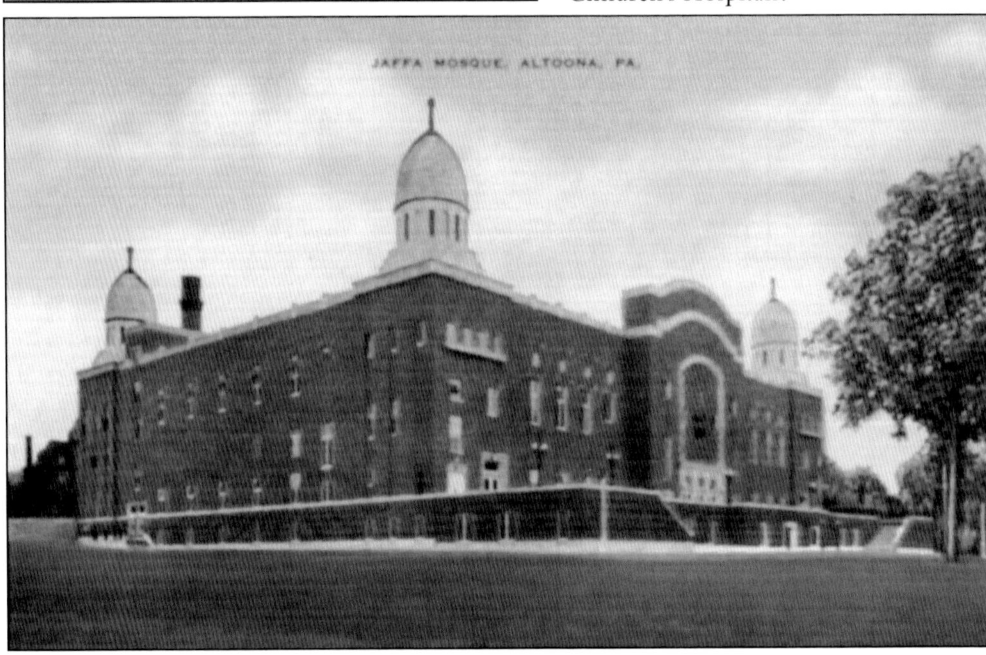

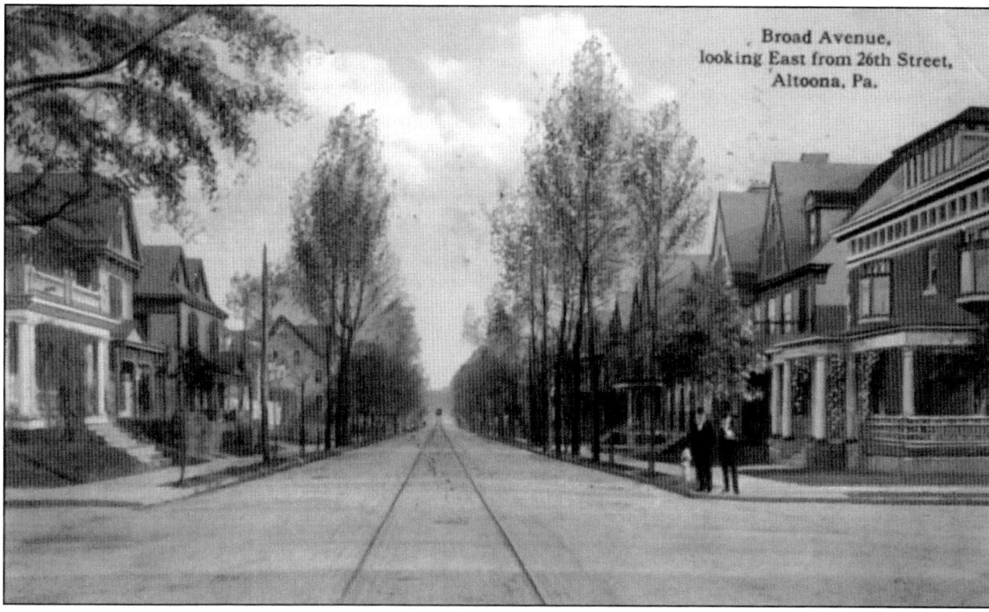

This view of Broad Avenue looks east from Twenty-sixth Street. Broad Avenue was noted for its upscale homes and mansions, yellow-brick paving, and a line of the Altoona and Logan Valley Electric Railway. The view is inbound to downtown, but the opposite direction is toward Hollidaysburg via Lakemont Amusement Park. This card is postmarked October 26, 1914.

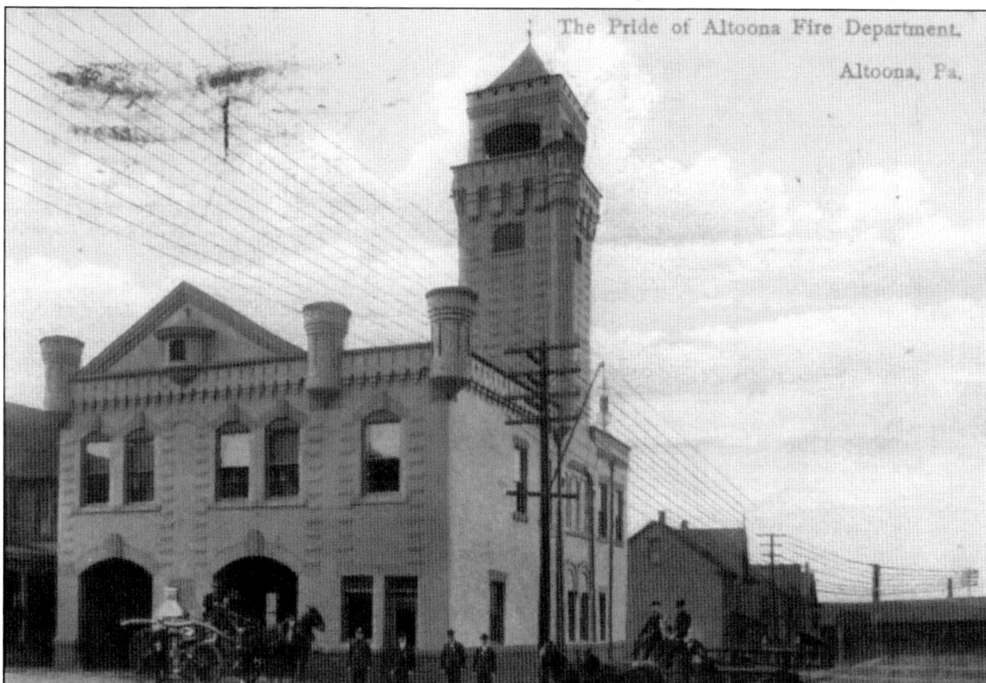

The Pride of the Altoona Fire Department was the firefighting station at Fifth Avenue and Third Street. Clearly visible is the horse-drawn pumper in front of the station in this view around 1900. This structure still stands, but it is no longer used for firefighting. This card is postmarked August 28, 1909.

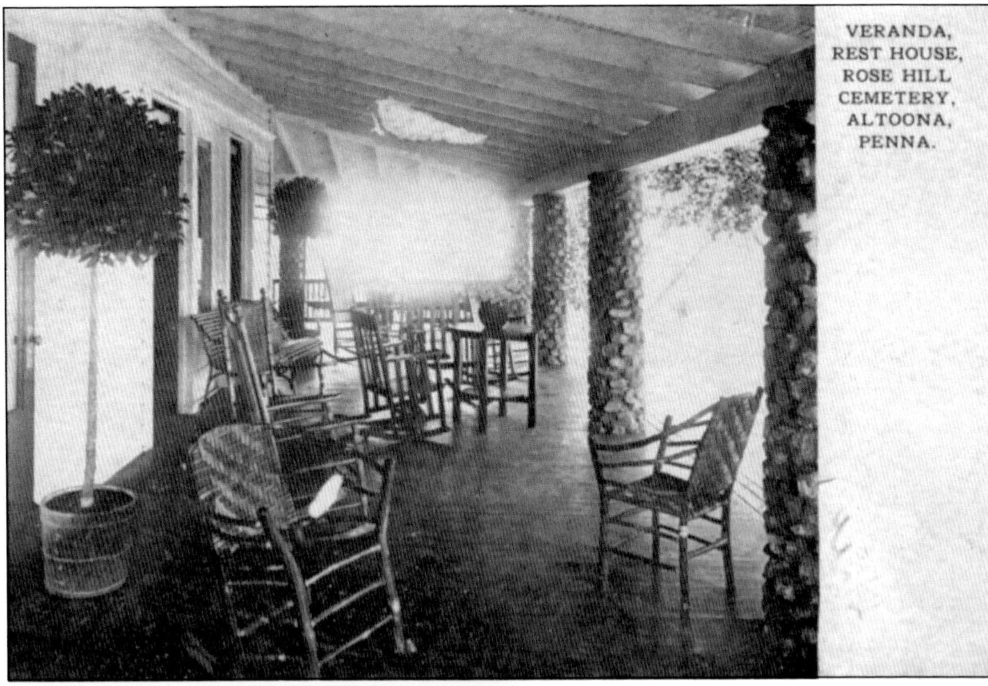

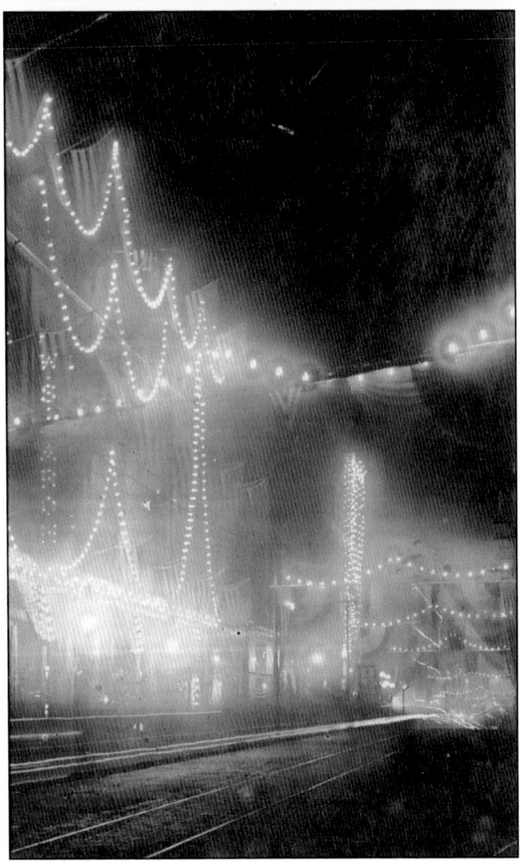

The veranda of the rest house at Rose Hill Cemetery is seen here. This cemetery on a hillside overlooking east Altoona was also served by the Altoona and Logan Valley Railway, whose tracks ended on South Street at the cemetery entrance. A special trolley was outfitted for funeral purposes to transport the deceased and family to the cemetery gate.

This is a rare vintage evening image of downtown Altoona at Christmastime. It is believed this image is of the W. S. Aaron Furniture Store on Twelfth Avenue near Fifteenth Street. A streak of light is that of a passing automobile as the tracks of the Altoona and Logan Valley Electric Railway glisten from the lights. The card is postmarked June 20, 1913, which may date the image to December 1912.

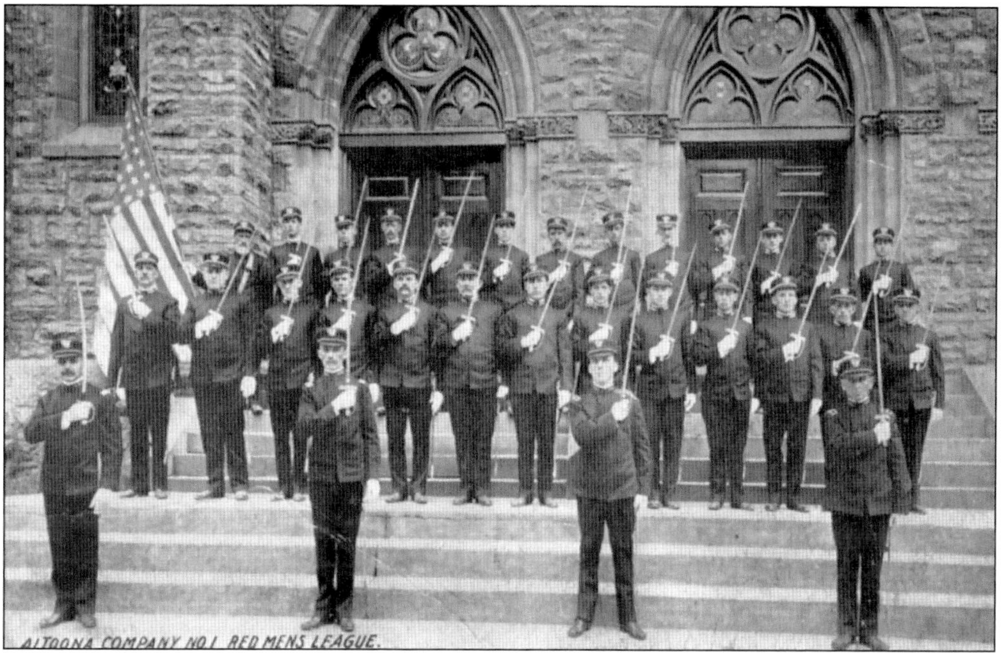

Altoona Company No. 1 of the Red Men's League poses on the steps of First Lutheran Church in downtown Altoona. Altoona, like most cities, had many fraternal organizations, especially pre-1950. This was likely a patriotic occasion, perhaps prior to or after a parade on Independence Day.

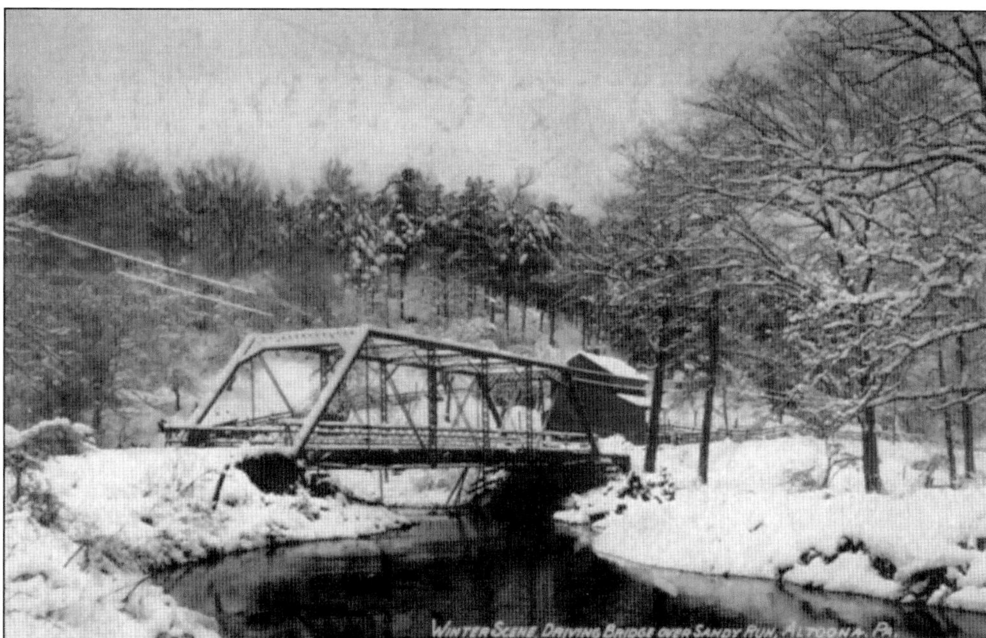

This winter scene illustrates the truss bridge over Sandy Run near Altoona. The industrial city of Altoona with its massive railroad shops and classifications yards had compact urbanization, surrounded by mountains and foothills, which made it possible for anyone to enjoy the rural elements with ease. This postcard is undated.

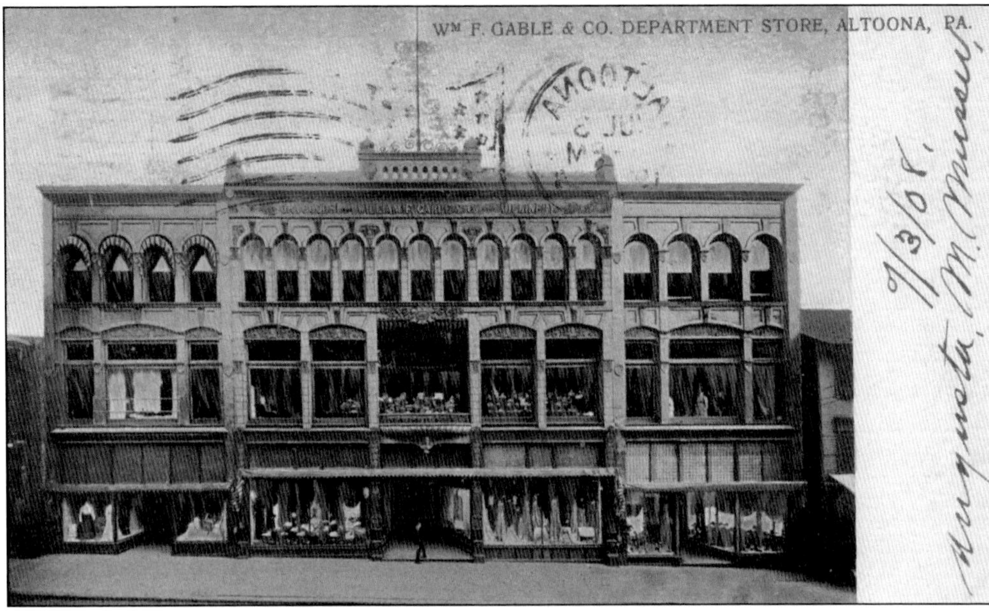

Known as "The Daylight Store," William F. Gable and Company began in a small 20- by 40-foot room at Eleventh Avenue and Thirteenth Street on March 1, 1884, and it continually expanded from there. In the early 20th century, this edifice in the 1300 block of Eleventh Avenue contained five floors and 45 departments. The business was the preeminent downtown Altoona department store until it closed in 1980. This card is postmarked July 3, 1908.

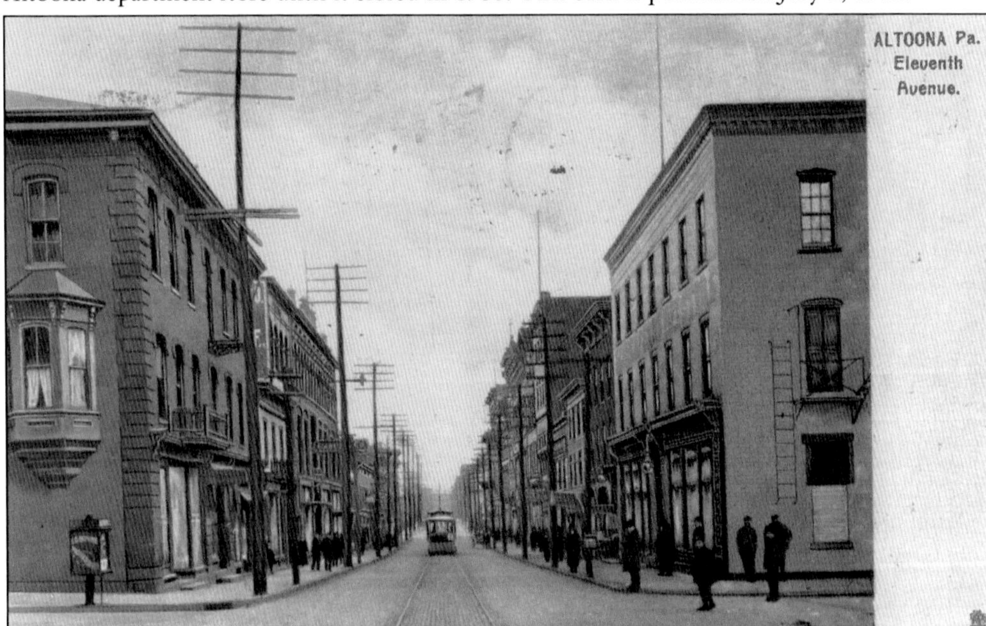

In this view of Eleventh Avenue, Altoona's main business district street, William F. Gable and Company is mid-block on the left. Later expansions demolished the corner structure on the left and two new buildings, facing Eleventh and Twelfth Avenues (back-to-back), each four stories high, became the focal point of the retail activity in center city. This card is postmarked Altoona, June 19, 1908.

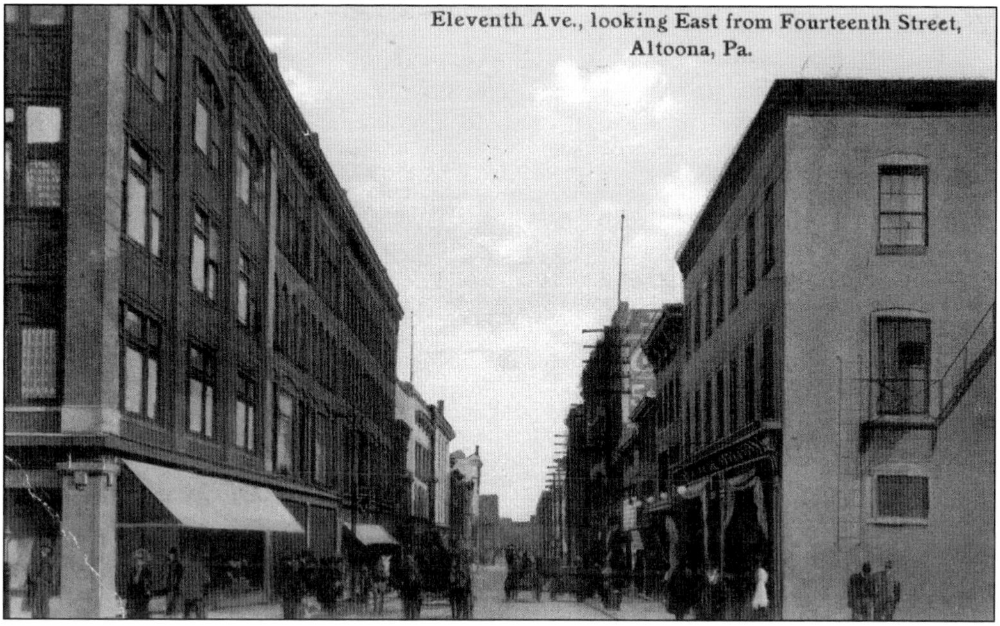

Succeeding the previous view, William F. Gable and Company has enlarged to the corner of Fourteenth Street on Eleventh Avenue. The new building dramatically expanded the number of departments and range of services, noted for everything from fine clothing and jewelry, to housewares and home furnishings. The arcade in the Twelfth Avenue building was popular with shoppers, as were the store's two restaurants. Groceries and fine meats were also offered through the World War II era. This card is postmarked November 12, 1911.

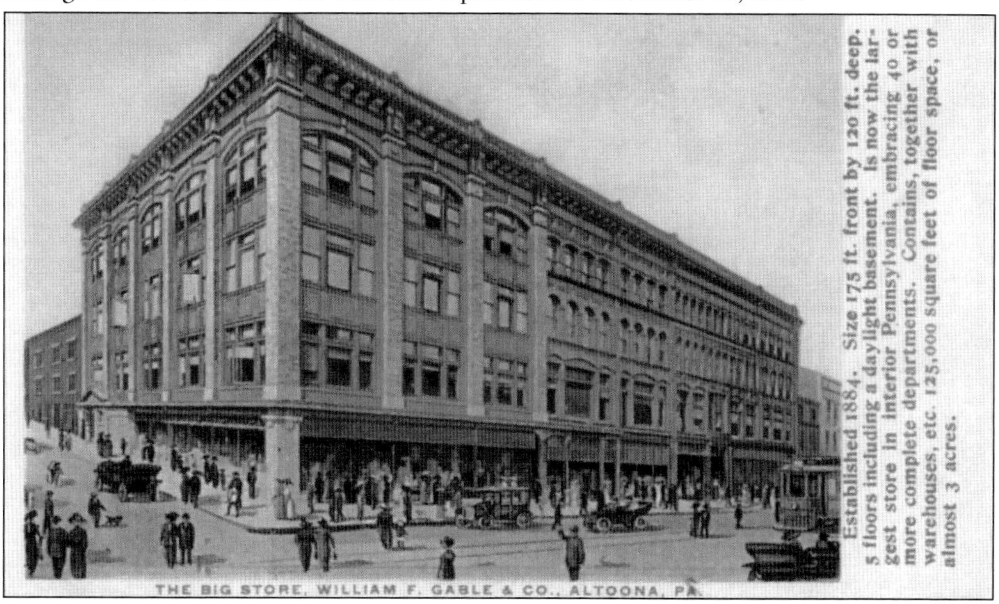

Later known as Gable and Company Department Store, this view has the new Eleventh Avenue building depicted in the second decade of the 20th century. The Twelfth Avenue building to the extreme left of the photograph has not yet been constructed. At one time, the sidewalk had glass blocks that permitted light into the basement salesroom where customers could hear pedestrians walking overhead.

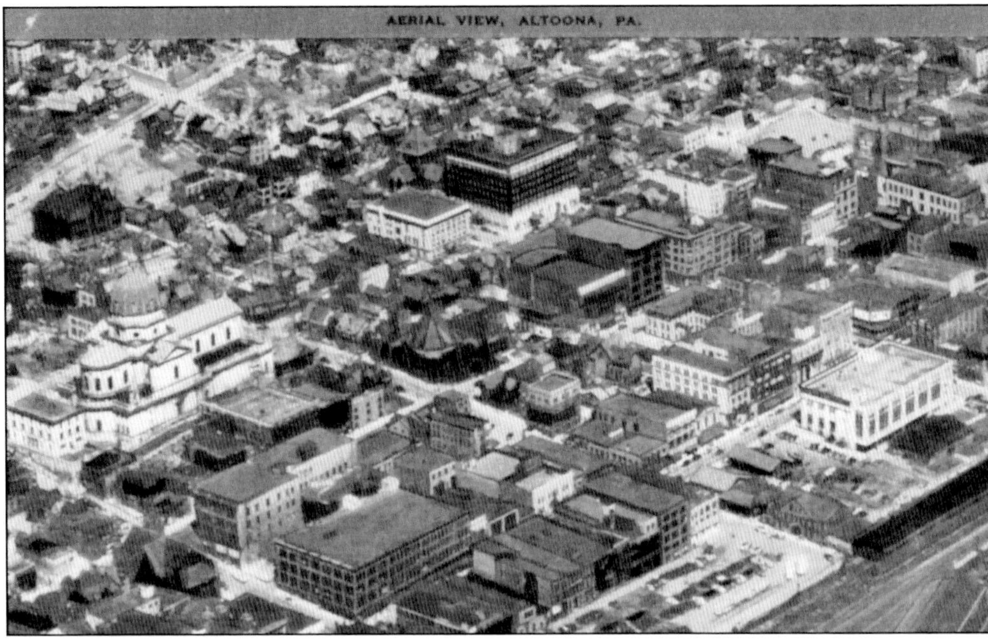

This aerial view of center city Altoona was taken around the 1950s. The Cathedral of the Blessed Sacrament is at the middle left and the PRR passenger station and post office are at the bottom right. City hall and the Penn-Alto Hotel can be seen at top center. The card is postmarked October 9, 1955.

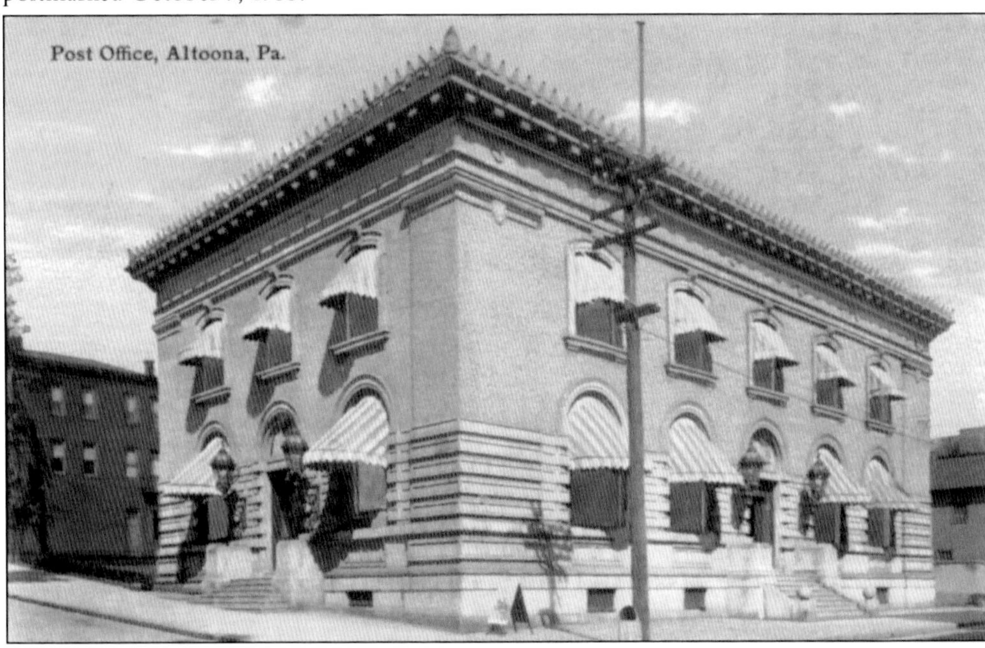

The old post office was constructed in 1901–1902 and demolished in 1933 when the new post office opened. It featured Second Renaissance Revival architecture with a rusticated ground level, a modillioned cornice, a monumental entry portal, and stone window frames. The architecture was remarkable, but the site became an Amoco full-service gasoline station in 1944. This postcard is postmarked December 12, 1913.

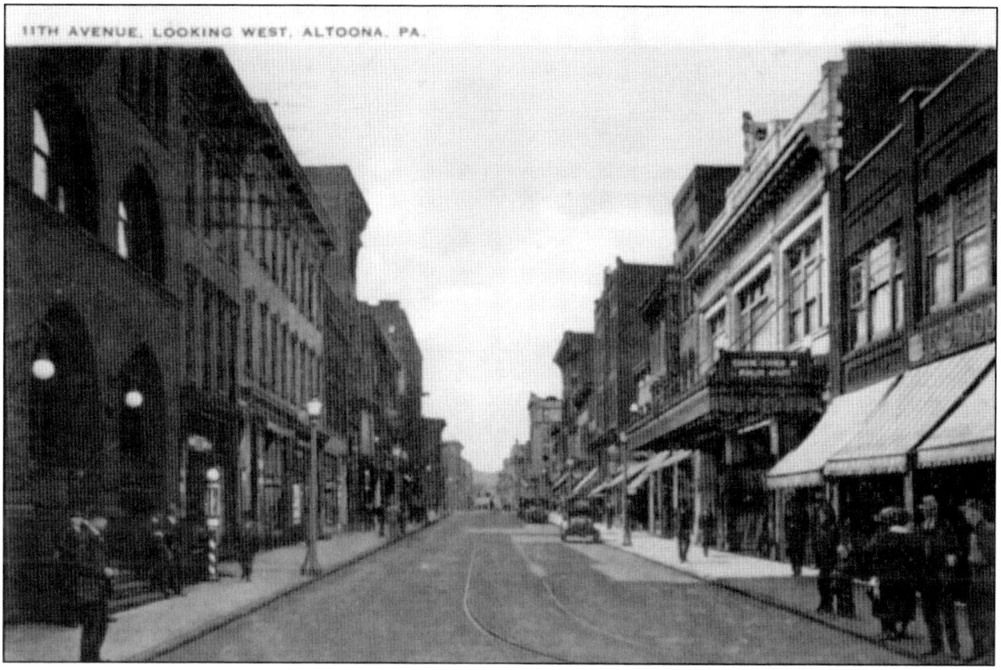

This view of Eleventh Avenue looks west from Eleventh Street. On the left is the Altamont Hotel. The buildings on the right replaced the Eleventh Avenue Opera House, which was destroyed by fire June 14, 1907. The building with the marquee is the new Olympic Theatre, built by the Alex Notopolous family. The card is postmarked August 23, 1923.

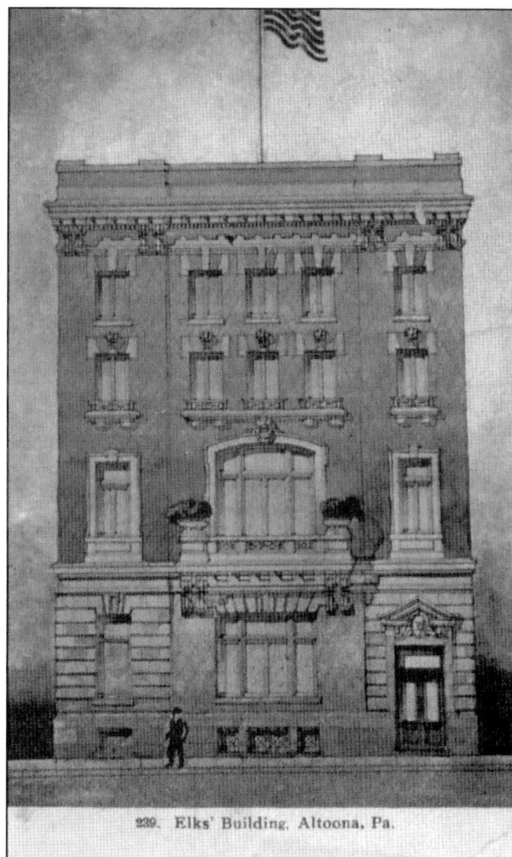

The front facade of the Benevolent and Protective Order of the Elks lodge on Twelfth Street near city hall is shown as built following a disastrous fire in October 19, 1906, which also destroyed the Rothert Department Store and the Mishler Theatre nearby. Today, the building has lost some of its architectural ornamentation and is home to the Altoona Community Theatre.

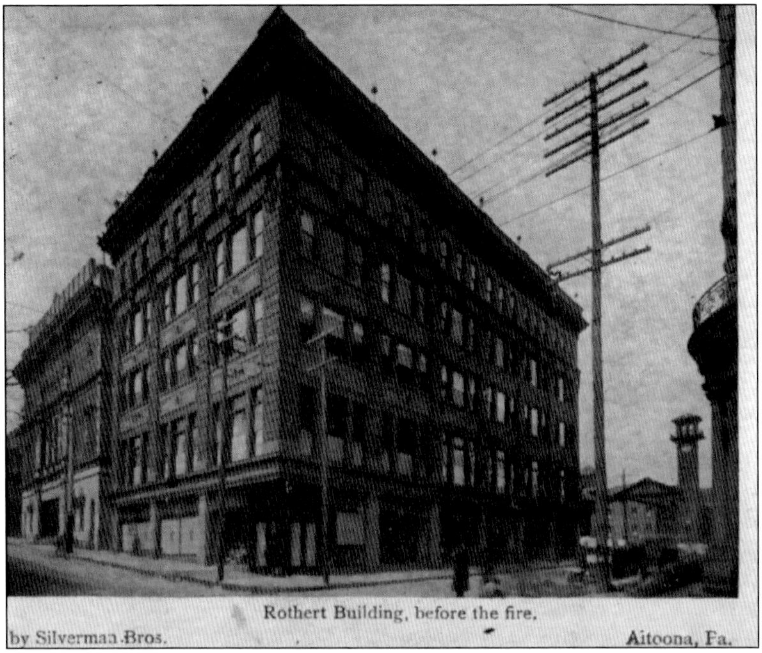

The Rothert Department store is shown prior to the October 19, 1906 fire that destroyed the store, the Mishler Theatre (left) and the Elks building (rear). The tower at the right side of the photograph is the hose tower of the Vigilant Volunteer Fire Company in the city building. The fire was one of Altoona's worst. The card is postmarked Juniata, July 23, 1914.

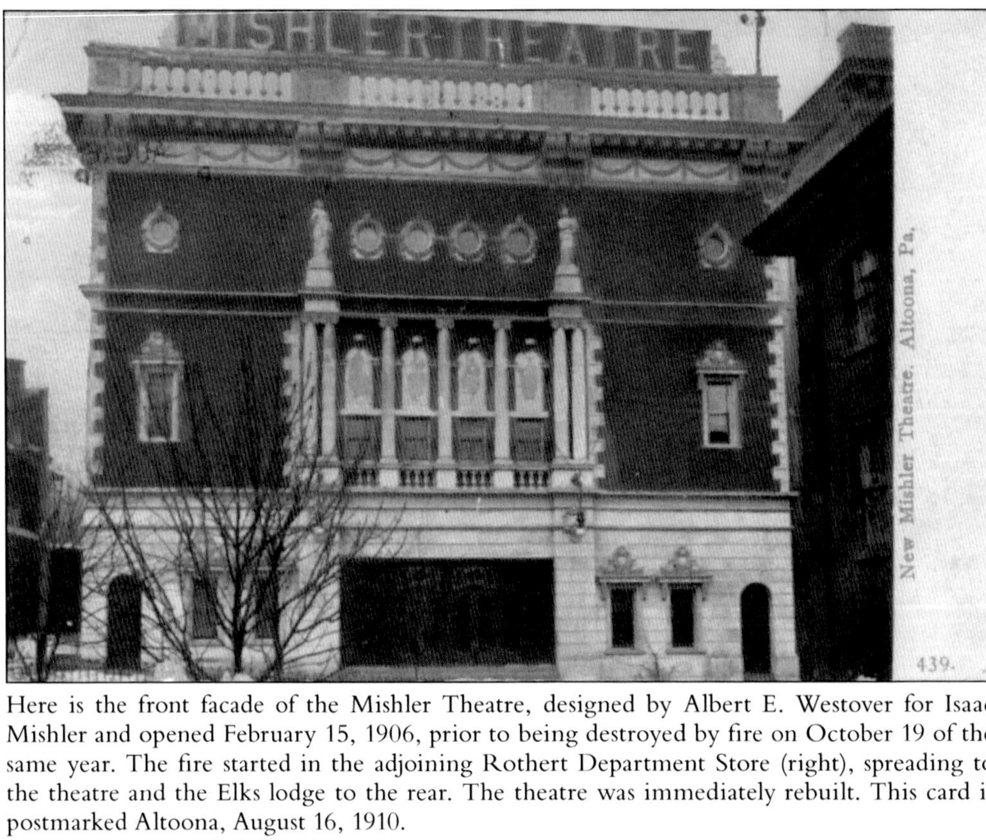

Here is the front facade of the Mishler Theatre, designed by Albert E. Westover for Isaac Mishler and opened February 15, 1906, prior to being destroyed by fire on October 19 of the same year. The fire started in the adjoining Rothert Department Store (right), spreading to the theatre and the Elks lodge to the rear. The theatre was immediately rebuilt. This card is postmarked Altoona, August 16, 1910.

This view west on Twelfth Avenue shows the Altoona Trust Company, Rothert Department Store, and the front facade of the Mishler Theatre prior to the fire of October 19, 1906.

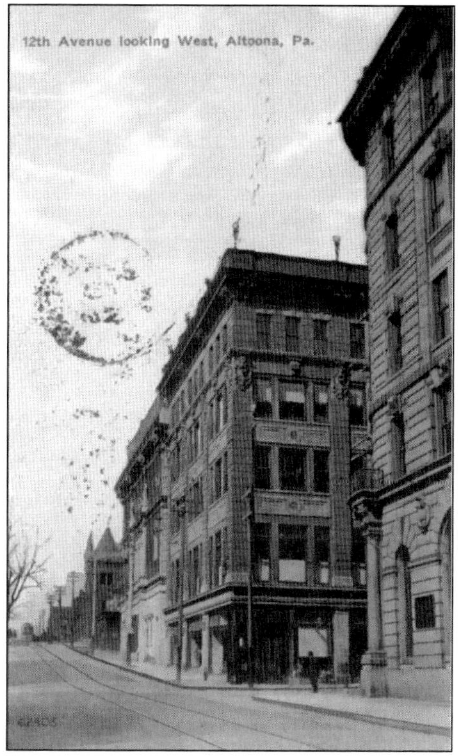

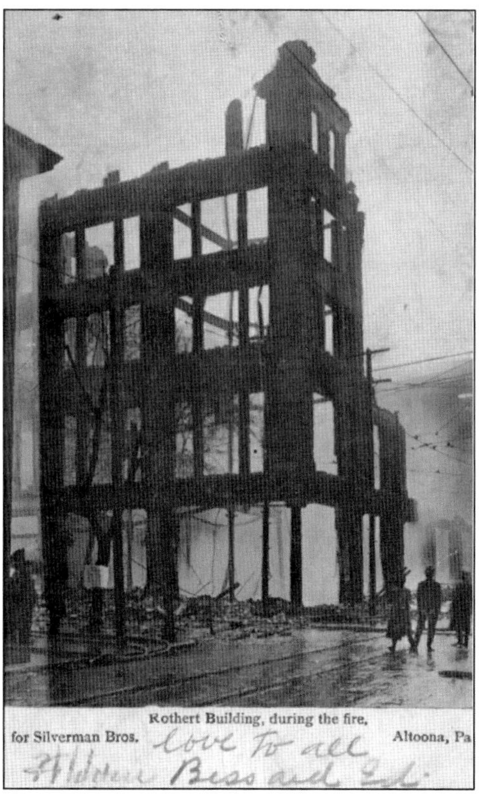

These are the ruins of the Rothert Department Store on October 19, 1906. The fire also consumed the adjacent Mishler Theatre to the left and the Elks building to the rear. The card is postmarked February 13, 1912, two months before the great steamship *Titanic* sank in the North Atlantic.

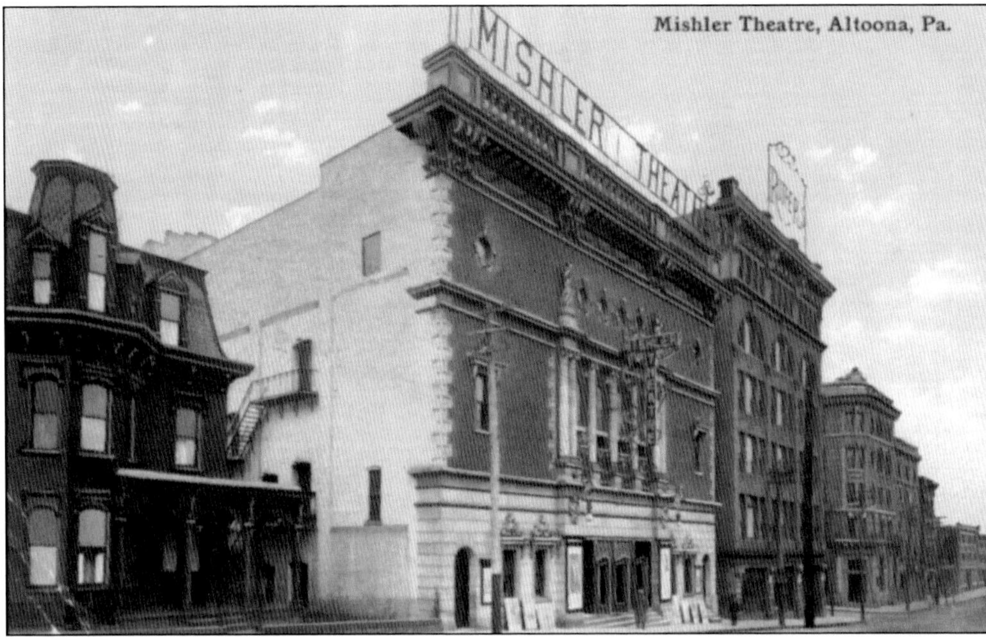

This easterly view on Twelfth Avenue shows the rebuilt Mishler Theatre and Rothert department store in 1907, following the fire that destroyed both on October 19, 1906. The arched windows in the department store are the architectural feature that changed from pre-fire images of square windows. Mishler Theatre today is home to the performing arts, but only after falling into disrepair and narrowly ducking the wrecker's ball in the late 1960s.

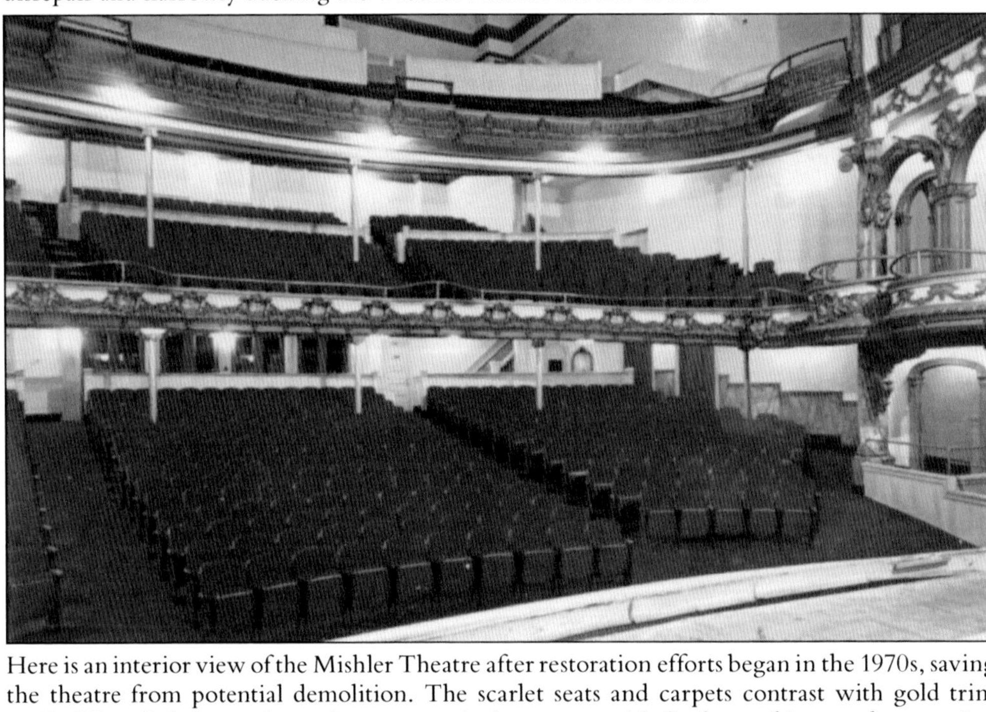

Here is an interior view of the Mishler Theatre after restoration efforts began in the 1970s, saving the theatre from potential demolition. The scarlet seats and carpets contrast with gold trim and brilliant lighting, enhanced even more in later years with further architectural restoration under the leadership of Altoona artist/preservationist John Rita.

The Orpheum Theatre on Eleventh Street is home to the Keith Vaudeville Company. Begun as Mountain City Theatre in 1887, which was destroyed by fire on March 5, 1888, it was rebuilt as the Lyric Theatre and reopened in 1906 but was destroyed by fire on February 24, 1907. The Lyric was rebuilt in 1908 and opened as the Orpheum but later changed its name to Embassy Theatre. In the 1930s, the Embassy became the Penn Theatre, which was razed in 1951. This card was postmarked November 29, 1911.

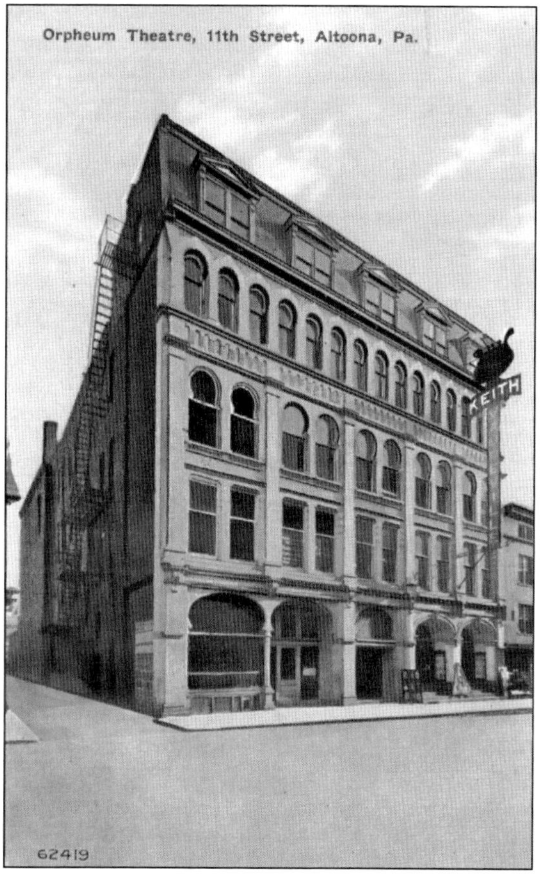

The Lyric Theatre, destroyed by fire on February 24, 1907, was previously the Mountain City Theatre, which was itself destroyed by fire on March 5, 1888. The Lyric was rebuilt in 1908 and renamed the Orpheum. Later name changes included the Embassy and the Penn Theatre (1930s). The building was razed in 1951. The card was postmarked April 17, 1907.

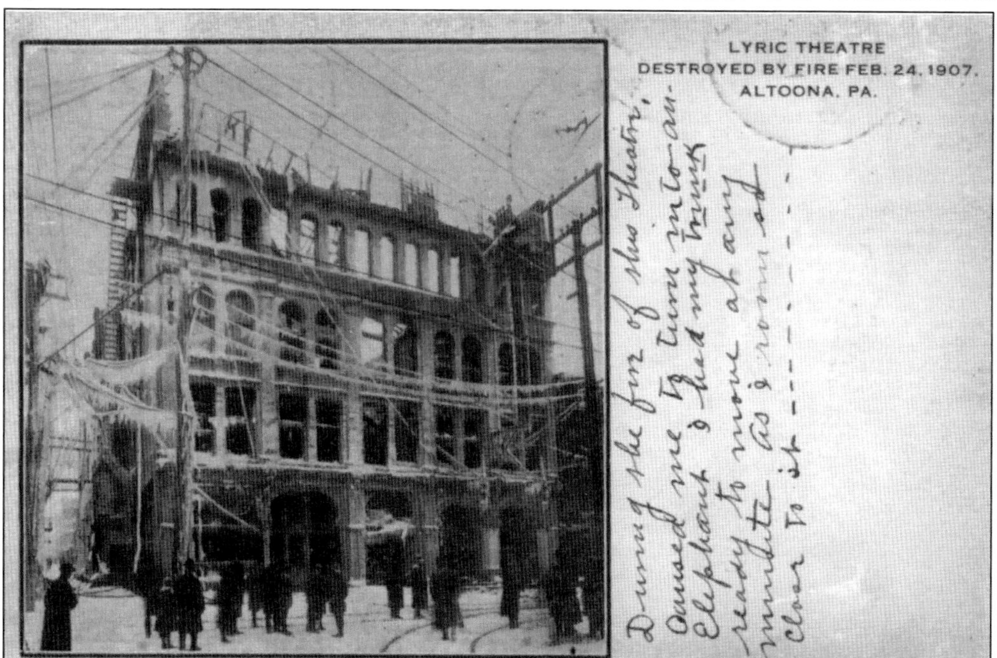

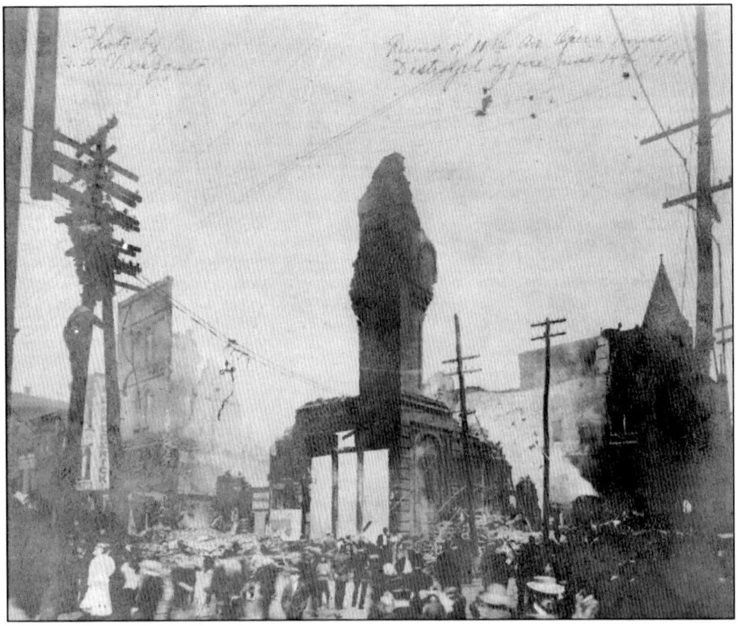

These are the ruins of the Eleventh Avenue Opera House, destroyed by fire on June 14, 1907. The first floor housed the Baltzell Department Store with the theatre on the second level. Originally built in 1868 as the Altoona Market House, it was remodeled in the 1870s to the Opera House by Charles B. Rouss. Closed for remodeling in the 1880s, it reopened October 1, 1888.

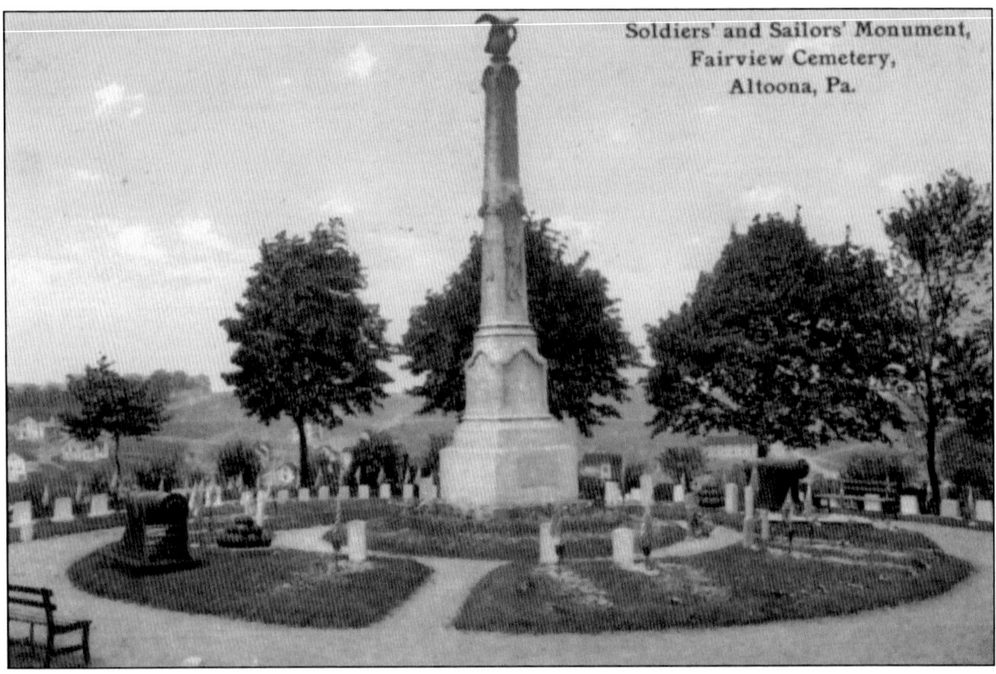

The Soldier's and Sailor's Monument in Fairview Cemetery sits at the pinnacle of a hill atop a central promenade approach, and contains the graves of honored veterans, many from the Civil War. Altoona's Memorial Day and Veteran's Day parades finished here until 1960, when the Robert E. Laws Veteran's Mall was constructed downtown. Fairview Cemetery is noted for many of Altoona's early founders, leaders, and railroad officials. This card is postmarked March 25, 1912.

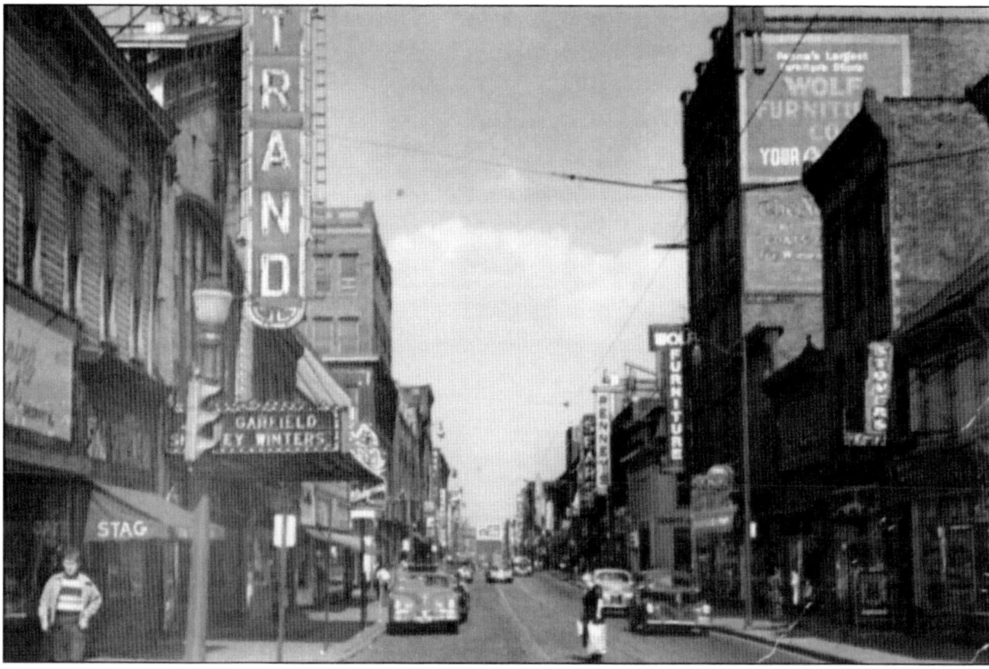

A 1951 view east on Eleventh Avenue from Sixteenth Street shows the elegant Strand Theatre on the left and the principal retail stores of local merchants. The tracks of the Altoona and Logan Valley Electric Railway were to be short-lived, with service ending in July 1954. In the 1980s, most merchants migrated to a new mall and downtown was never the same.

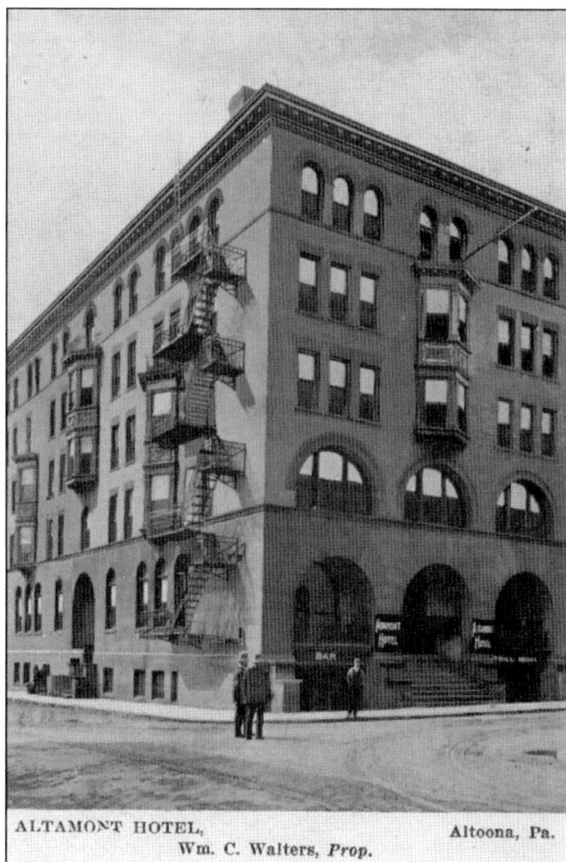

The Altamont Hotel is shown at the corner of Eleventh Avenue and Eleventh Street. Known in its history as the Corrine Hotel and Wayne Hotel, it was razed by the 1950s. Located just two blocks from the PRR passenger station, it was easily accessible to travelers.

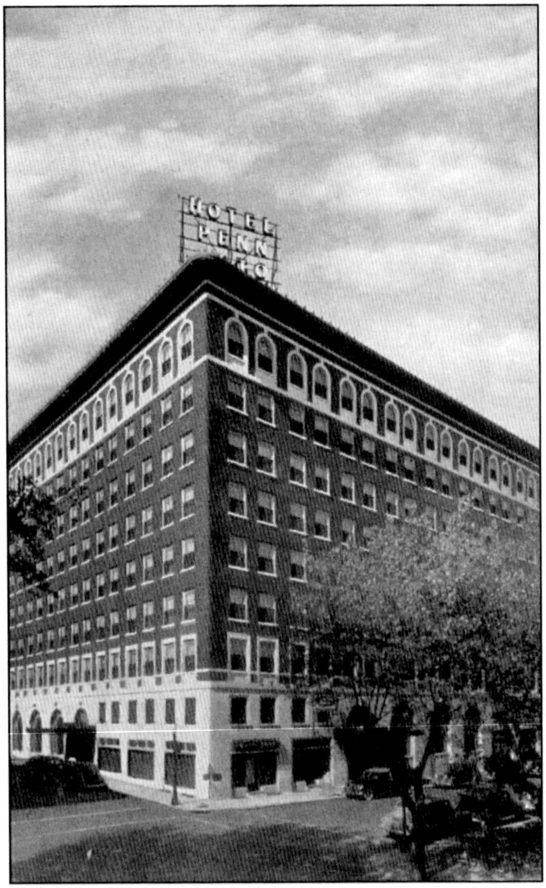

Altoona's premier luxury hotel, the Penn-Alto was constructed in 1919–1920 in the Second Renaissance Revival style, and it became the focal place for premier lodging conventions and Altoona society events. The first and second stories were faced with Bedford limestone, denoting the public spaces in the building. It was designed by George H. Stevens and Company of New York and Chicago.

The large and spacious lobby of the Hotel Penn-Alto (below) suggests luxury at every turn. This card advertised the Mayfair Room entertainment with Ruth Gillmore, "Queen of the Keyboards" on organ and piano; the Mayfair Room cocktail hour, and the Sunday evening smorgasbord in the Logan Room. Herbert A. Hanson was the manager. The card was postmarked February 7, 1952.

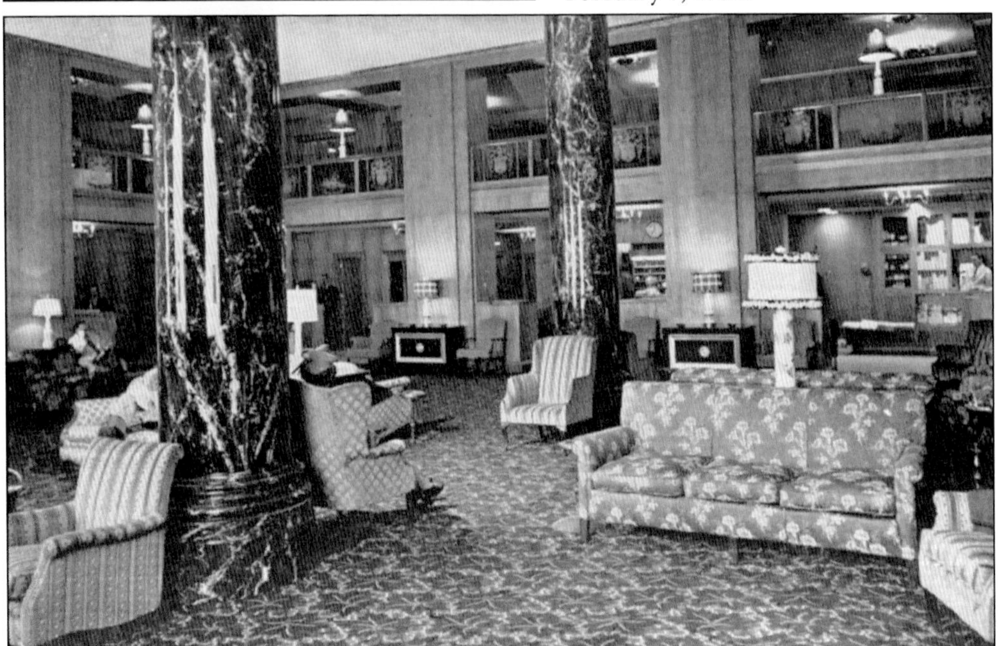

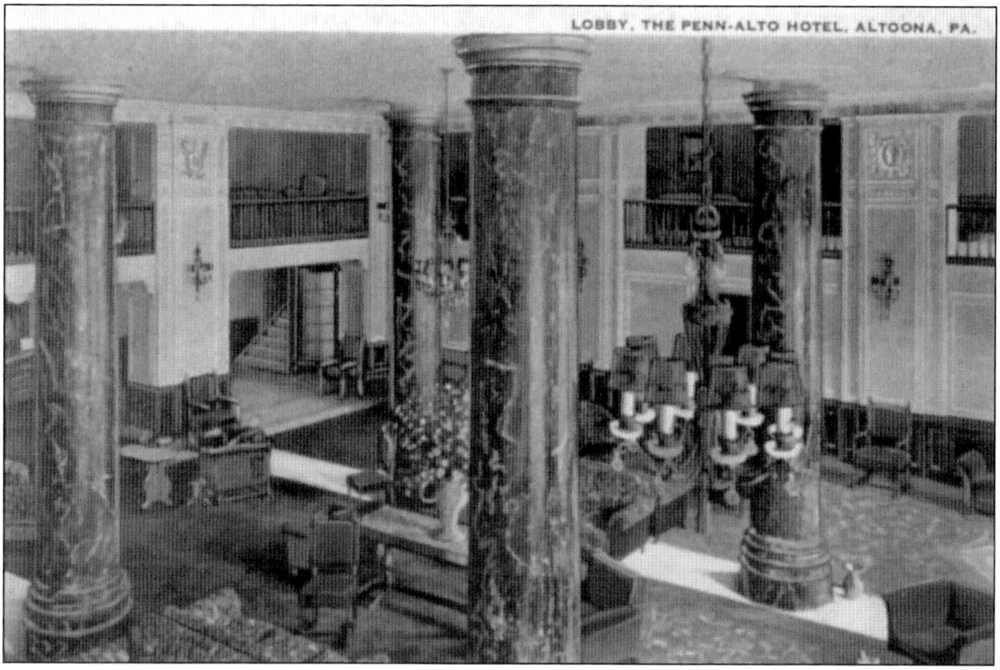

Here is another view of the luxurious Hotel Penn-Alto lobby, taken from the mezzanine level. The mezzanine level accessed the Logan Ballroom and private party or meeting rooms. The Lincoln Room and the Oneida Room were always popular for smaller groups. This card is postmarked February 23, 1928, when the hotel was just eight years old.

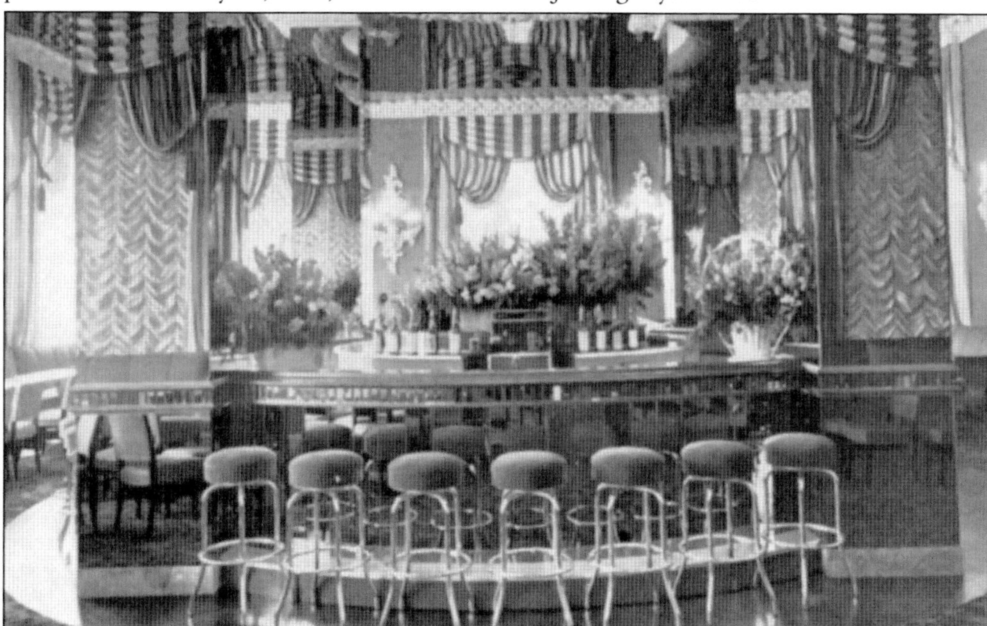

The elegant Mayfair Room of the Hotel Penn-Alto is shown in the art-deco 1930s era. Noted for entertainment and deluxe amenities, the Mayfair Room was a focal center for Altoona society. In the 1950s it was renamed the Continental Room and was quite popular with area citizens and hotel guests. It is now a convenience store space and the hotel is residential.

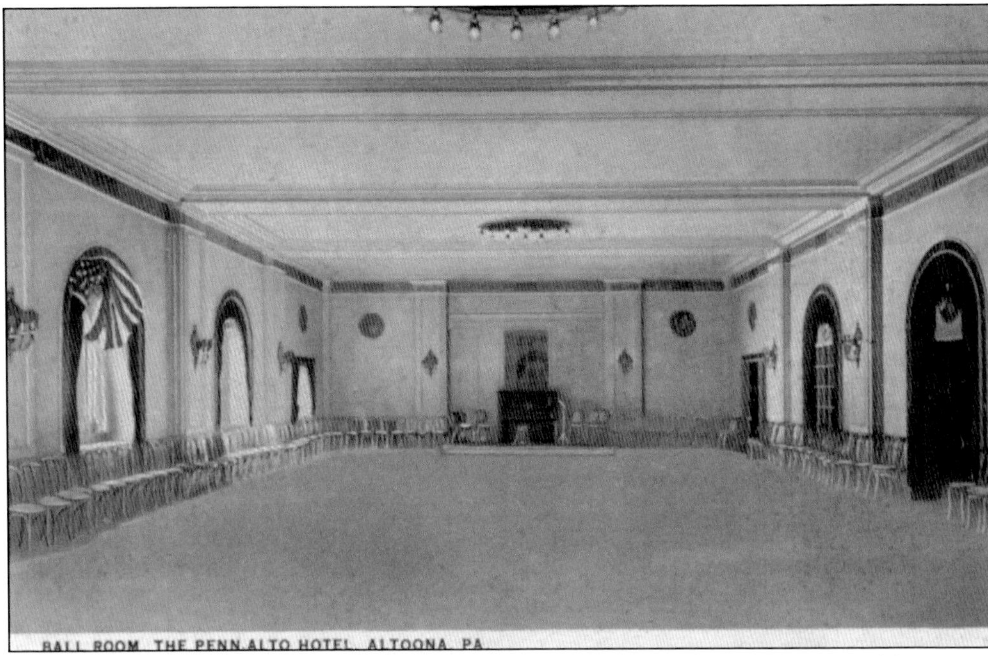

The Logan Room ballroom of the Penn-Alto Hotel was elegant in every respect in the early years. Enhanced in later years with ornate sculpted chandeliers, this room hosted most of the important social events for over half a century, providing a venue for corporate events, conventions, and elaborate weddings. Dining here was an occasion with service to match. Harry Truman's vice president, Alben Barkley, helped celebrate Altoona's centennial here in August 1949, as did Altoona-born actress Janet Blair and Admiral James E. VanZandt.

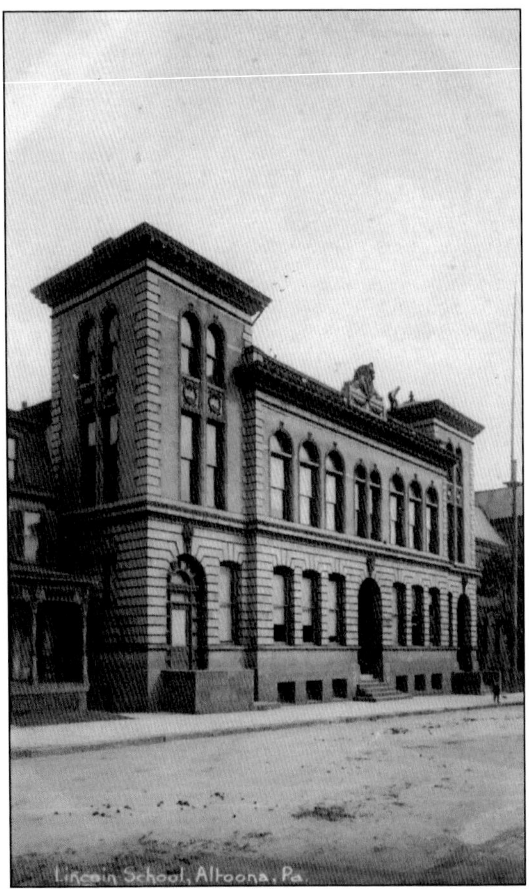

Lincoln School is pictured in the 1400 block of Seventh Avenue. Once used as a high school and later an elementary school, it served the Altoona School District into the 1950s, as did the adjacent (right) Emerson School, a former elementary that transitioned into a vocational trade school. This card is postmarked September 13, 1907.

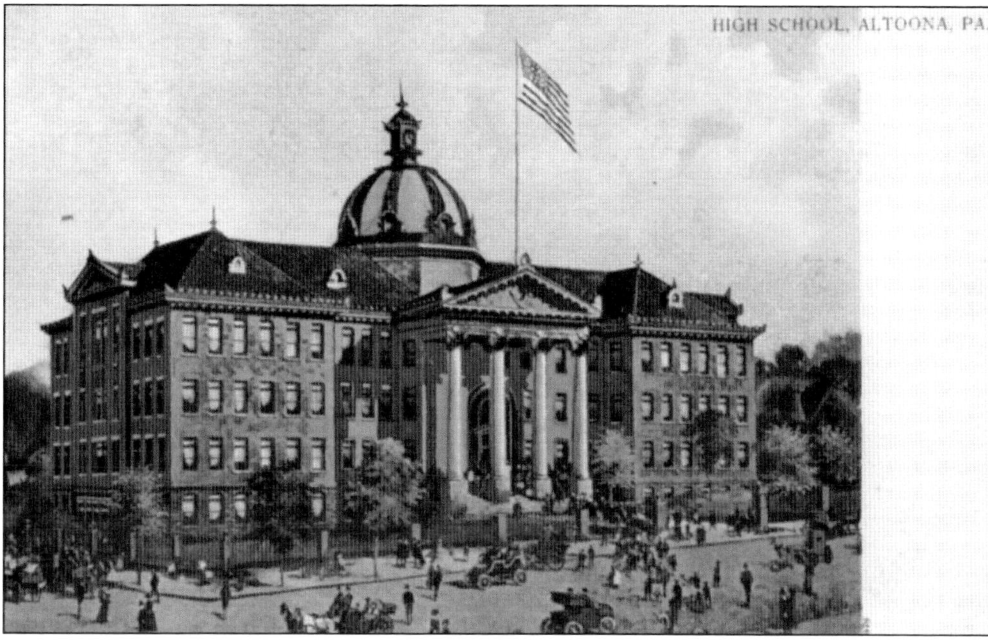

The second Altoona High School, constructed in 1905 in the neoclassical style, was characterized by Hummelstown Brownstone, colossal portico, and glass dome with Ionic columns. The central interior vault under the dome also had open spheres between floors under the dome. This structure was demolished in 1974 for a new high school, over the pleas of preservationists.

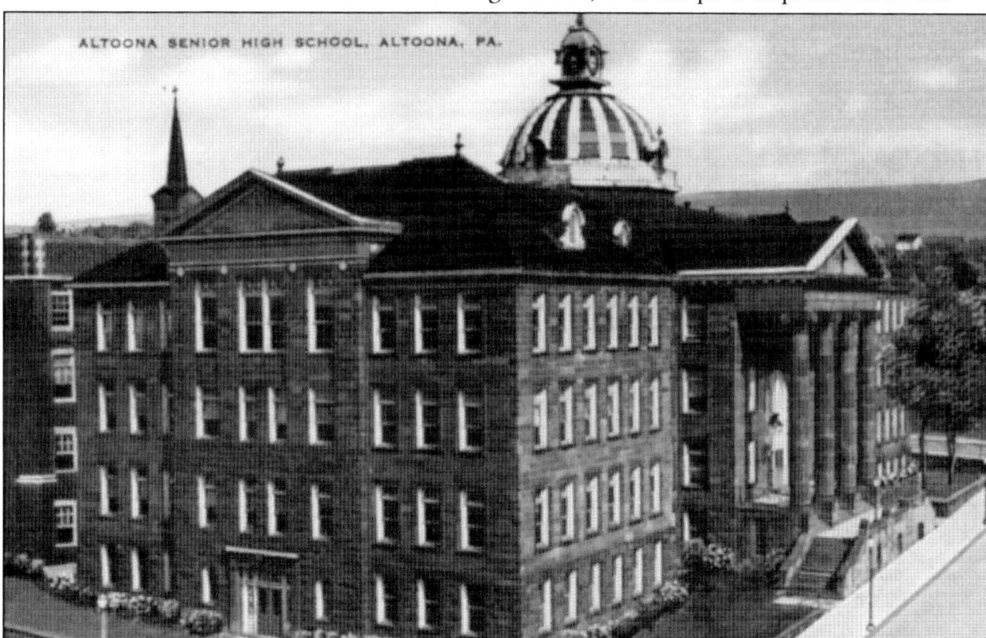

This is a *c.* 1940s view of the Altoona Senior High School on Sixth Avenue and Fifteenth Street. A modernization of the dome in later years removed the coronation crown appearance, to be replaced by glazed green tile free of ornamentation. The addition (left) was added around 1927 to double the size of the high school. The brownstone portion was razed in 1974.

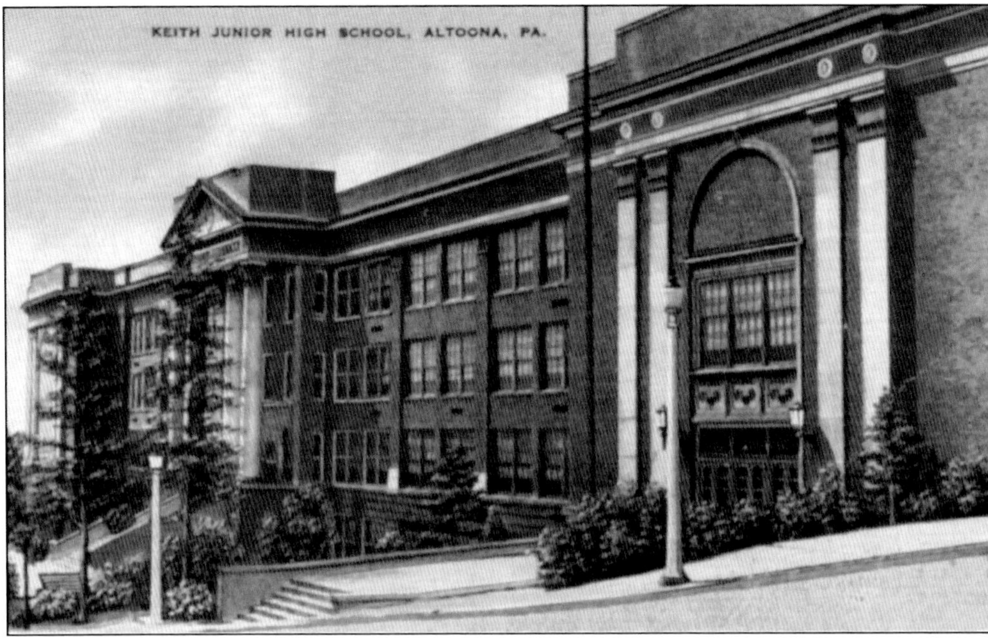

Keith Junior High School stands atop the Calvert Hills promontory, covering a full city block from Thirteenth to Fourteenth Streets and Nineteenth and Twentieth Avenues. This facade faces Nineteenth Avenue with commanding views of the city below. Built in 1930 on the McCartney farm, it was named to honor David Scott Keith, superintendent of schools (1879–1918). Decommissioned in 2007, the historic structure is being converted into residential units for senior citizens.

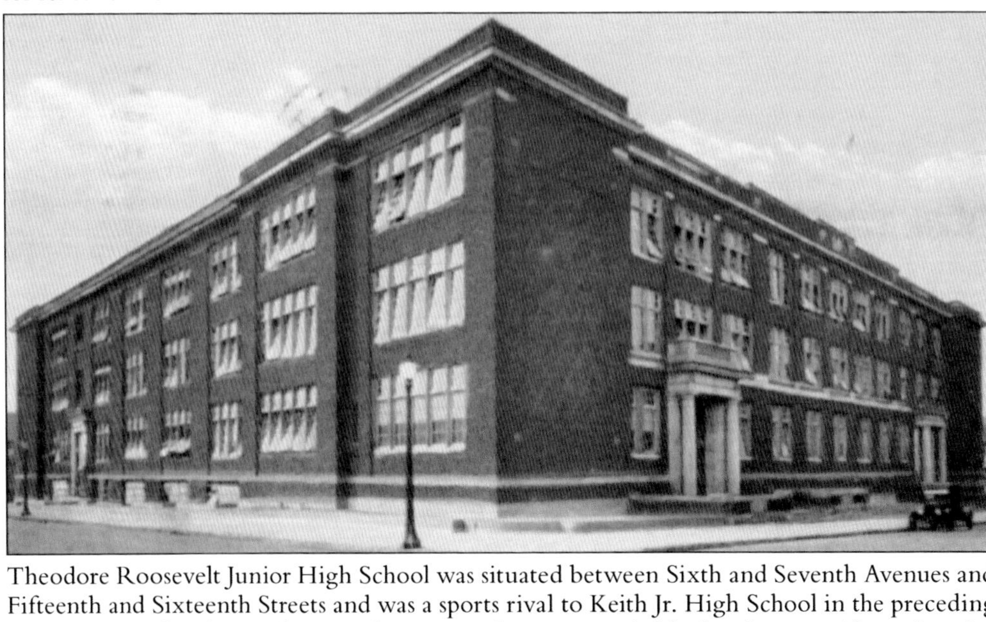

Theodore Roosevelt Junior High School was situated between Sixth and Seventh Avenues and Fifteenth and Sixteenth Streets and was a sports rival to Keith Jr. High School in the preceding image. Somewhat larger than Keith, Roosevelt was remarkable for the magnificent interior auditorium with two balconies, which hosted international stars of stage, screen, and symphony. Closed in 2007 along with Keith Jr. High School, this structure was sadly demolished to make way for an athletic practice field for the new Altoona Area Junior High School nearby.

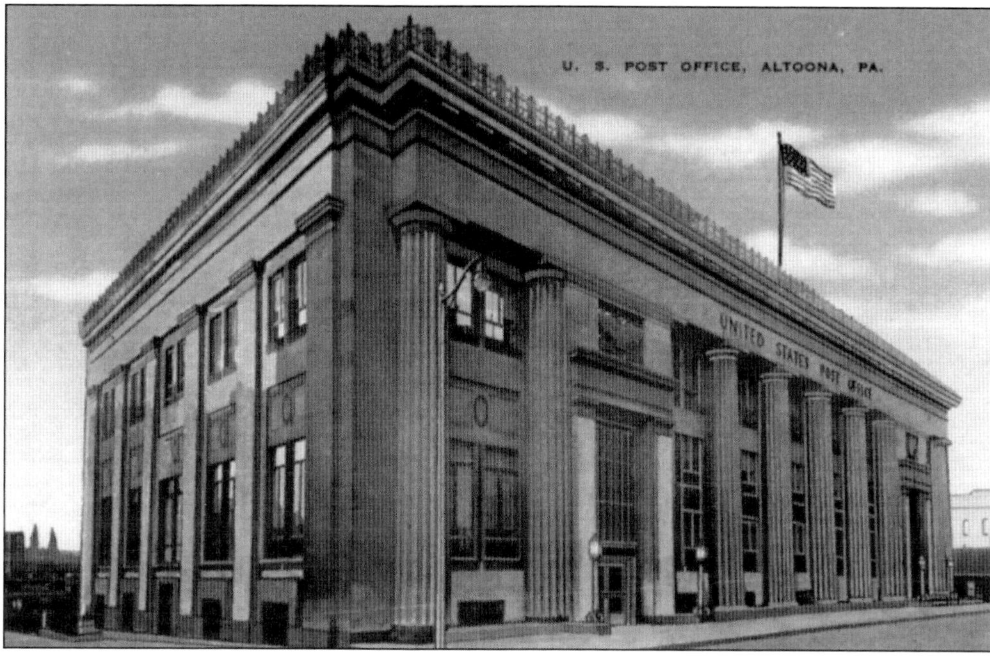

Altoona's U.S. Post Office Building opened in 1933, replacing the former post office on page 59. Ground was broken for it in 1931 by former postmaster Hambleton P. Wilson, on the site of the PRR's Logan House Hotel. The lobby of this structure is adorned with remarkable murals from the era of the Works Progress Administration depicting Altoona's early history.

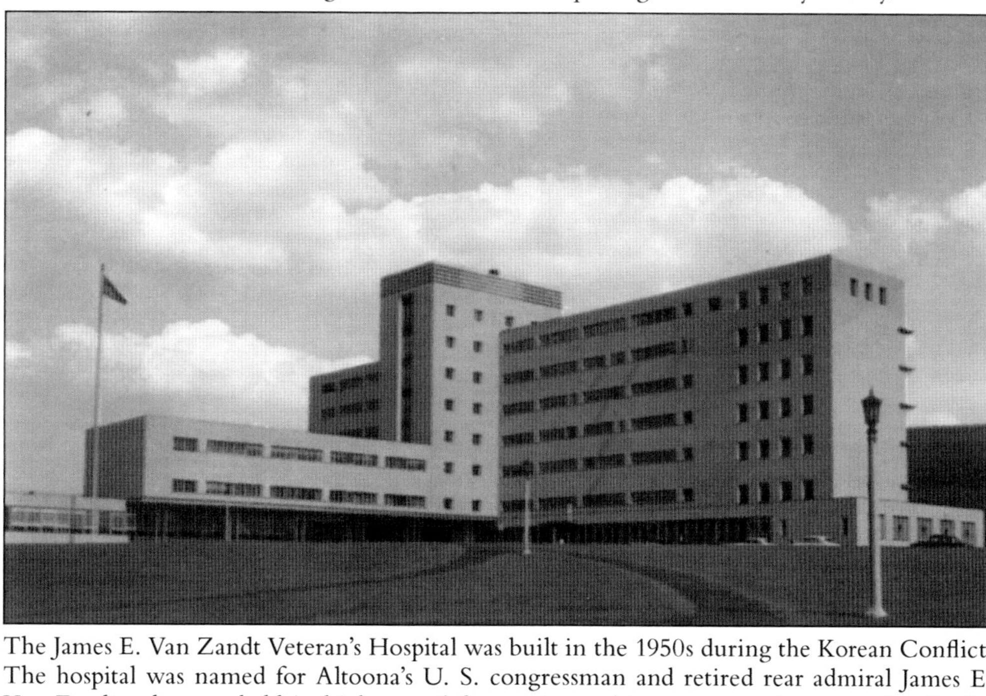

The James E. Van Zandt Veteran's Hospital was built in the 1950s during the Korean Conflict. The hospital was named for Altoona's U. S. congressman and retired rear admiral James E. Van Zandt, who was held in high regard for service to his country and community. In the late 1990s, the expansive front lawn was enhanced by a scale replica of the Vietnam Veteran's Memorial Wall. The wall is now a local tourist destination of honor and respect.

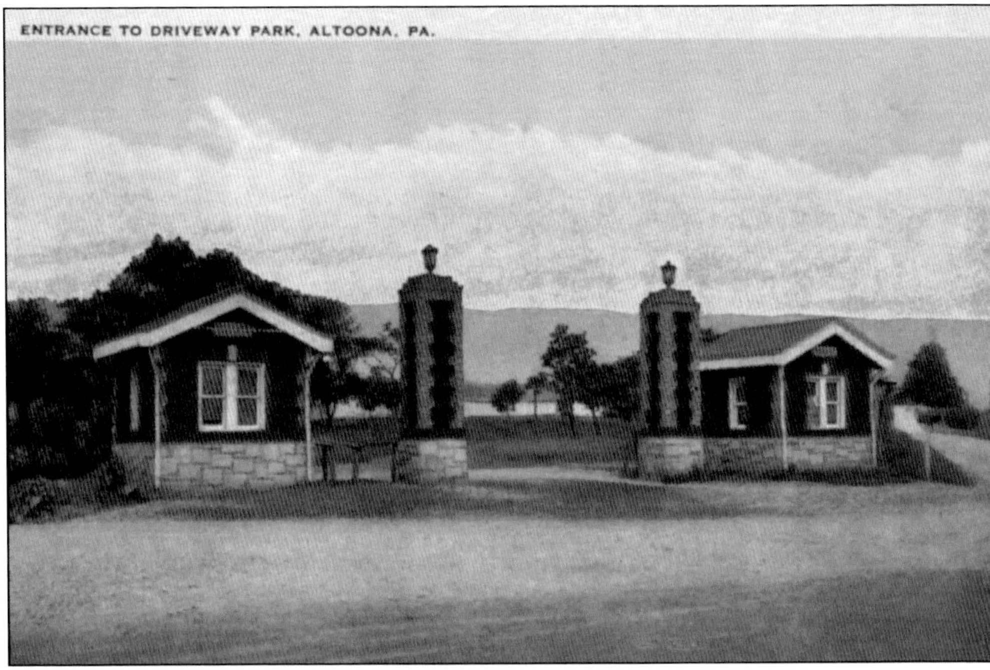

This card proclaims the entrance to Driveway Park, but this was actually the Driving Park, a raceway at the junction of Plank and Frankstown Roads. The area was known for sulky-style horse races and early county fairs. It was very popular in the first decade of the 20th century, as can be seen in the succeeding view.

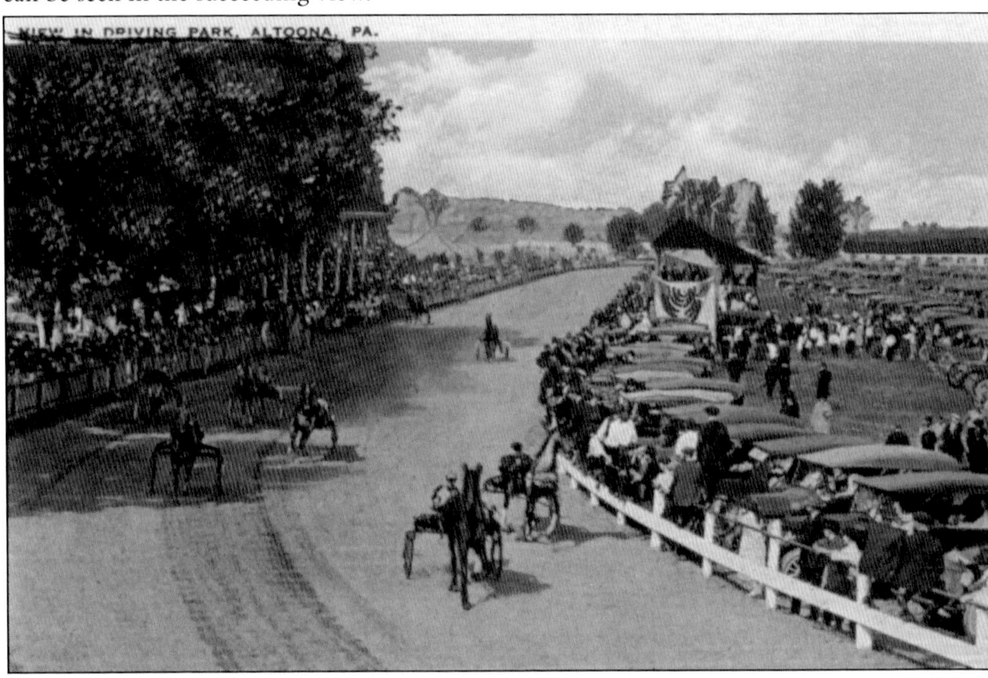

This view was taken in Driving Park in the early 20th century when automobiles were relatively new. In the second half of the 20th century, the park became the Pleasant Valley Shopping Center, the first of Altoona's strip shopping centers. It is still popular today.

Two

Altoona's Railroads

Altoona was founded by the Pennsylvania Railroad (PRR), which consequently had unparalleled influence on Altoona's development, growth, and history for over 100 years. The PRR provided employment. This new town of Altoona (1849) was similar to a frontier town with little population; therefore, the much-needed labor force came from European immigrants whose crafts and skills could serve the needs of this new railroad company. The success of the PRR in linking Philadelphia and Pittsburgh, providing a major connection in the development of a transcontinental railroad, and the founding and selection of Altoona for shops and yards to maintain (and later build new) trains, enabled Altoona to grow rapidly in the early years of the Industrial Revolution. Over the years, railroad employment in Altoona had its share of periodic layoffs as different economic circumstances prevailed at any given time (fluctuations in the coal, steel, or railroad industries affected each accordingly), but the PRR was the prime economic force and lifeblood of the city. The end of the steam era in the 1950s had tragic effects on Altoona's economy, eliminating jobs, crafts, and skills. While Altoona scrambled to diversify its employment base, the successor railroad employers (Penn Central Railroad, Consolidated Rail Corporation, and Norfolk Southern Railroad), while no longer the predominant employers in Altoona, continued to provide very significant employment for the greater Altoona economy with its principal locomotive repair shops.

Altoona was also served by the Altoona and Logan Valley Electric Railway (1882–1954) and its subsidiary, the Logan Valley Bus Company. Both provided public transportation for Altoona and nearby communities. For more information, see *Altoona and Logan Valley Electric Railway* from Arcadia Publishing's Images of Rail series.

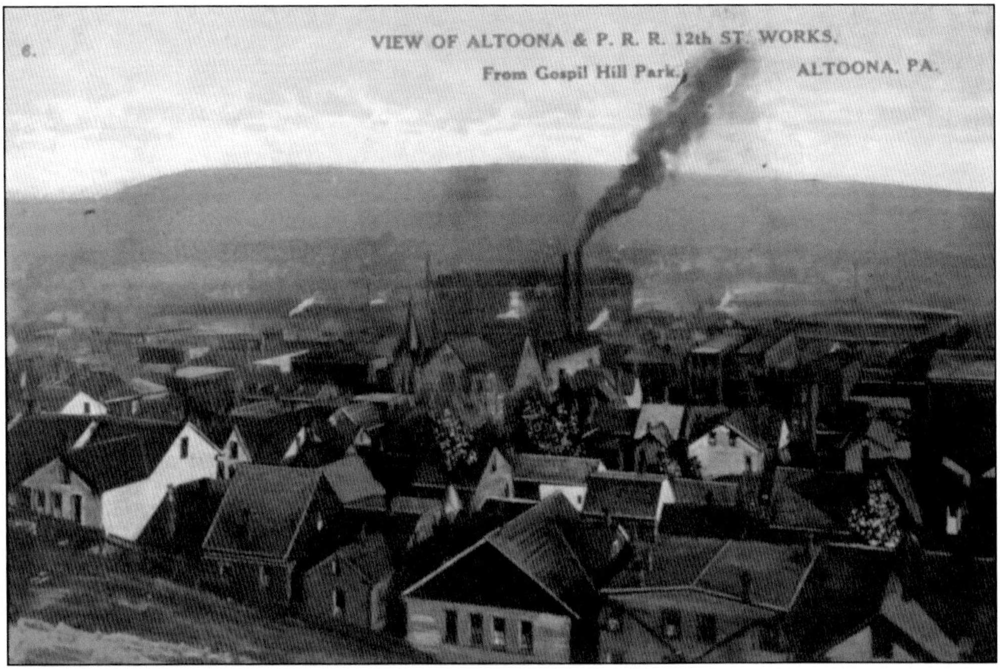

Here is a view of Altoona and the PRR's Twelfth Street Works from Gospel Hill Park. The century of railroad steam technology in Altoona (shops, power plants, and locomotives) was all coal fired. As such, Altoona was dirty and smoky, but it also meant employment and economic stability. In this view the Altoona Works dominates the downtown skyline.

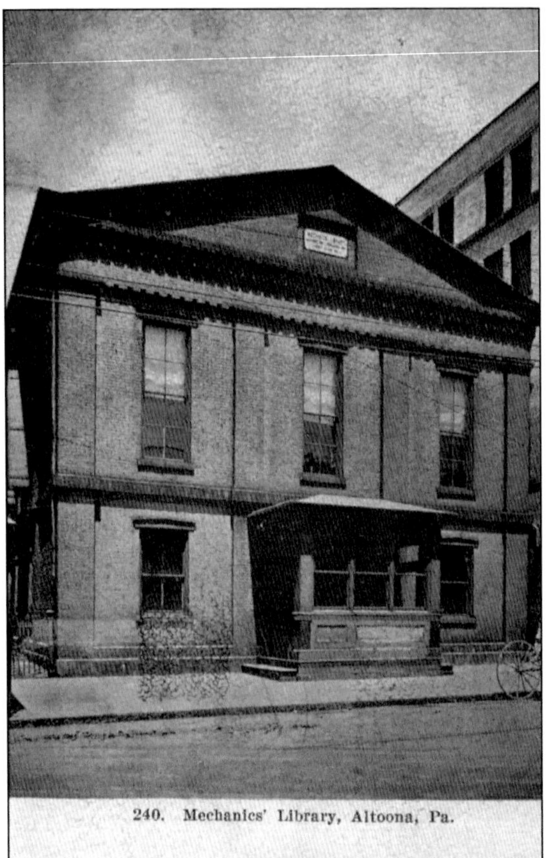

The Altoona Mechanics Library and Reading Room was originally the First Presbyterian Church and was transformed into the Mechanics Library for the education of PRR apprentices. Organized in 1858, it operated in several locations but was in this facility from 1900 to 1924. Some 75,000 volumes were then transferred to the Altoona School District, forming a basis in later years for the Altoona Area Public Library. This card is postmarked July 15, 1911.

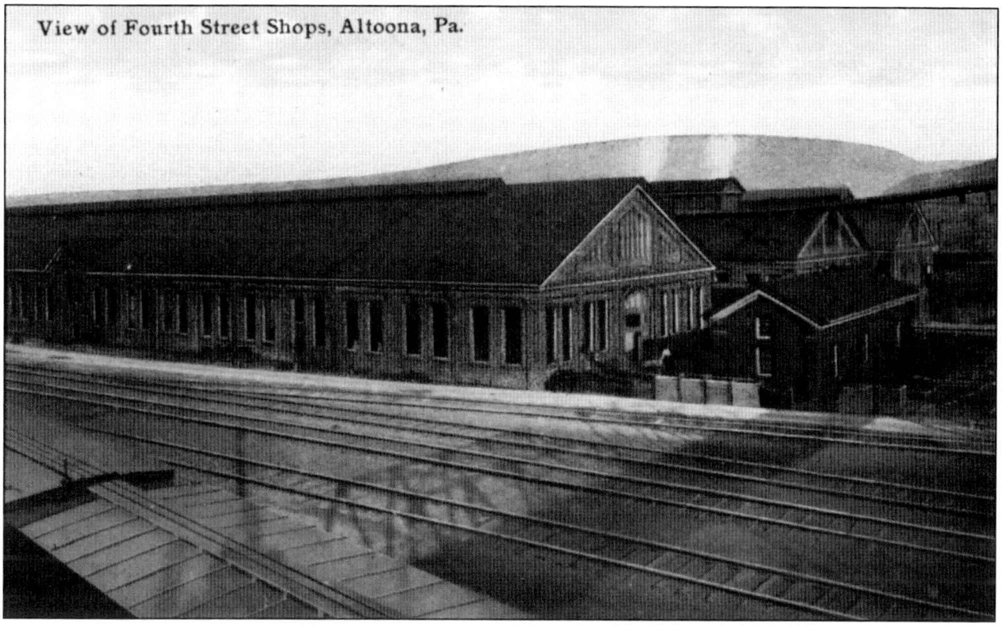

This view of the Fourth Street Shops of the PRR looks east from the Fourth Street pedestrian bridge. A series of shops paralleling Chestnut Avenue as part of the Altoona Car Shop department, these support facilities were near the west end of the Altoona classification yard and passenger car shops. This building is now occupied by Lumax Industries, a manufacturer of commercial lighting fixtures. The card is postmarked May 2, 1912.

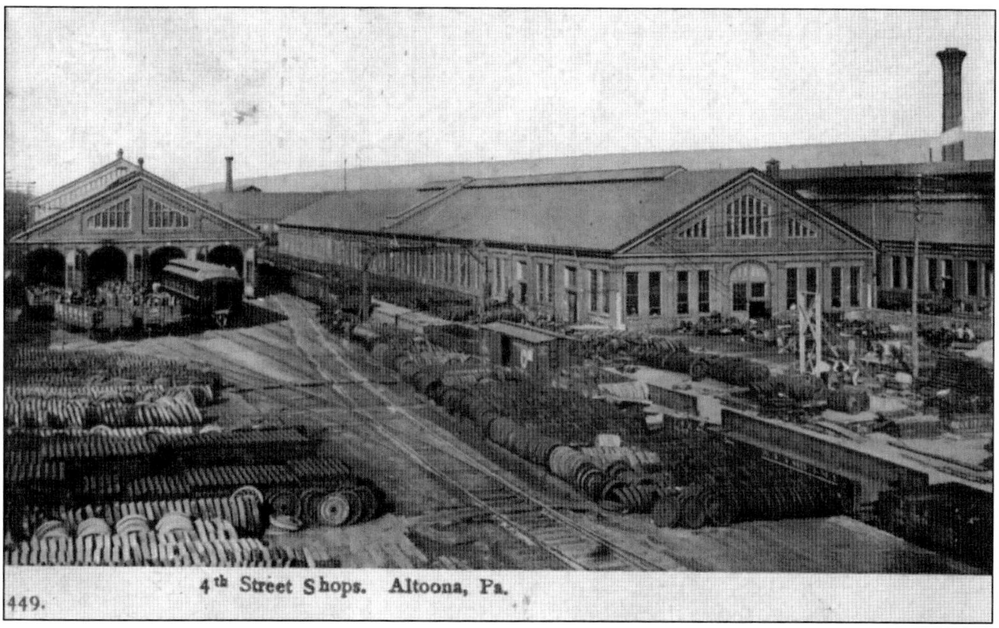

Another view of the Fourth Street shop complex illustrates the substantial inventory of wheels for passenger and freight car repair for the Altoona Car Shop department. The shop building construction is the classic design often used by model railroaders seeking period structures. The passenger car paint shops were immediately west of this location. The card is postmarked September 2, 1908.

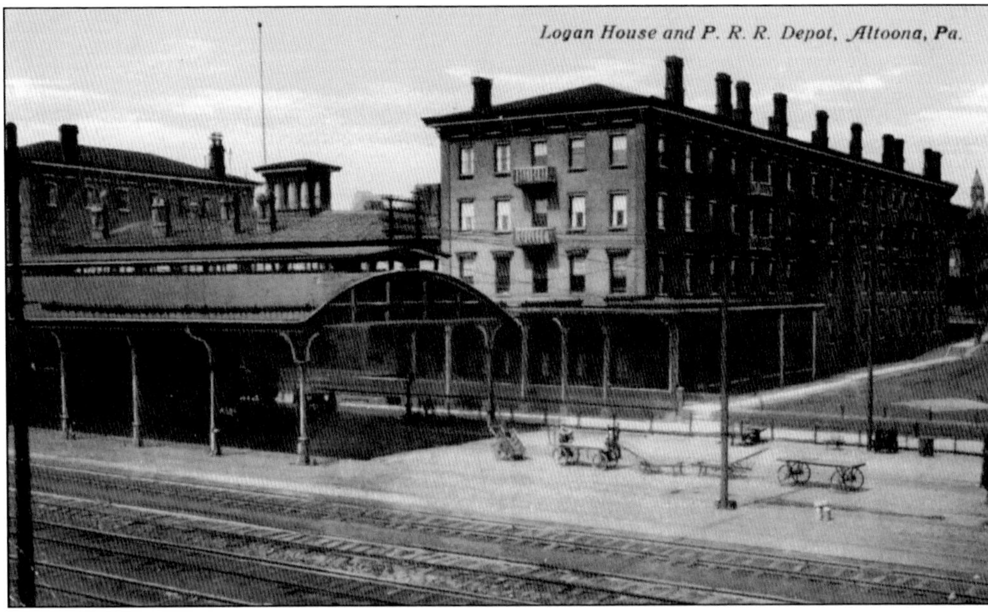

The gateway to Altoona via the PRR was the passenger station and wrought iron train shed adjacent to the railroad's Logan House Hotel. The Logan House was constructed around 1854, the same year the Horseshoe Curve and lines west over the Allegheny Mountains opened connecting Philadelphia and Pittsburgh, providing travelers with excellent accommodation, especially in Altoona's infancy.

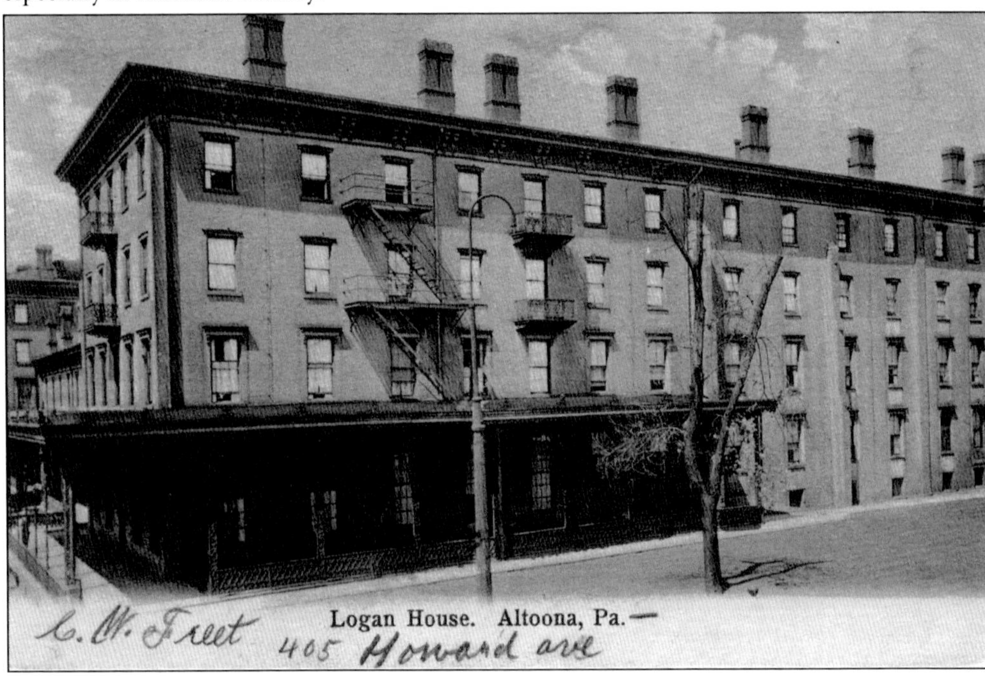

PRR's Logan House Hotel was constructed in the renaissance revival style and ranked as one of the best in the country in its early history. In 1862, the Loyal (northern) War Governors met here under the leadership of Pennsylvania governor Andrew Gregg Curtin to affirm their allegiance to President Lincoln during the Civil War. The card is postmarked September 25, 1906.

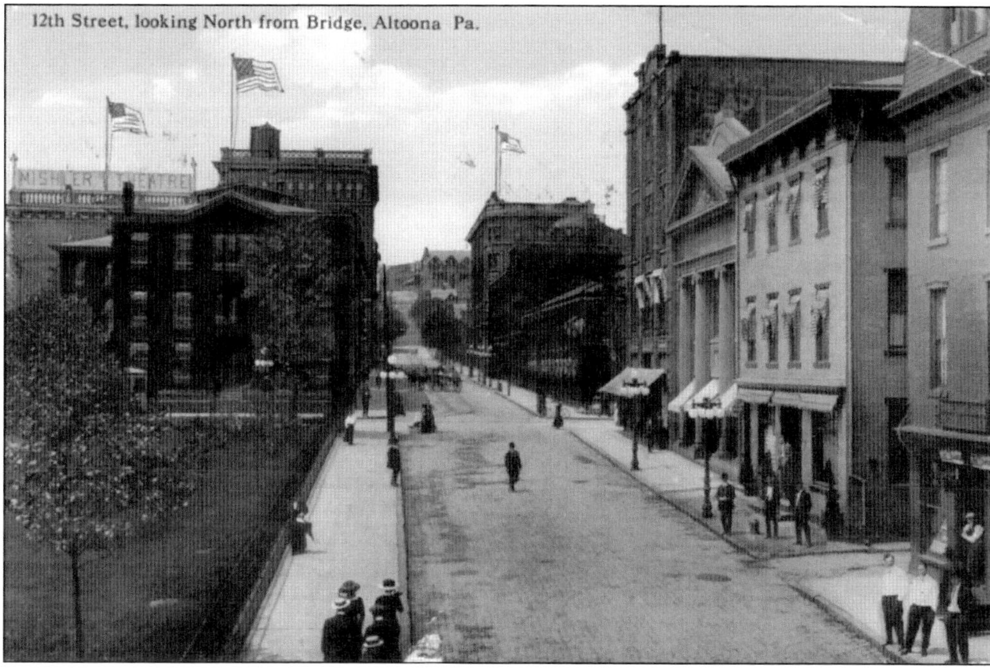

Here is a northerly view of Twelfth Street from the PRR mainline. On the left is the lawn of the railroad's Logan House Hotel. Facing the lawn is the PRR office building on the corner of Eleventh Avenue. The Mishler Theatre may be seen at the top left. The card is postmarked July 29, 1914.

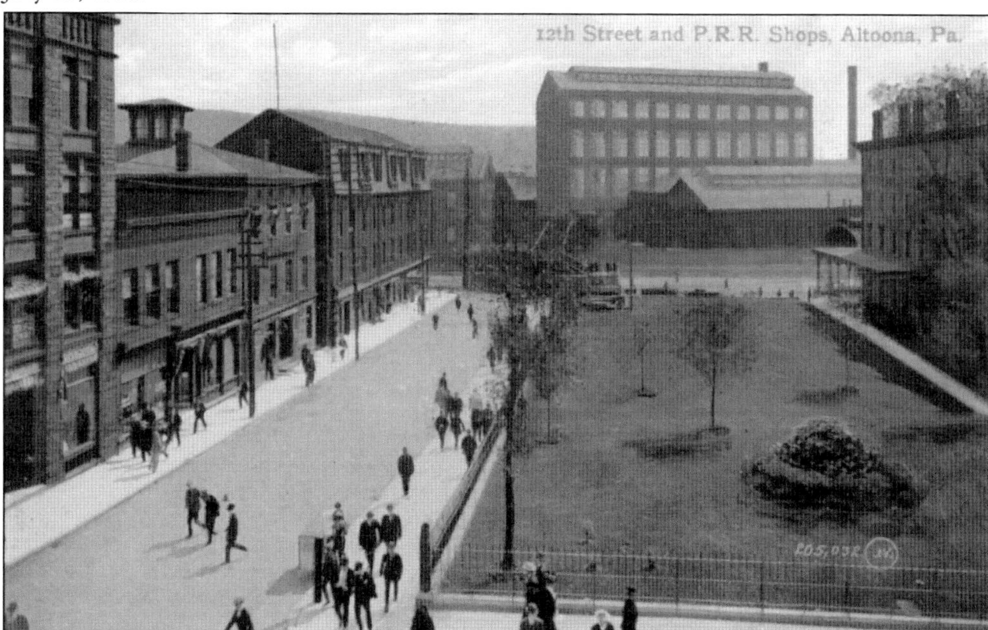

This is an opposing view of the scene in the preceding image, taken from the PRR office building. The Logan House Hotel lawn is in the foreground and in the distance, on the opposite side of the railroad mainline, are the shops of the Altoona Works that were destroyed in a spectacular Christmas vacation fire on December 27, 1931.

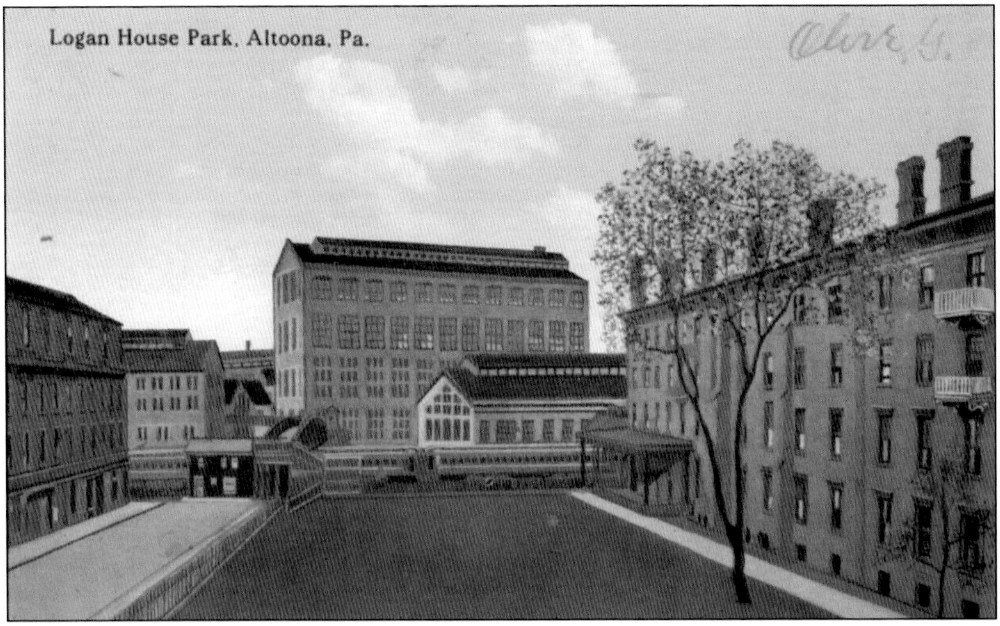

A somewhat similar view as in the preceding images, this scene illustrates the Logan House Park and Hotel, as well as the Altoona Works complex. Note the passenger train in the station. The Logan House Hotel was the hub of Altoona society for the second half of the 19th century primarily. It was razed in 1931 to make way for a new post office. This card is postmarked November 17, 1912.

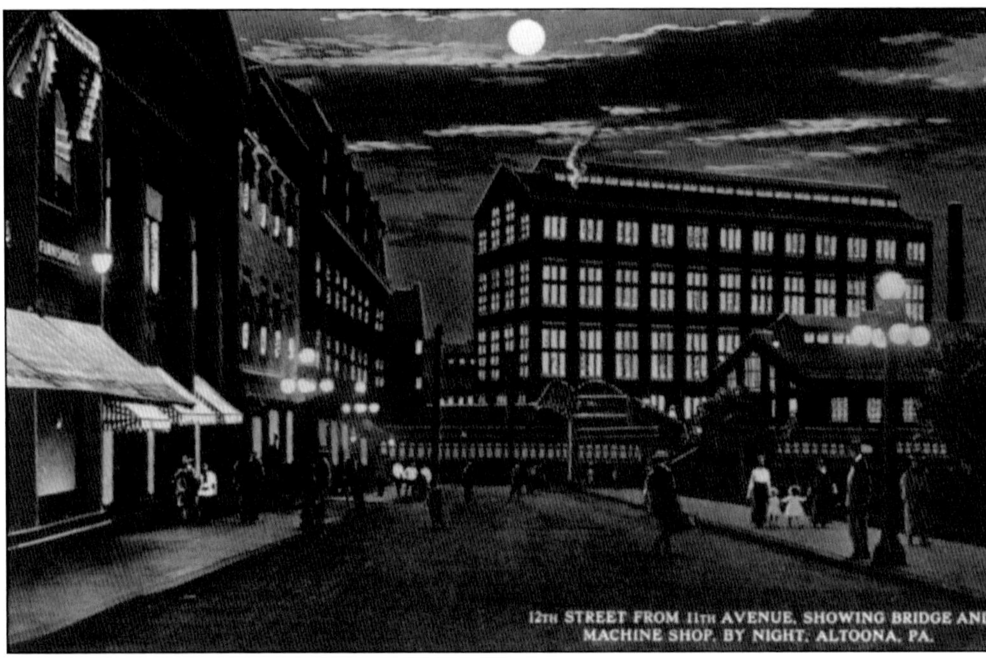

This night scene on Twelfth Street looks from Eleventh Avenue toward the railroad mainline and Machine Shops of the Altoona Works. The machine shops were destroyed by fire on December 27, 1931, resulting in the loss of buildings and machine shop equipment and displacing many workers. Note the passenger train in the station.

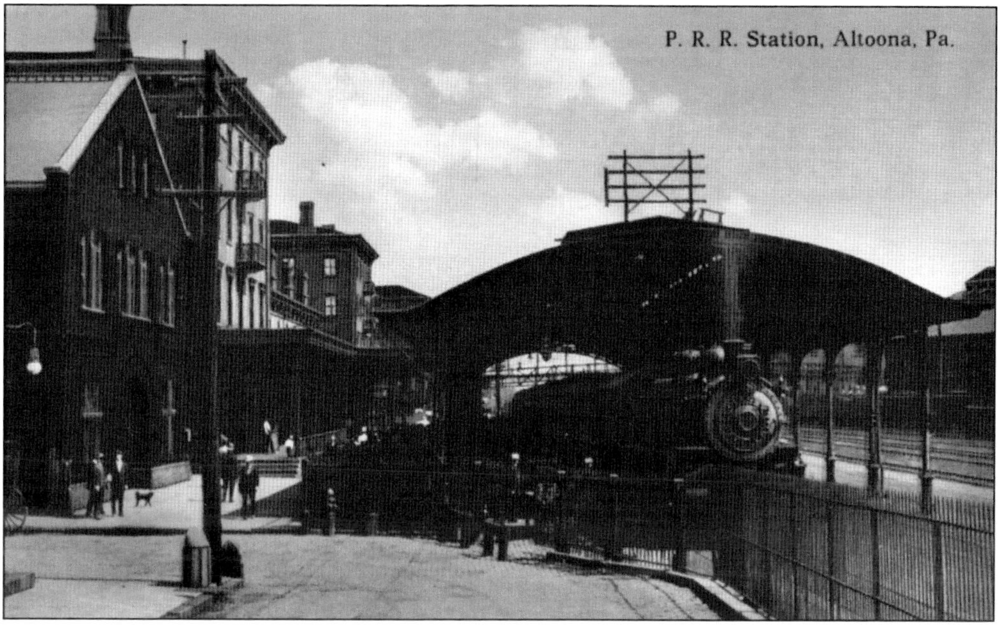

The PRR passenger station at Tenth Avenue (paved with yellow brick) and Thirteenth Street is seen here. The station building (1887) is at left with the railroad's Logan House Hotel adjacent. The wrought iron train canopy, which was razed in 1961, shelters a westbound train around the 1920s.

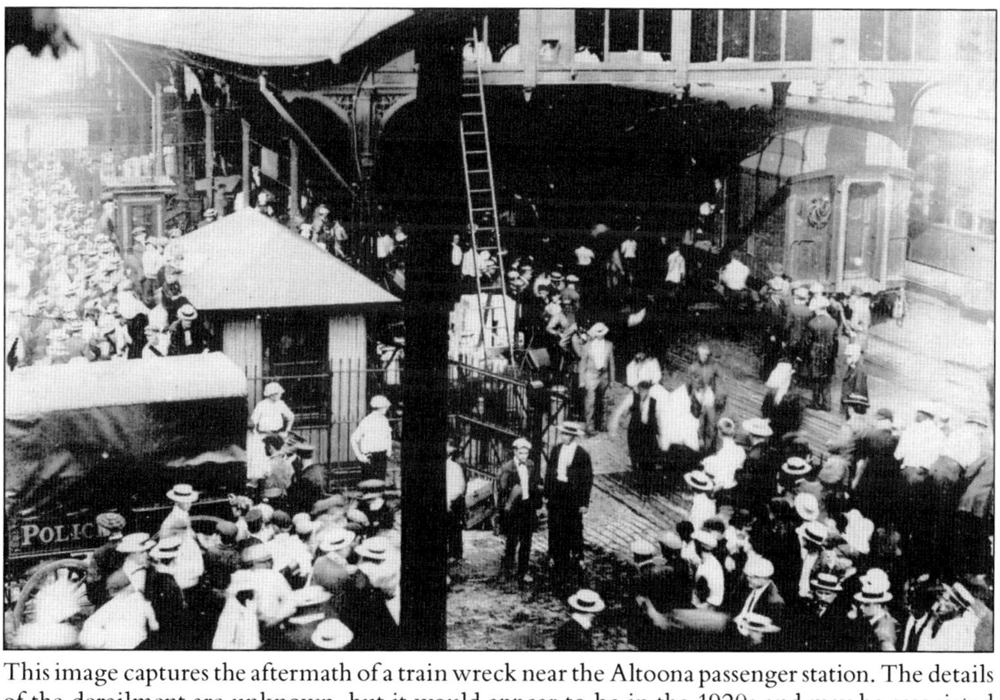

This image captures the aftermath of a train wreck near the Altoona passenger station. The details of the derailment are unknown, but it would appear to be in the 1920s and may be associated with the Seventeenth Street wreck of November 29, 1925, caused by an eastbound runaway train that descended the mountain into Altoona. This limited view seems to show a freight train on the south side of the station, away from the station canopy and passenger equipment.

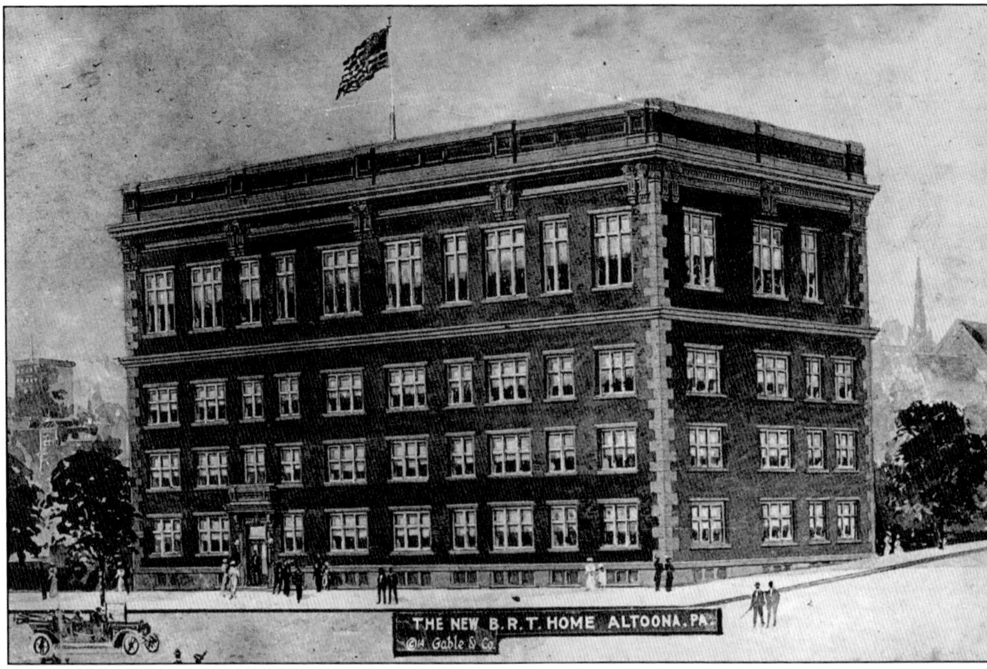

The Brotherhood of Trainmen building at Eighth Avenue and Eleventh Street had lodge meeting rooms and a ballroom on the fourth floor and a dormitory for transient crews in the basement. Floors one through three were apartments. This structure is still in use today, although the Brotherhood of Trainmen has no presence in the structure.

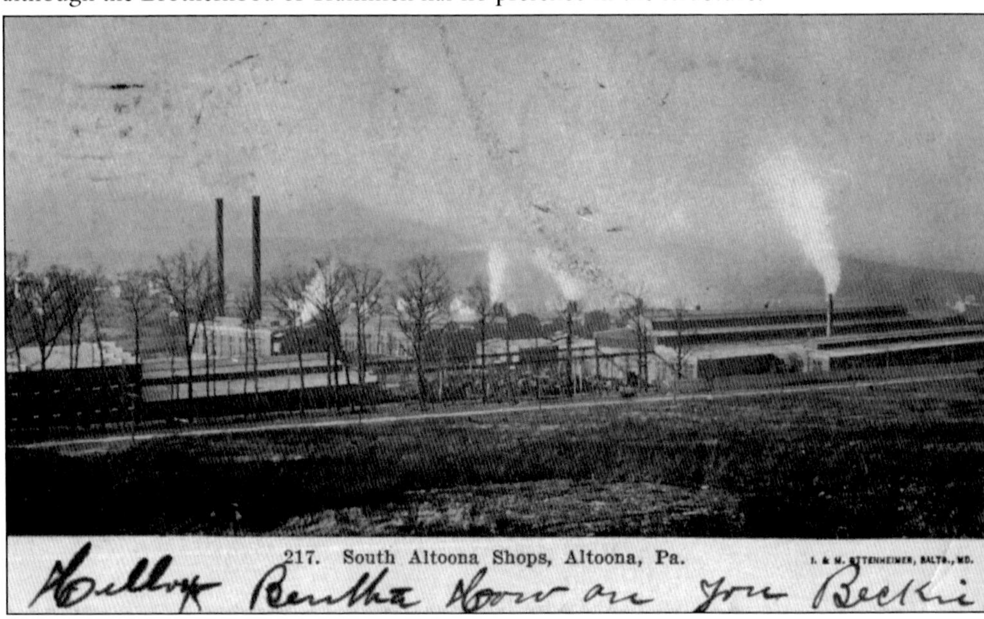

The South Altoona Shops of the PRR in the vicinity of Sixth Avenue and Forty-first Street were the principal foundry operations that manufactured castings for steam locomotive components, similar to any steel mill operation. These facilities were closed in the 1950s at the end of the steam era, and some buildings are used by other industries today. This card is postmarked September 27, 1908.

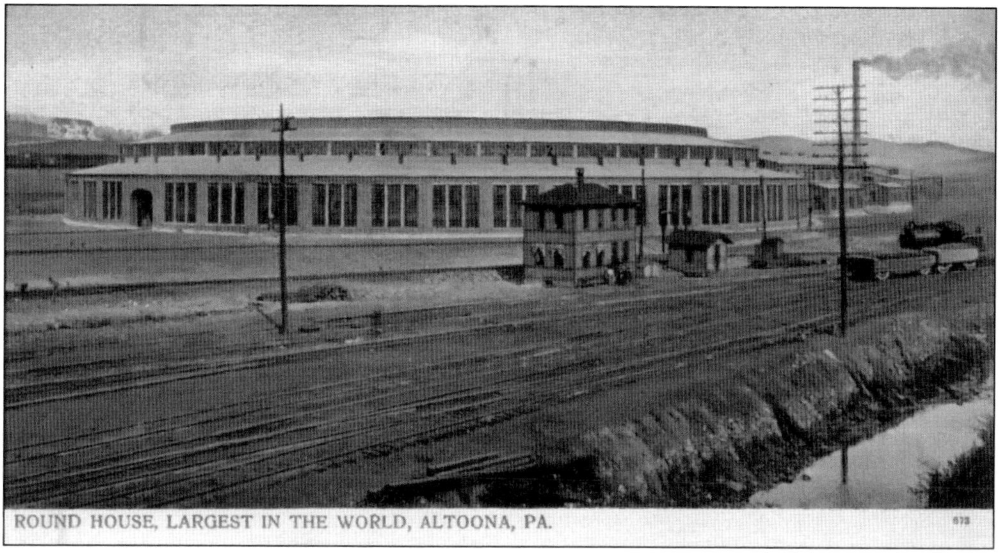

The East Altoona Roundhouse, known as the largest in the world at one time, was comprised of 50 stalls and boasted a 110-foot turntable in its center during World War II to accommodate the enormous length of World War II–era locomotives. Ready tracks in the vicinity served locomotives of the Pittsburgh and Middle Divisions. A huge concrete coaling station was situated east of the roundhouse.

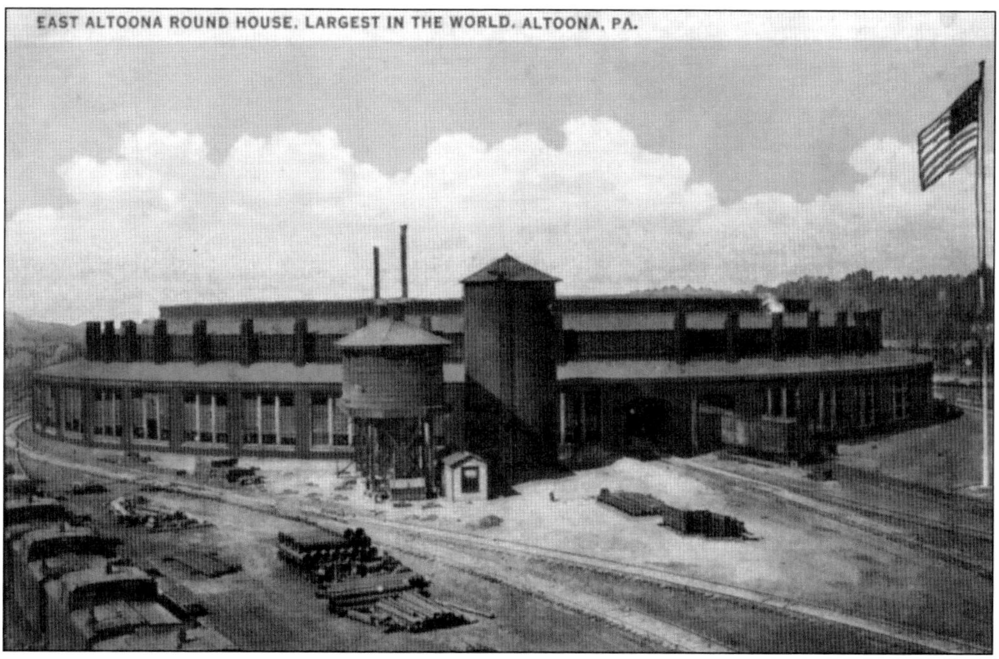

Pictured is another view of the East Altoona Roundhouse on the north face with caboose track in the foreground. On the PRR, cabooses were referred to as cabins where the conductor and brakemen worked aboard ensuring the safety of their train and observing passing trains for defects such as loose lading or hot boxes, a fire involving a wheel and axle in the days of friction-bearing truck assemblies for the wheel sets.

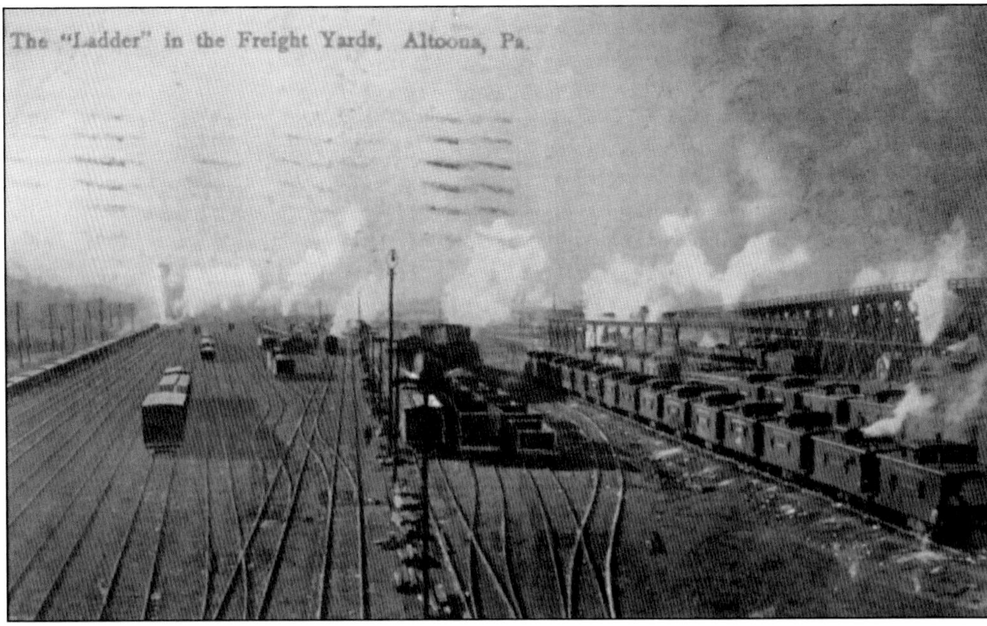

This is referred to as the "ladder" in the freight yards of the PRR immediately west of the East Altoona Roundhouse. On the left is the eastbound classification yard, where cars were sorted according to their destinations. A cabin (caboose) car track and ash pits are on the right. Steam and smoke are part of the East Altoona skyline in the fossil-fuel age, around 1900. This card is postmarked July 3, 1909.

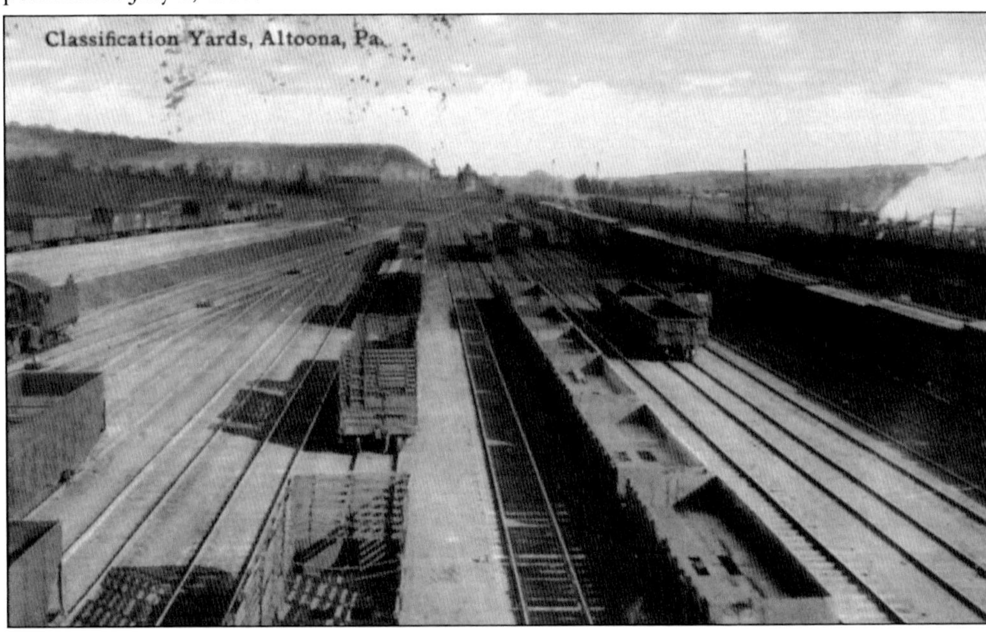

Viewed eastward, this is the westbound classification yard around 1900. In the distance is the WJ hump-tower whose crews classify trains for other westbound destinations. After the Rose Tower Yard opened on November 17, 1907, cars would be advanced there for further travel westward. The westbound yard was on a higher elevation than the parallel eastbound yard. This card is postmarked Juniata, May 4, 1911.

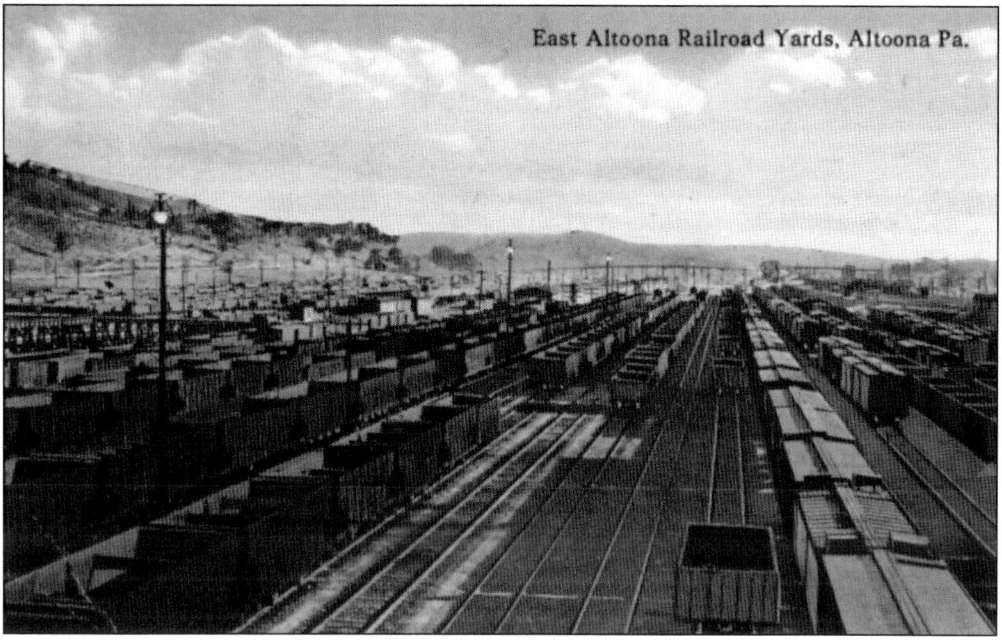

Viewed westward, the westbound classification yard is depicted in this scene from the early 1900s. The cars seen here have just been classified by WJ Tower and will be advanced to Rose Yard in the distance. Altoona was a major classification center for freight, as well as a crew change for most trains. The card is postmarked April 23, 1917.

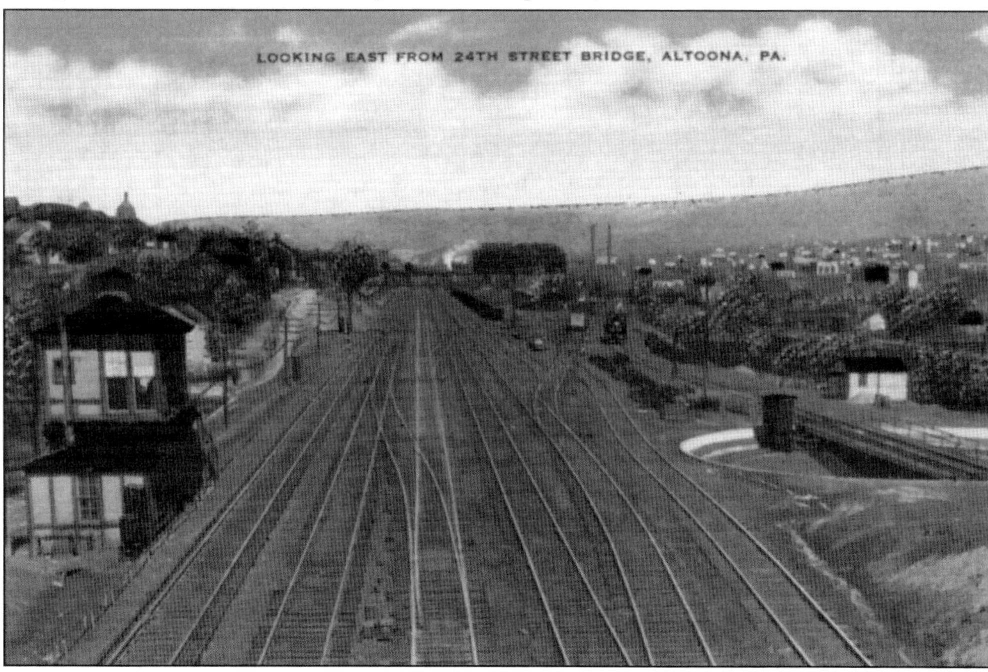

This view looks east from Twenty-fourth Street Bridge. "Slope" Tower on the left marked the end of the Pittsburgh Division and the start of the Middle Division on the PRR in Altoona. Opposite is a table to turn passenger steam locomotives with center city Altoona and the Altoona Works about 10 blocks distant.

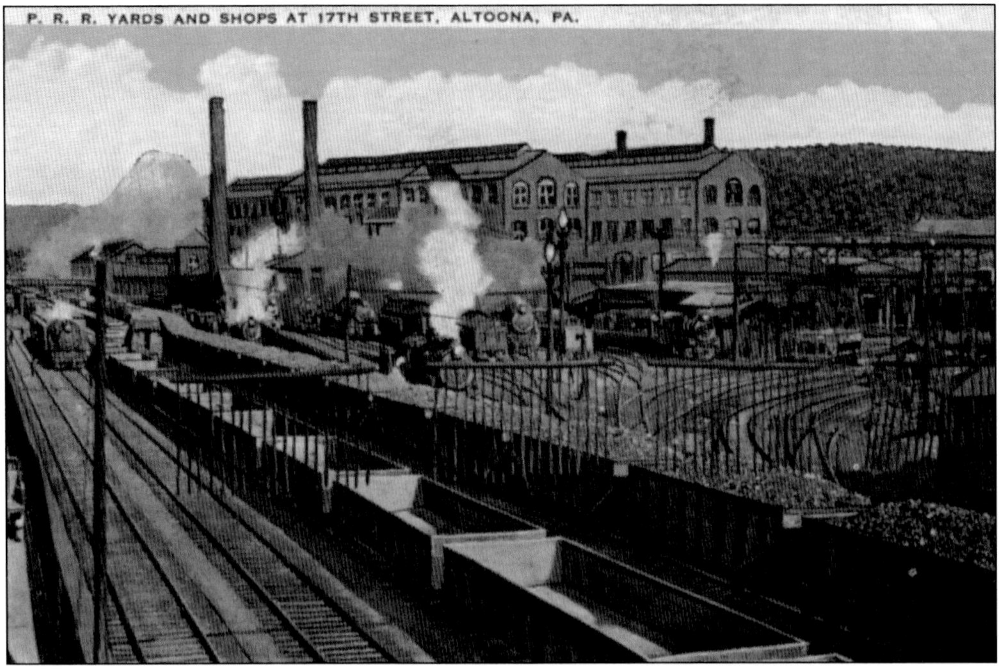

The PRR Yards and Shops at Twelfth Street are seen here, facing eastward. The Altoona Works on the right were razed about 1970; today the site is home to Station Medical Center and Railroader's Memorial Museum. The vertical ropes hanging from the cable were used to alert brakemen on top of cars about an approaching bridge with a low overhead clearance.

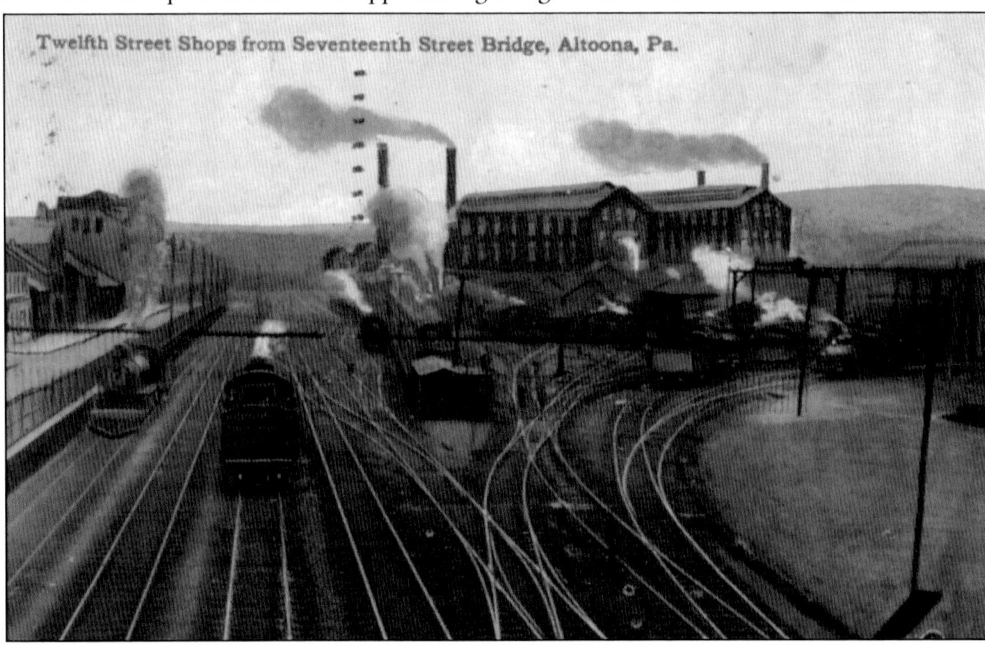

Here are the Twelfth Street Shops, seen looking eastward from the Seventeenth Street Bridge sometime around 1900. The Altoona Works of the PRR stands on the right, as does Western Roundhouse No. 3. The buildings at left, just west of the passenger station, are rooming houses, hotels, and bars—known collectively as Whiskey Row. The card is postmarked July 2, 1911.

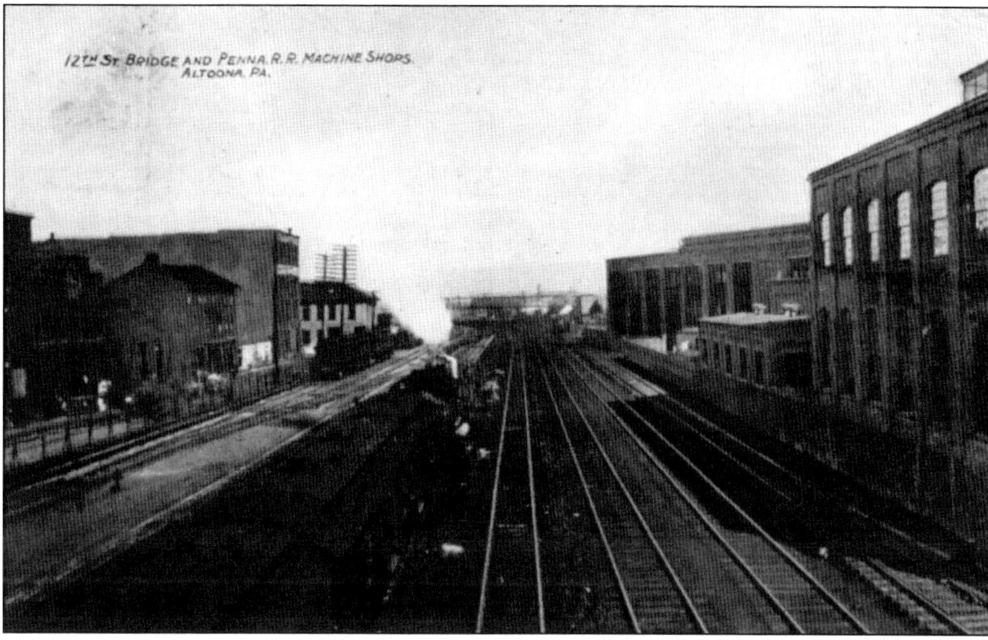

The bridge and PRR Machine Shops are viewed looking eastward from Twelfth Street to Ninth Street. The passenger train is just departing the passenger station eastbound and the freight station is left center near the telegraph poles. Much of the shop complex (right) is now home to Altoona Pipe and Steel Company. The card is postmarked August 1908.

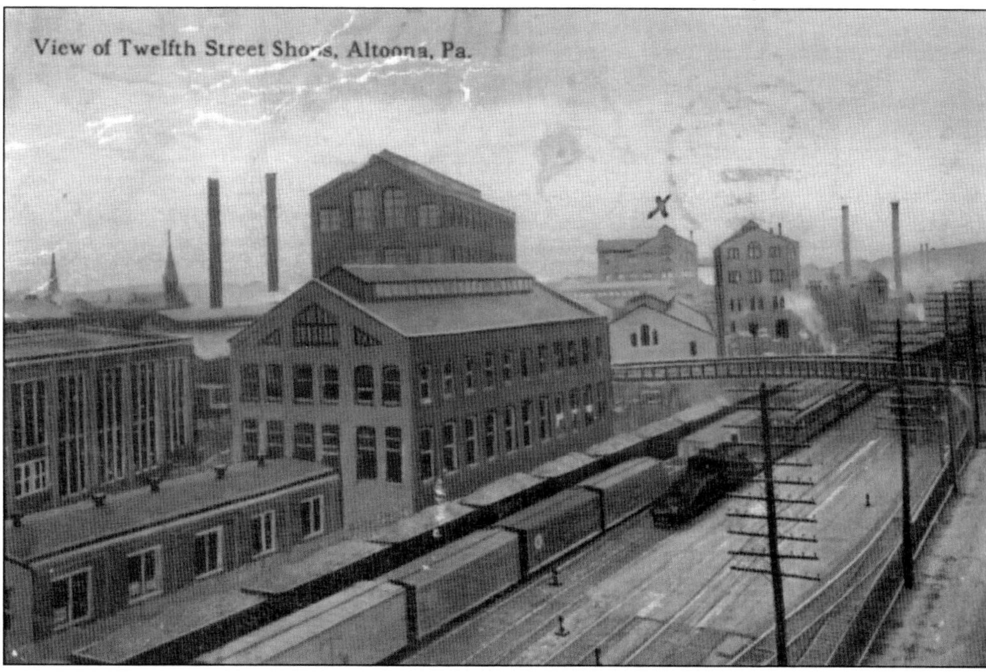

This is a reverse view of the preceding image showing the Twelfth Street Shops of the PRR. The mainline is visible and the passenger station is middle right at the bridge. The industrial might of the railroad was Altoona's lifeblood via transportation, shops, and classification yards. This card is postmarked December 28, 1912.

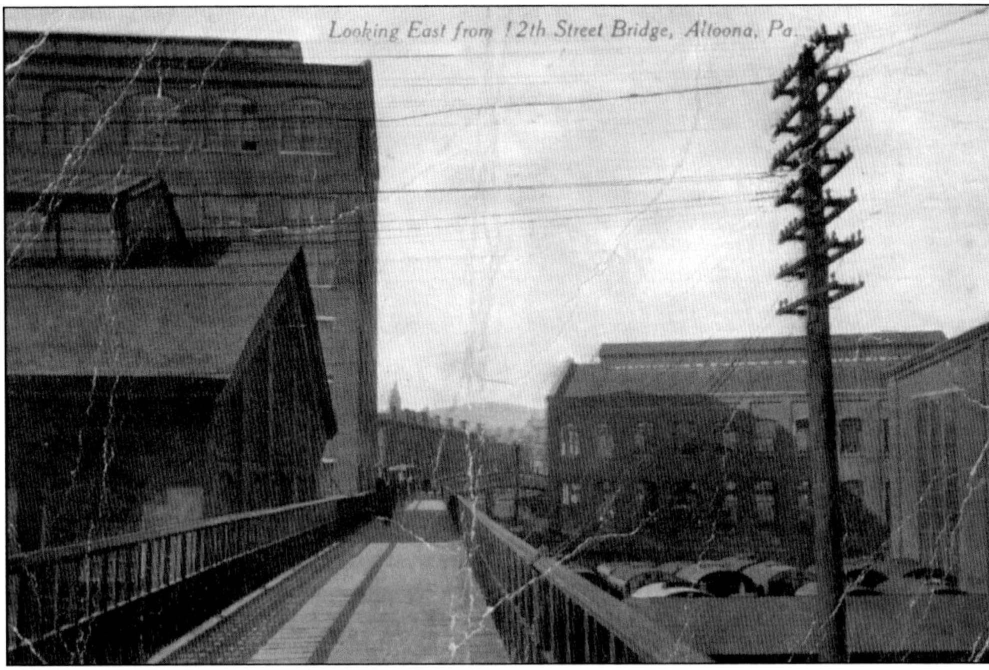

The Twelfth Street pedestrian bridge crossed from the PRR passenger station to the south side of town, but it served all the principal shops of the Altoona works. The buildings on the left were destroyed by a massive fire on December 27, 1931.

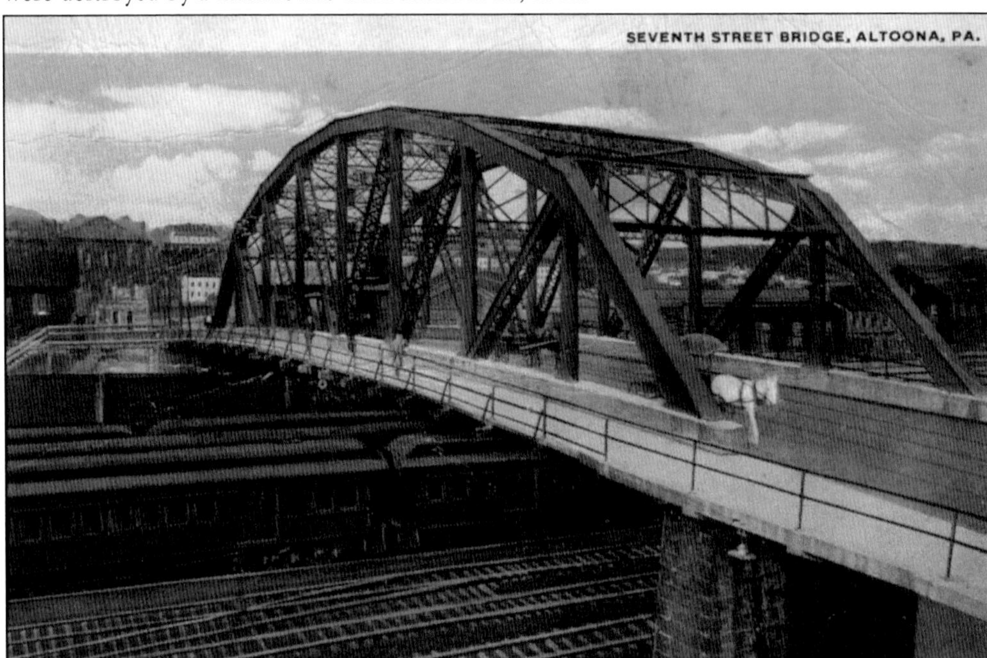

The PRR mainline passes under the Seventh Street Bridge, which opened in 1913 as a project between the city of Altoona, the Altoona and Logan Valley Electric Railway, and the PRR. It connected the north and south sides of the city in the vicinity of the Altoona Hospital. The Seventh Street Bridge was replaced in 2007.

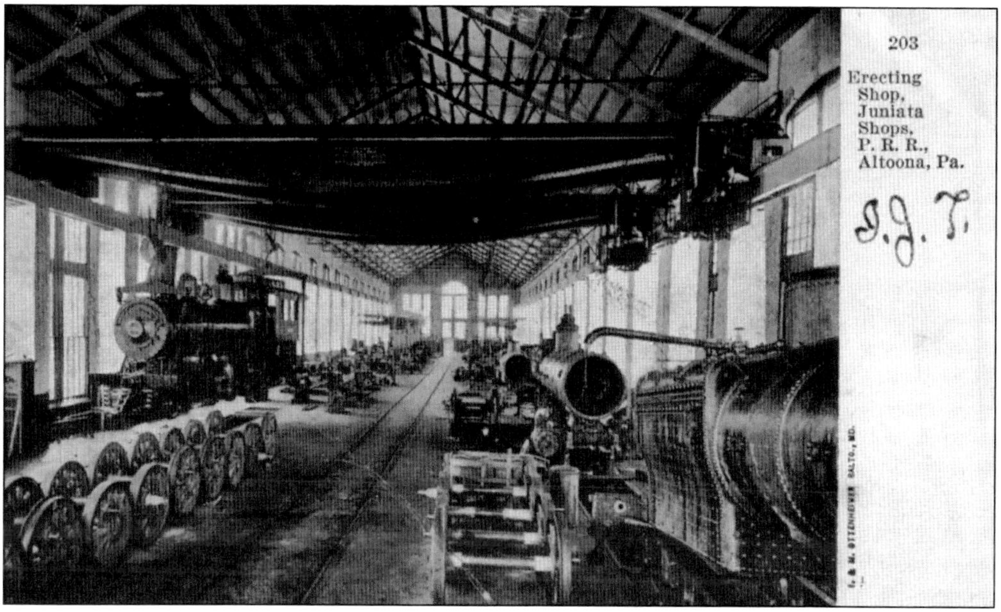

The Erecting Shop, Juniata Shops, and PRR are seen here. The locomotive works were originally 1 mile west at the Altoona Works, but the Juniata expansion moved locomotive repair and locomotive building there after 1890. Characteristic of the PRR was the Belpaire firebox attached to the boilers (squared off) seen right. This card is postmarked March 19, 1908.

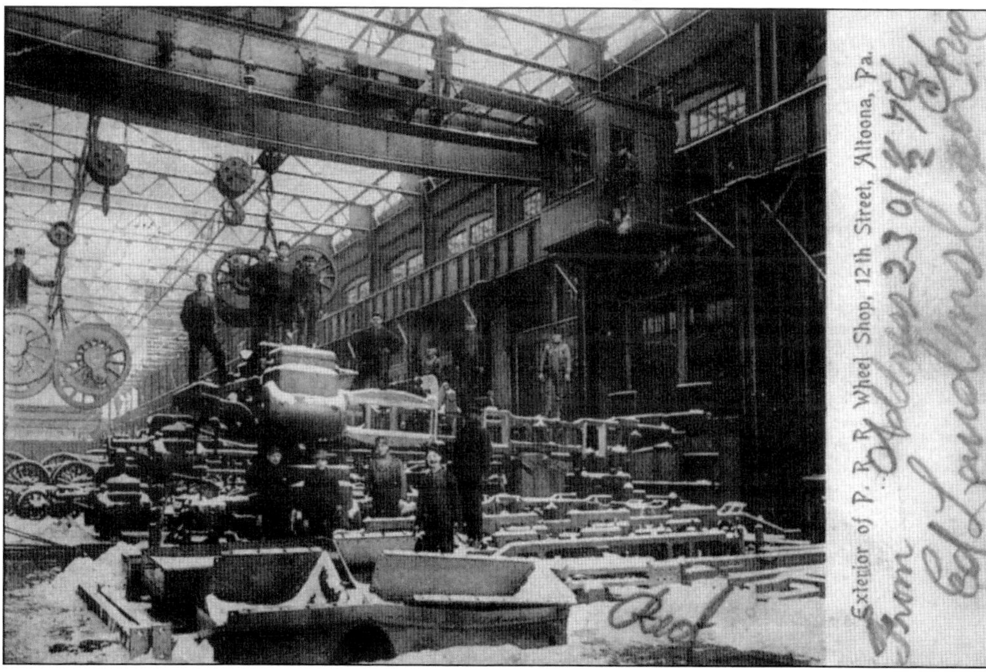

Shown is the exterior of PRR Wheel Shop, Twelfth Street. Seen under the gantry crane are locomotive driving wheels, as well as truck frames and cylinder heads. Maintaining steam locomotives was labor intensive, but it provided Altoona with its economic life blood and sustained European immigrants arriving for employment. As more and more families were established, the city grew. This card is postmarked August 19, 1905.

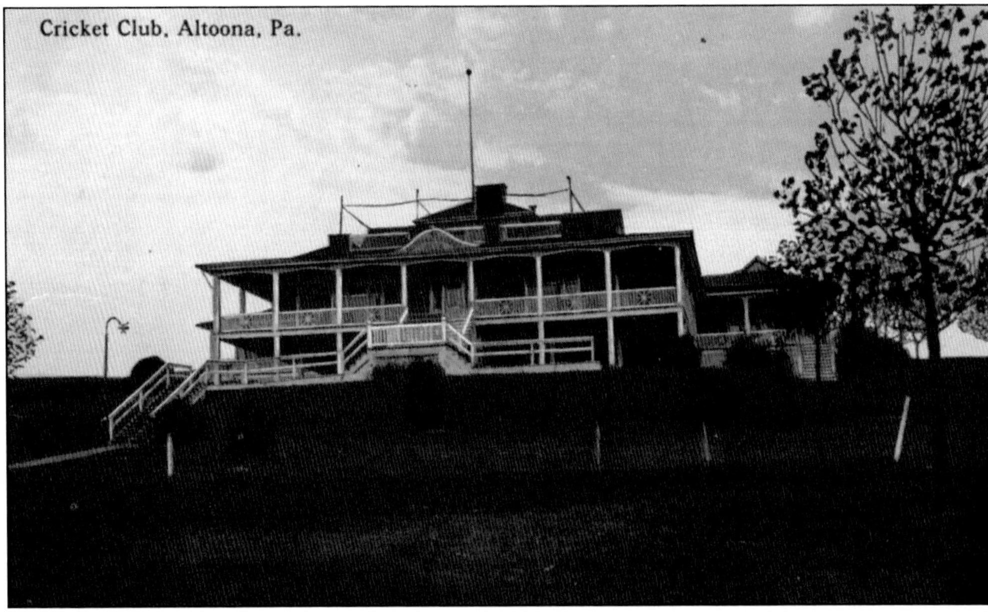

The Juniata and Altoona Pennsylvania Club House (known as the "Cricket Club") was located on Golf Hill between Altoona and Juniata. This club was for management of the PRR and wealthy citizens who enjoyed cricket in Altoona's infancy, as well as tennis and golf. Today, the land is no longer used for recreation but has been subdivided for commercial enterprises, as well as encroaching roadways.

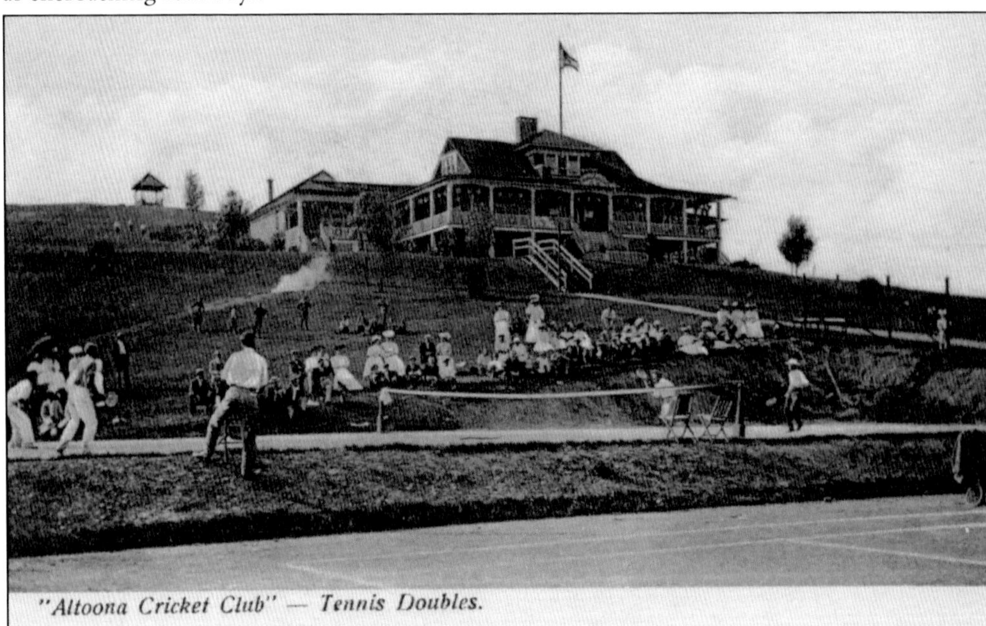

Here is a view of the Altoona Cricket Club's tennis doubles tournament. Designed for the recreation of PRR management and other prominent citizens, this club differed from the Cricket Field about six blocks west, which was a general sports stadium for all railroad employees and the general public. Cricket Field was well suited for baseball and all other sports. Today, that property is all commercial.

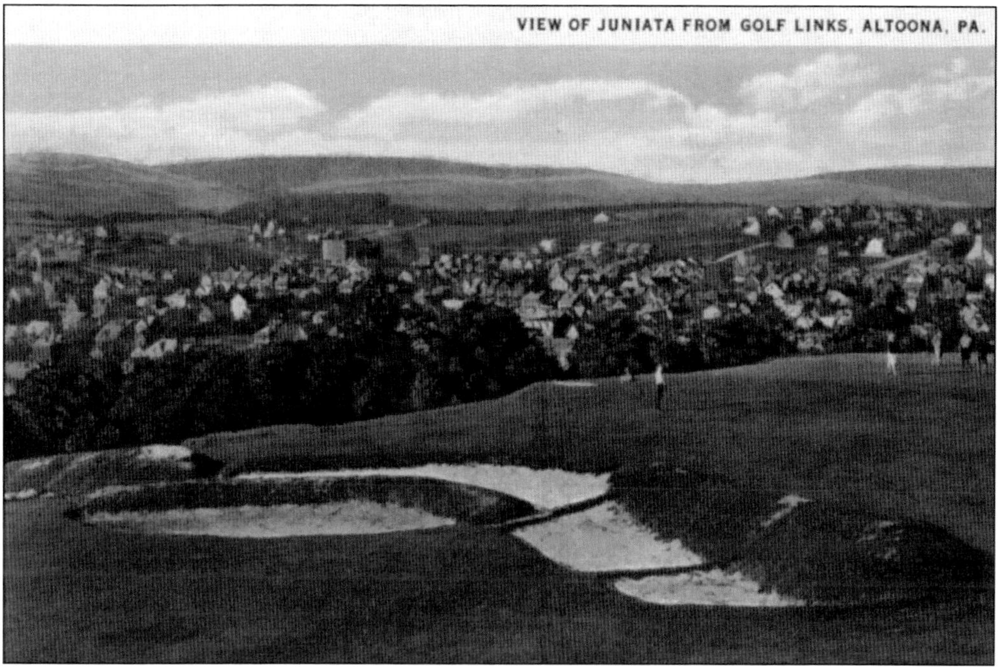

This is a view of Juniata from the Golf Links, part of the Cricket Club for management personnel of the PRR. This was a nine-hole golf course on a hill overlooking Juniata and the railroad's locomotive shops and car shops. It is now subdivided for commercial property and split by the relatively new Juniata Gap Road extension to Chestnut Avenue.

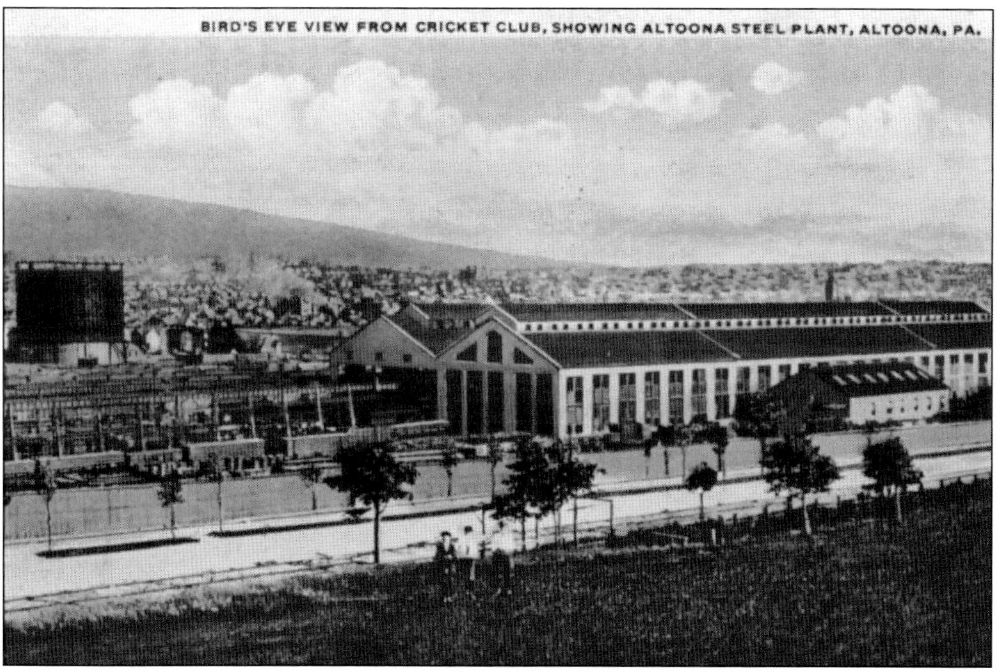

Here is the PRR's Altoona Car Shop as seen from the golf course of the Cricket Club. Freight and passenger cars were built or repaired here for a century prior to a decline following the end of the steam era. The card is postmarked July 22, 1925.

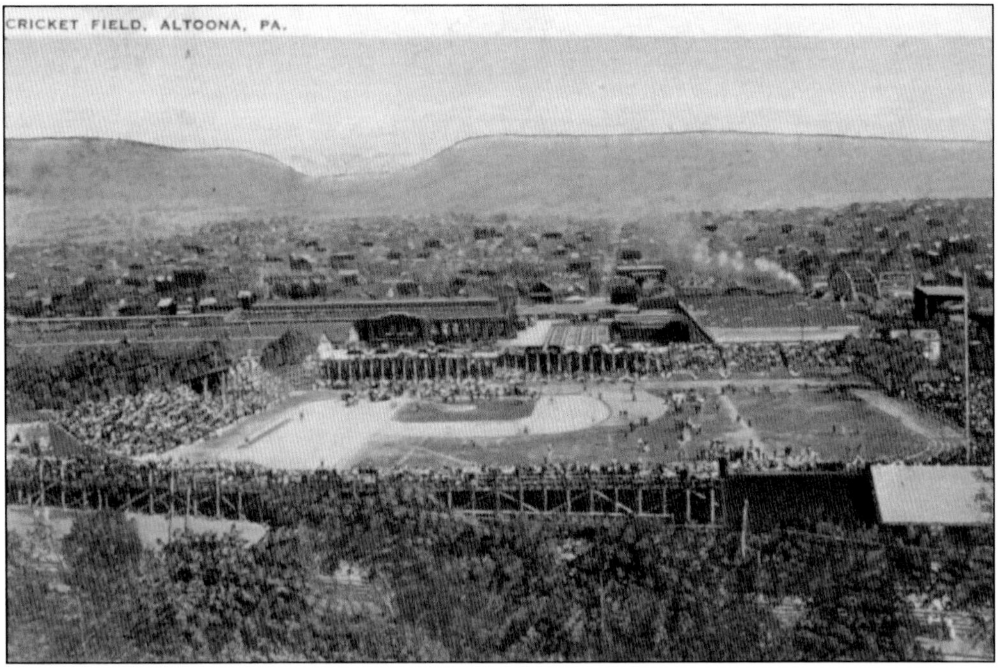

The Cricket Field, a sports stadium open to the public, was built and maintained by the PRR. Employees were sometimes recruited for sports ability much like colleges do today, as shop and division meets were commonplace here. Babe Ruth also played an exhibition baseball game here, belting a home run onto nearby Lexington Avenue.

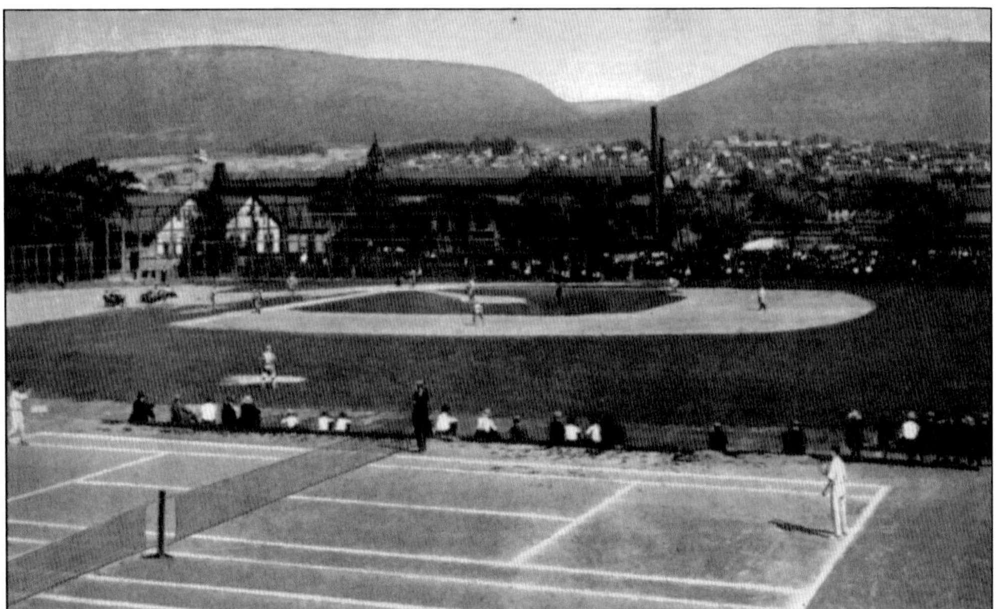

Summer recreation is shown at the Cricket Field. Tennis is played in the foreground while baseball is played on the adjoining field. This stadium was popular through the early 1960s before being dismantled. The area is now a shopping center with an office parcel. Parochial League football was popular here until its closing.

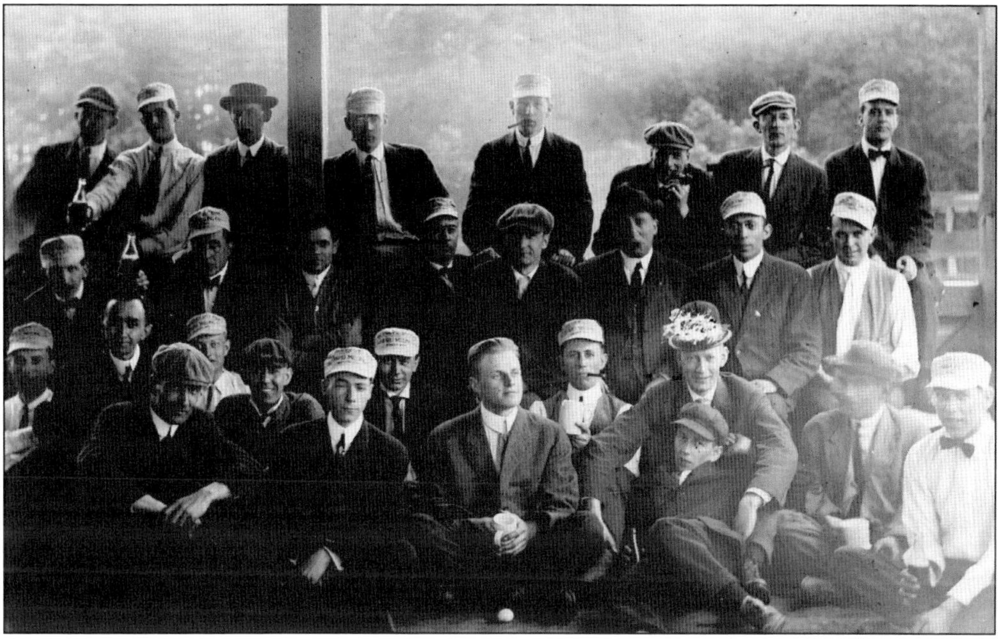

This is believed to be a group of PRR locomotive engineers, meeting in Altoona at the railroad's athletic venue, the Cricket Field. This sports stadium was located at Chestnut Avenue and Seventh Street, opposite the passenger car paint shops on the south and Altoona Hospital on the north. The railroad recruited employees for their sports prowess, much as colleges do today.

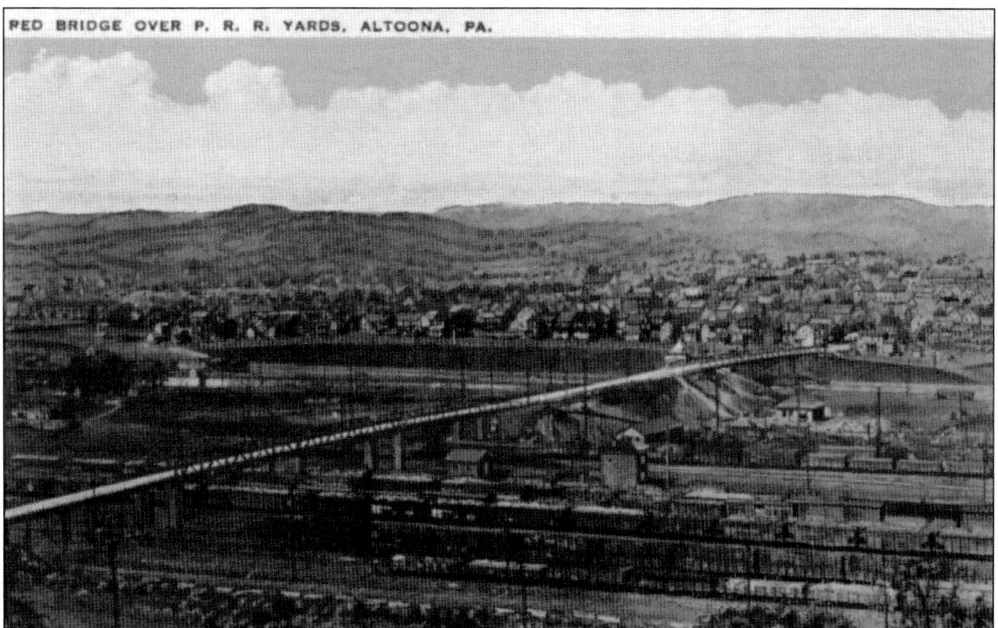

Here is a partial view of the PRR's classification yards in Altoona's Juniata section. The bridge spanning the yards was known as Red Bridge because of a red lead oxide paint used on the wrought iron in the early years. The massive east-west classification yard is a memory today, with only local shifting services and some re-crewing operations remaining.

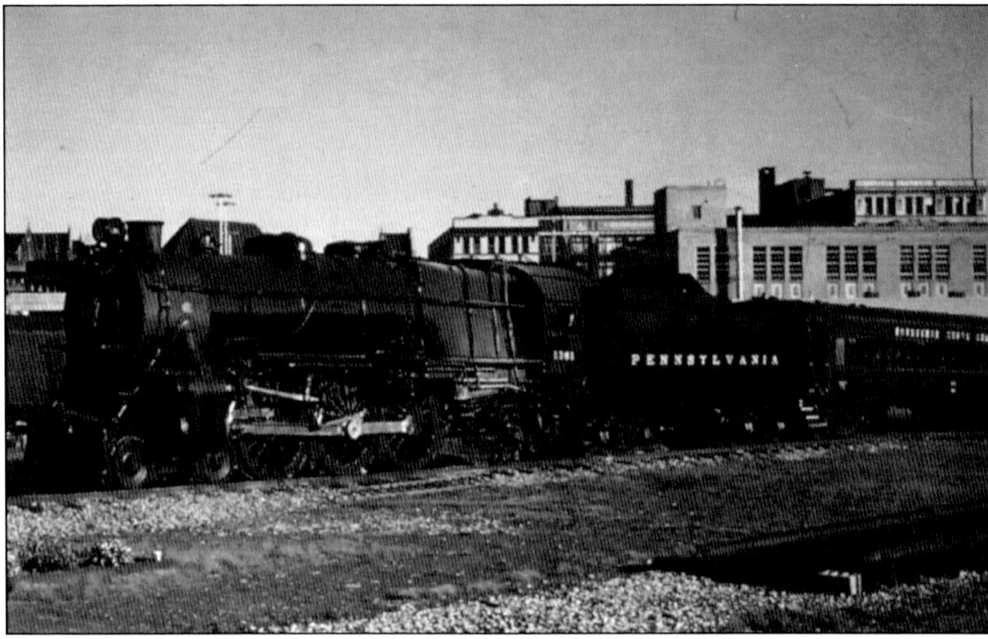

PRR steam locomotive No. 1361, Class K-4s, is exhibited at Railroader's Memorial Museum on May 17, 1987, following restoration and 28 years as a static display on Horseshoe Curve west of Altoona. One of 425 units of this class, it was the mainstay of the passenger services. This view is the former location of the original Altoona Works when Altoona was founded. (Photograph by Joe Glath, published by Mary Jayne's Railroad Specialties, Inc.)

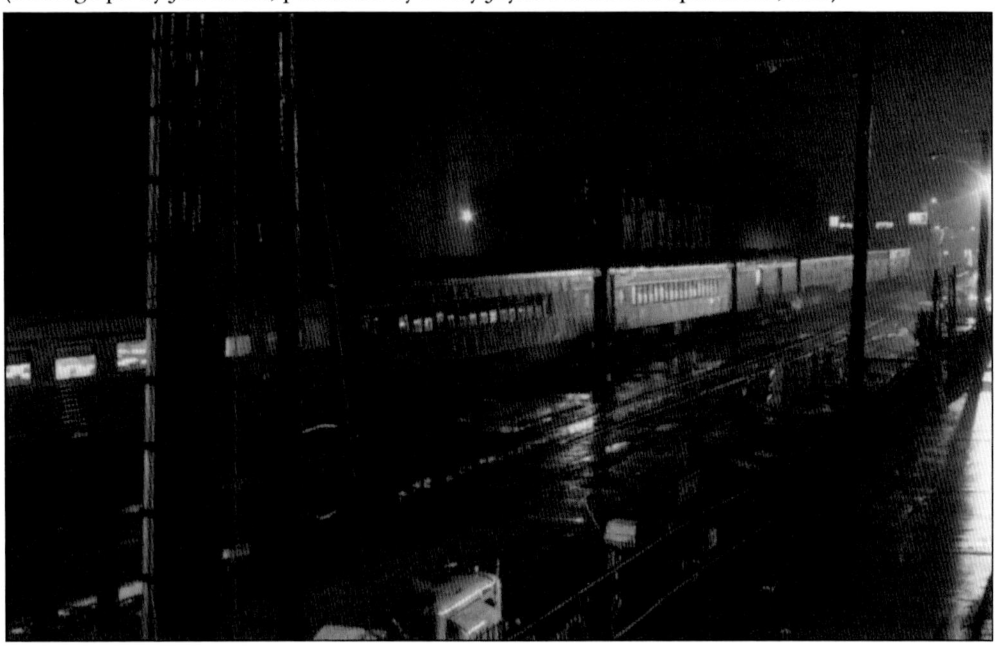

This view of the Manhattan Limited at Altoona station was taken in November 1968, nine months after the PRR's ill-fated merger with the New York Central Railroad. This train is westbound to Chicago. The closed shop buildings of the famed Altoona Works are in the background. (Photograph by the author and published by Mary Jayne's Railroad Specialties, Inc.)

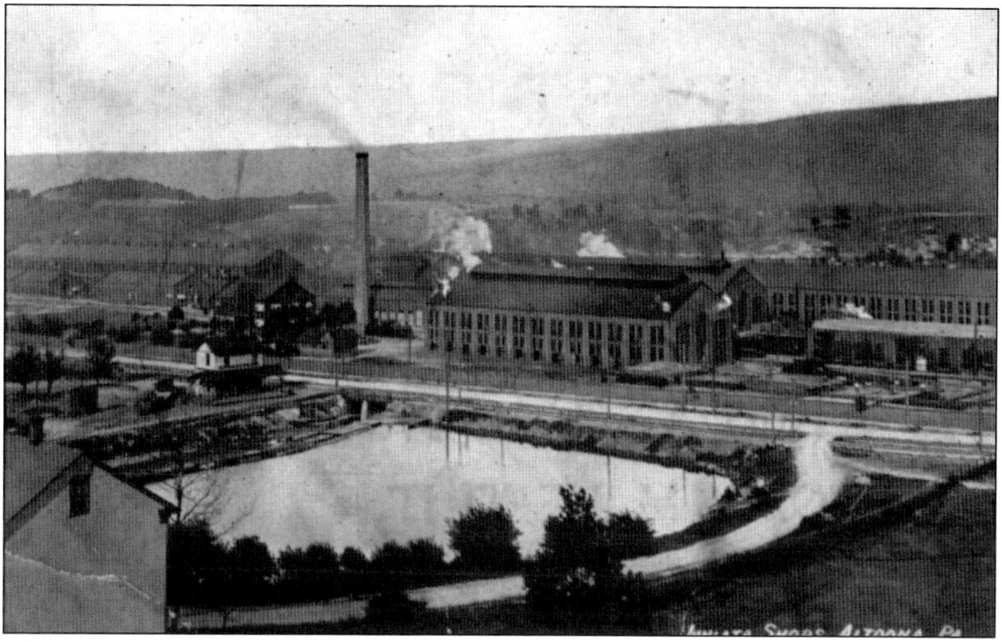

The Juniata Shops are pictured around 1910 as seen from golf hill of the Cricket Club. On the far side of the pond (Juniata Reservoir) is the terminus station of the Altoona Northern Railroad, a small short-line that traversed northward to crest scenic Wopsononock Mountain and which was popular with local residents. The pond is now filled in and was converted to commercial use, currently as Thompson's Pharmacy.

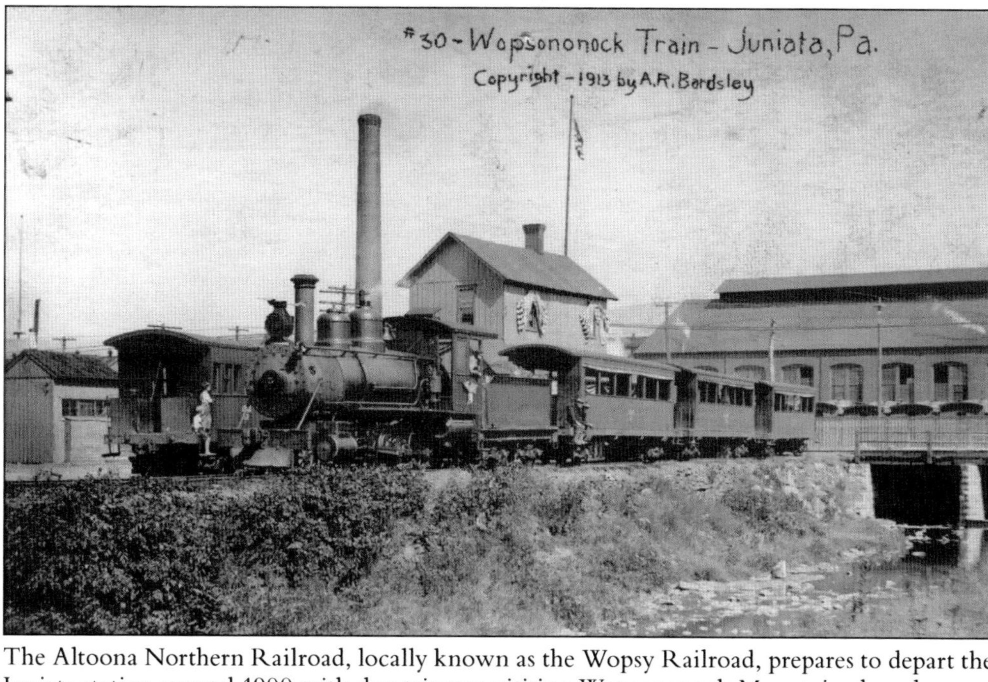

The Altoona Northern Railroad, locally known as the Wopsy Railroad, prepares to depart the Juniata station around 1900 with day-trippers visiting Wopsononock Mountain aboard an ex-PRR Class "R" locomotive. The railroad also served coal mines and lumbering operations on the mountain. (Courtesy of Elaine Conrad.)

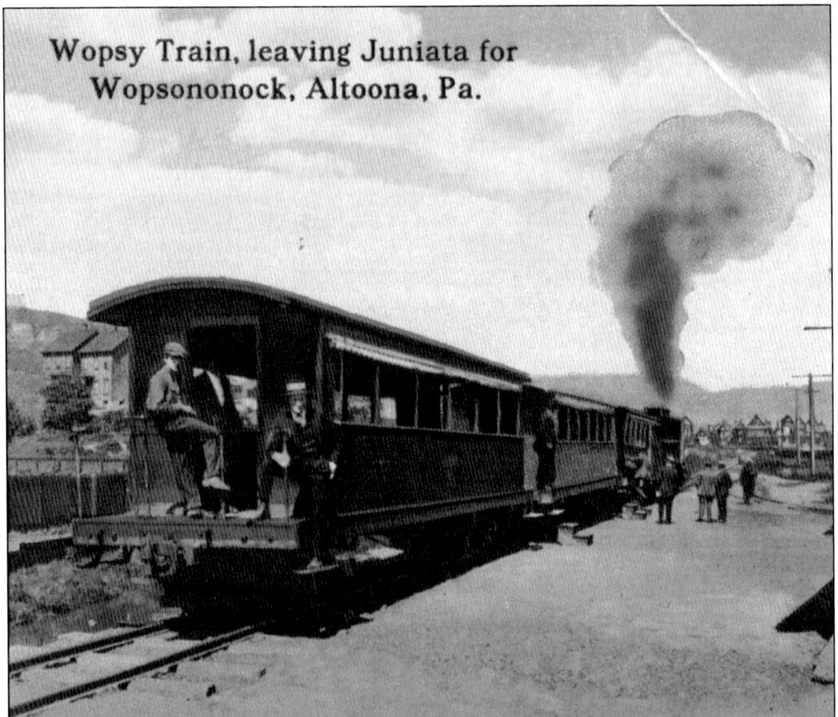

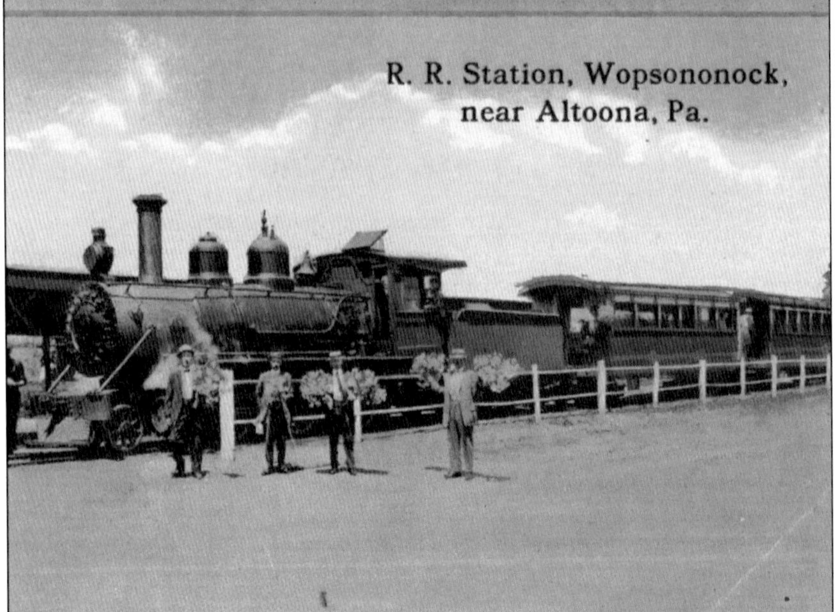

The Wopsy Train leaves Juniata for Wopsononock in the uppermost photograph. Immediately above is the railroad station at Wopsononock. The Juniata terminus was opposite the PRR's Juniata Shop complex, while Wopsononock was about 5 miles north on the plateau table of the mountain. The line passed through land that later became Ivyside Amusement Park and served a resort hotel and a spectacular lookout until a disastrous forest fire in 1905.

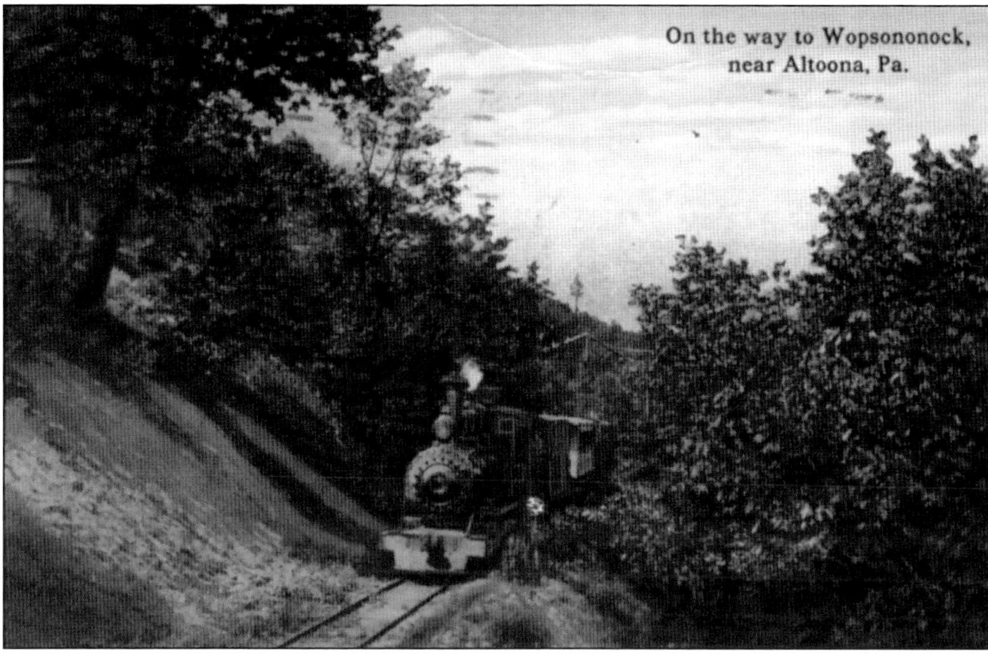

The Altoona Northern Railroad on the way to Wopsononock. This scenic line operated from Juniata to the plateau of Wopsononock mountain for passengers seeking relief from the summer heat or for patrons of the Wopsononock Resort Hotel. Although the line also transported coal and lumber, business fell off after the burning of the hotel and the surrounding forest in 1905, and the railroad closed in 1921. This card is postmarked August 9, 1917.

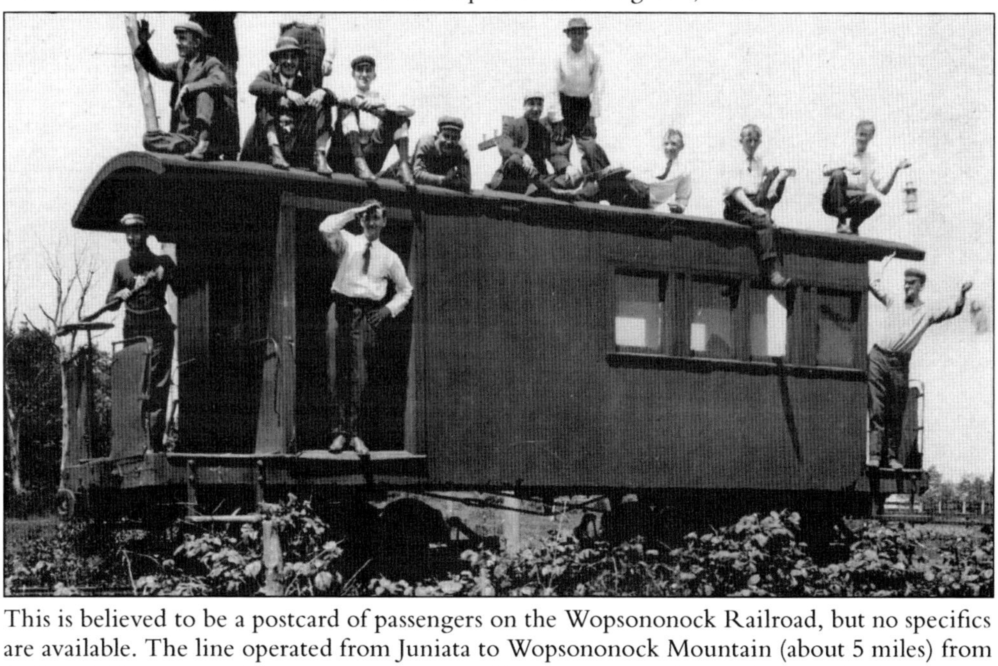

This is believed to be a postcard of passengers on the Wopsononock Railroad, but no specifics are available. The line operated from Juniata to Wopsononock Mountain (about 5 miles) from 1891 to 1921, and the fare on the last trip was 70¢ per person. The gradient on the line was 4 feet to the mile, steep for the equipment of the day. Note the brakeman using the brake-club on the handbrakes.

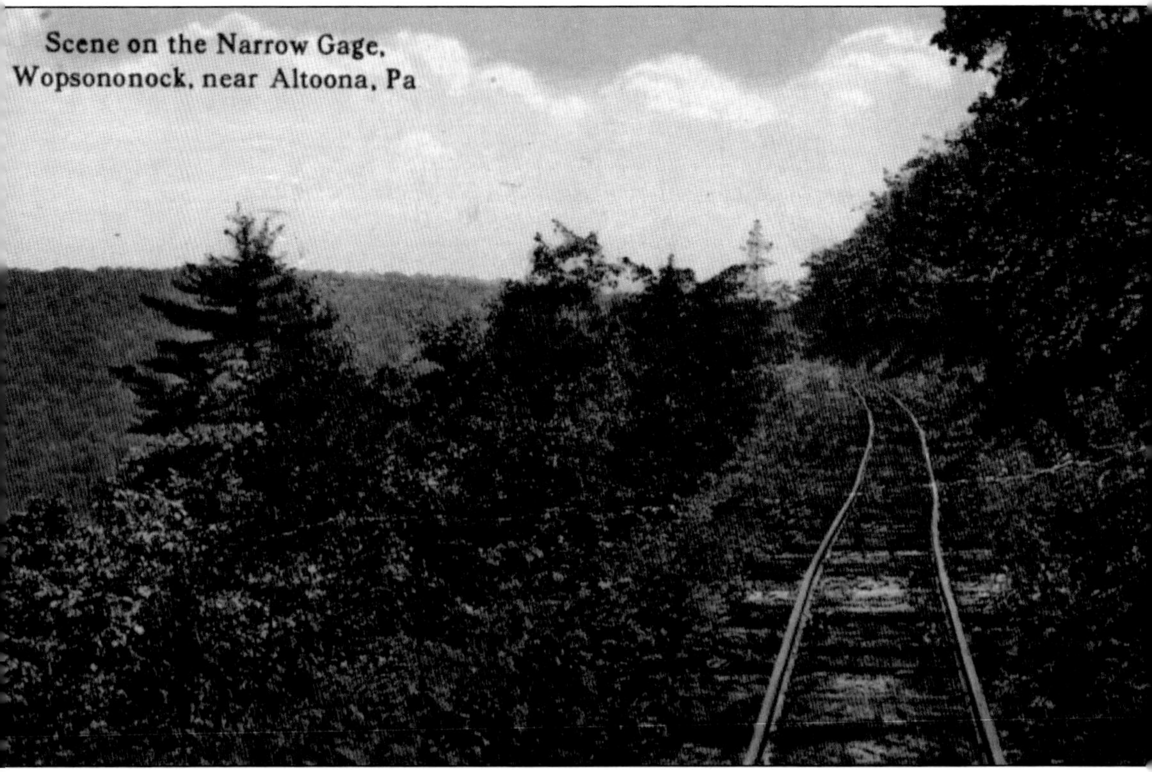

Here is a scene on the narrow gauge Wopsononock near Altoona. This line, although constructed as a narrow gauge starting in 1889, was converted to standard gauge in 1900. The line was reported to have operated two R-class locomotives from the PRR and five Baldwin moguls for heavy hauling on the steep grades. Wopsononock was known for the resort hotel, restaurant, dance pavilion, photograph gallery, picnic grounds, tennis courts, and a lookout tower, which afforded a 22-mile view. The lookout lasted until 1921 when another forest fire destroyed the structure. It was 40 feet in height. Prominent visitors to the area were various PRR officials from Philadelphia, as well as Andrew Carnegie and Charles M. Schwab, titans of the steel industry. Schwab would visit when staying at his summer estate at Loretto in neighboring Cambria County.

Three

Horseshoe Curve

The phrase "World-Famous Horseshoe Curve" is a common term in Altoona's postcard labels and tourism literature. The town's most famous geographical landmark may seem to function as a tourist destination, but it also serves as a vital link in the transcontinental railroad system. Horseshoe Curve was designed by a team of engineers led by J. Edgar Thomson, who faced the challenge of fitting a railroad line to the terrain, enabling the railroad to cross a mountain range. Five miles west of the newly founded town of Altoona, engineers were confronted by unusual terrain—a sort of gap between three mountains. Bridging this gap would result in a gradient in excess of 2 percent, which was unacceptable. Instead, Thomson and his crew detoured into a type of cul-de-sac formed by these three mountains, slicing off ledges on the easterly and westerly sides, as well as the face of Kittanning Point in the center. Using the fill from these excavations, streams and a road were bridged on either side of Kittanning Point, enabling the railroad line to gain gradual elevation (or descent). This engineering came to be known as Horseshoe Curve because of its shape. The design was revolutionary for its time, with far-reaching impact, as the method enabled railroads everywhere to conquer mountain terrain previously thought to be impassable.

Horseshoe Curve and the approximately 12-mile line from Altoona to Gallitzin summit was constructed during the period 1850–1854. Constructed primarily by 450 Irish laborers who left Ireland during the potato famine, using picks, axes, shovels, mules, wheelbarrows, and black powder, the line crested the Eastern Continental Divide at Gallitzin. The railroad line west of Altoona climbs or descends the Allegheny Mountain at a gradient of 2 percent or less at an average rate of 91 feet to the mile. Originally constructed in single-track form, it rapidly expanded to four tracks. During the Conrail period of the 1980s, it was scaled back to three tracks, using modern technologies and signaling. Horseshoe Curve remains vital into the 21st century and is a national landmark.

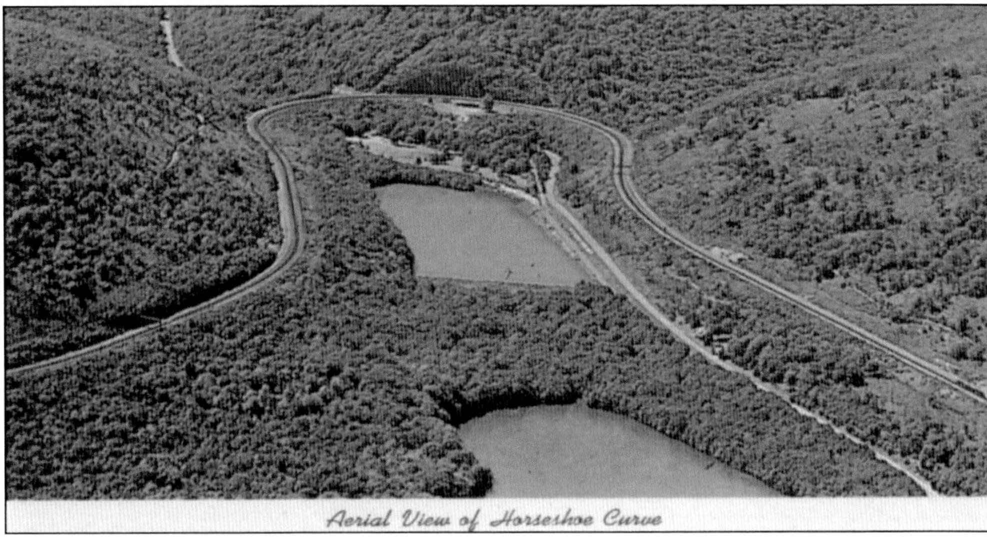

This aerial view of Horseshoe Curve clearly illustrates the dramatic route the PRR chose to ascend the east slope of the Allegheny Mountains west of Altoona. This line started with one track but rapidly grew to four, creating the famed "broad way," which their premier passenger train Broadway Limited traveled for decades between New York and Chicago. A bridge spanning the chasm would have been too steep for trains to navigate.

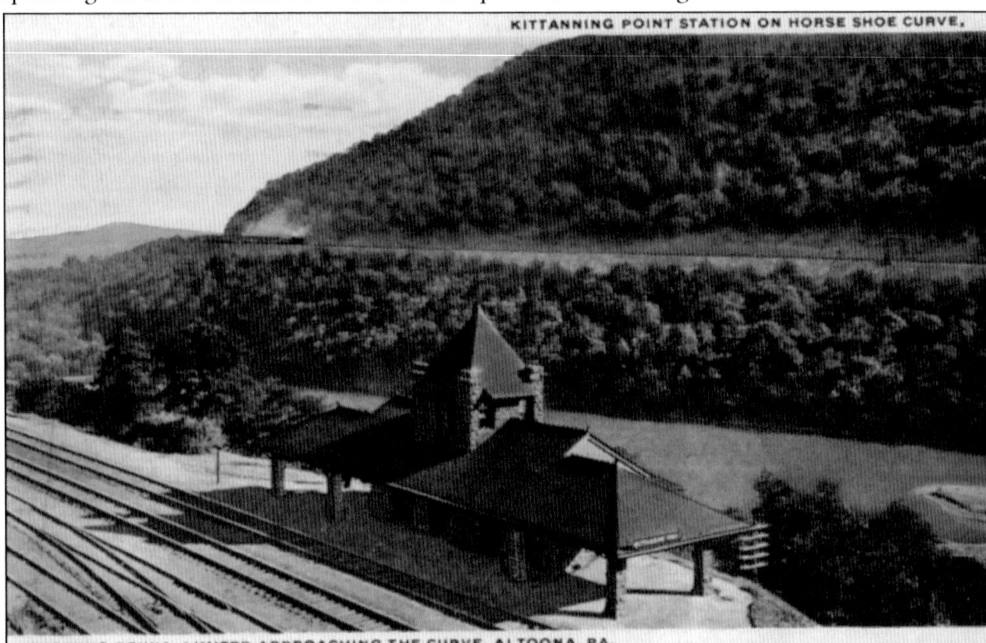

This view of the Kittanning Point Station shows the Pennsylvania Limited approaching the curve on the PRR 5 miles west of Altoona. Closed and razed prior to World War II, this station served small mining communities near the curve such as the village of Glen White. The Glen White mine and its namesake village no longer exist; the station site is today the approximate location of a signal bridge. Norfolk Southern Railroad owns and operates the railroad today, succeeding Penn Central and Consolidated Rail Corporation. This card was postmarked December 1, 1920.

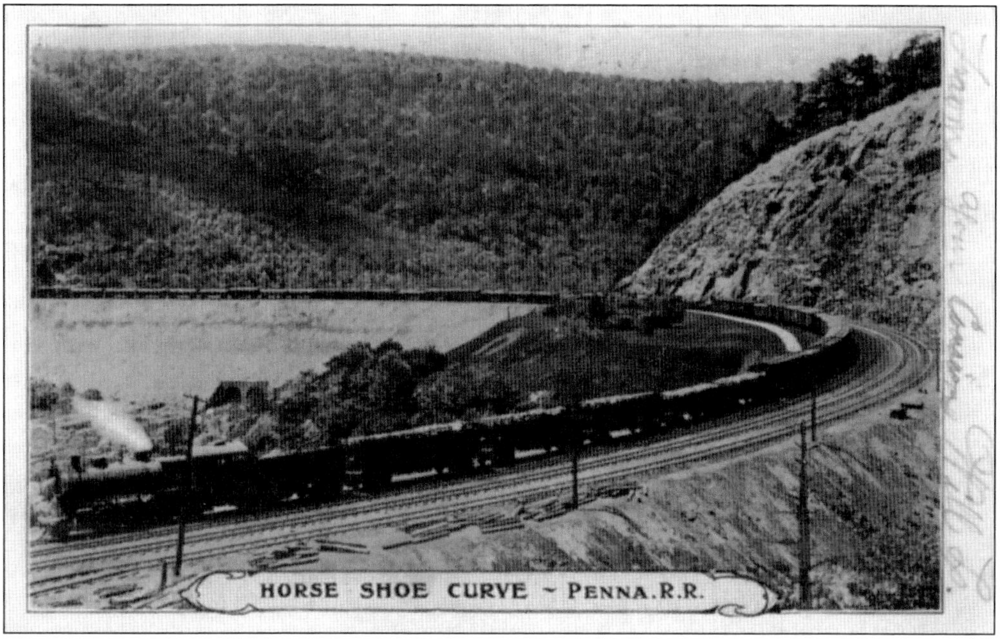

A PRR freight train descends the Allegheny Mountain around Horseshoe Curve in this early 1900s view. The railroad has reached its four-track profile and the low vegetation of steam-locomotive days gives an expansive view of Horseshoe Curve. Encroaching vegetation today somewhat diminishes this commanding view. The card is postmarked September 11, 1906.

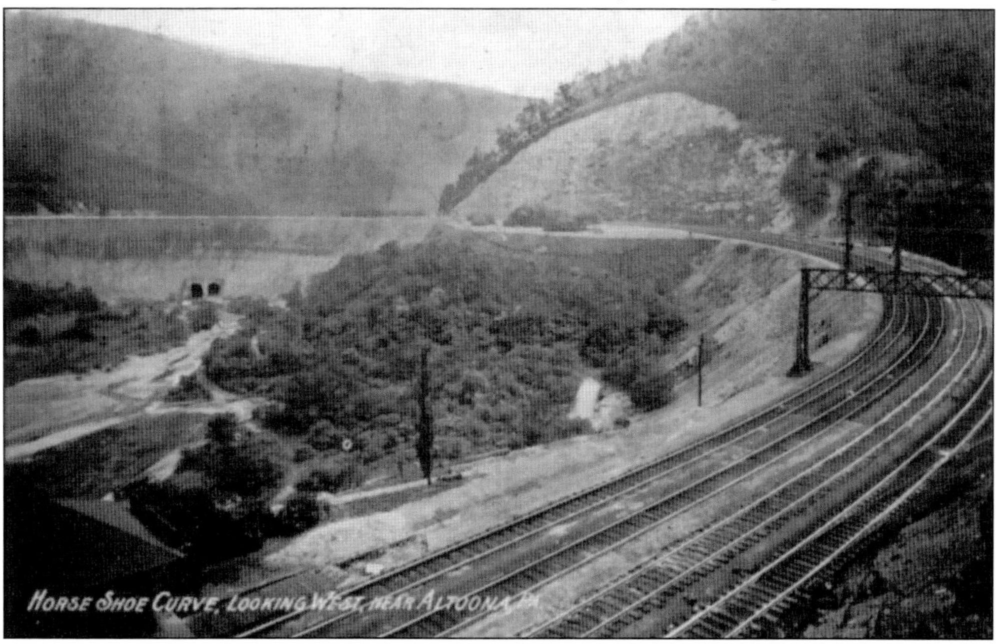

This view of Horseshoe Curve looks west in the first decade of the 20th century. Note the corner of Kittanning Point station (lower left) with semaphore signal masts on the bridge frame. The face of Kittanning Point Mountain was sliced off with basic hand implements and black powder to fill in the side ravines to provide passage; the project was the first of its kind. This card is postmarked April 28, 1908.

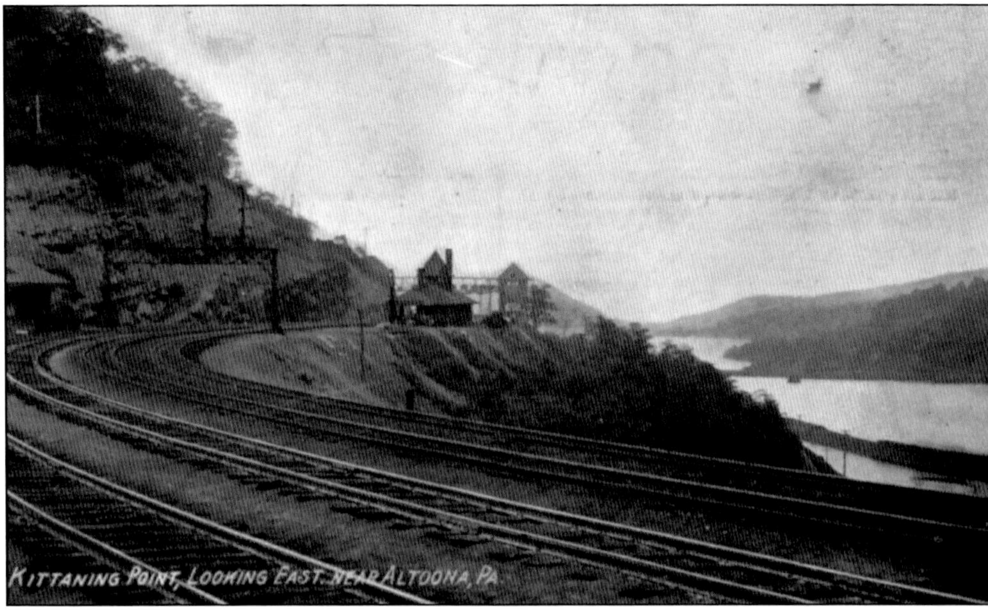

J. Edgar Thomson is credited for surveying the route that became Horseshoe Curve and he became president of the PRR. In this *c.* 1900s view easterly on Horseshoe Curve, the Kittanning Point Station can be seen in the distance with the three reservoirs in the valley below supplying the city of Altoona.

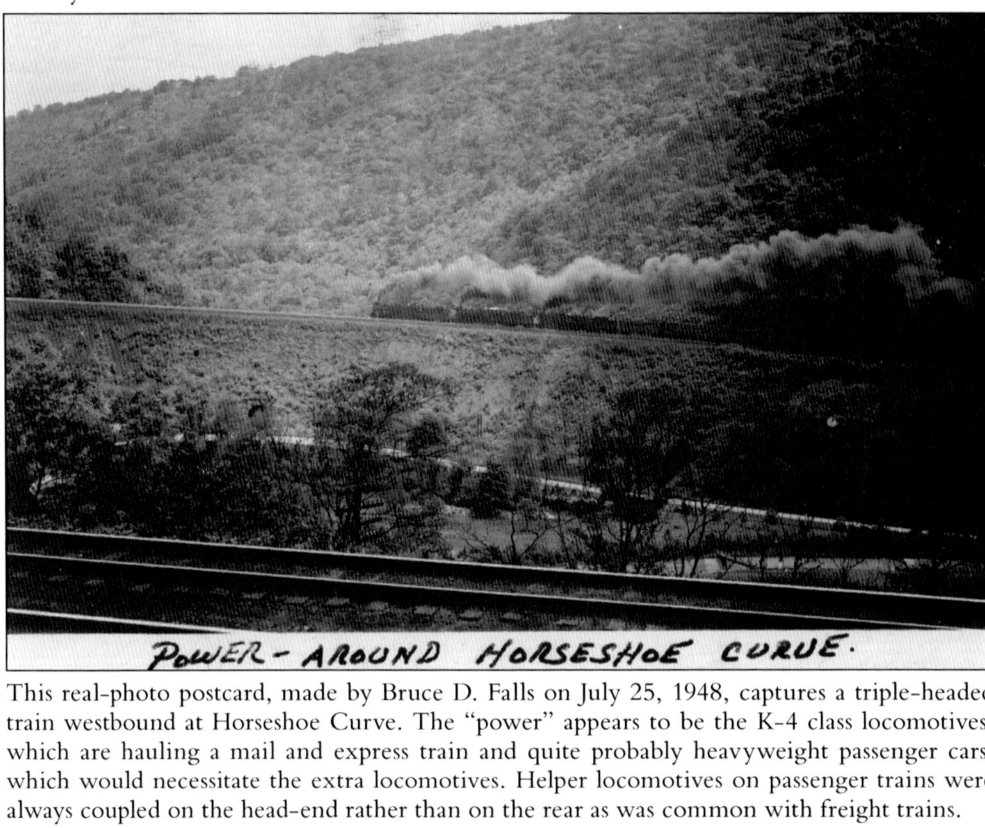

This real-photo postcard, made by Bruce D. Falls on July 25, 1948, captures a triple-headed train westbound at Horseshoe Curve. The "power" appears to be the K-4 class locomotives, which are hauling a mail and express train and quite probably heavyweight passenger cars, which would necessitate the extra locomotives. Helper locomotives on passenger trains were always coupled on the head-end rather than on the rear as was common with freight trains.

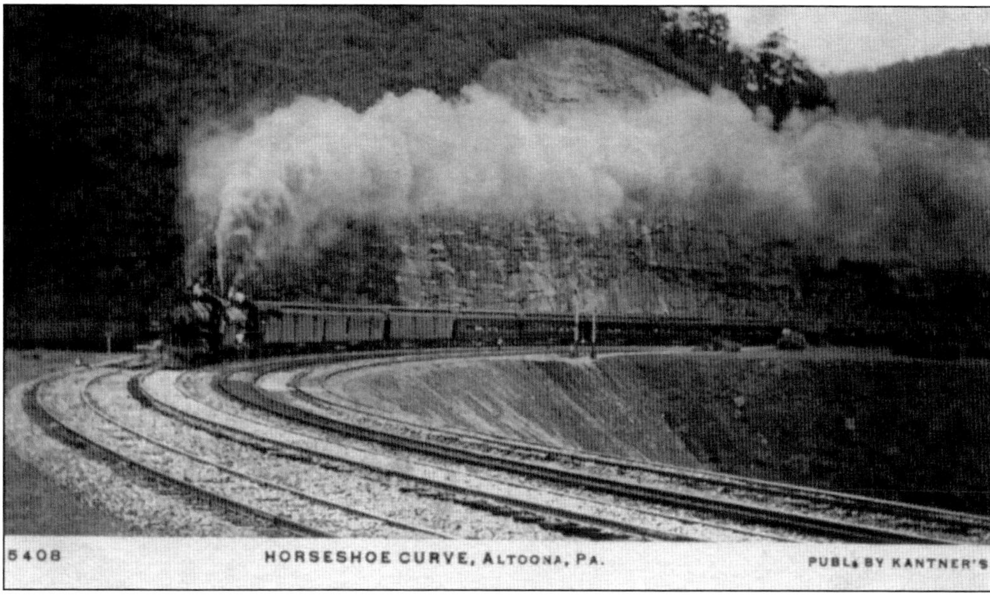

This is an early 20th-century view of a dual-locomotive passenger train westbound on Horseshoe Curve. Westbound trains worked hardest in the effort to climb the 91 feet to the mile elevation gain on the mountain, and passenger trains often had extra locomotives on the front in contrast to freight trains with helper locomotives on the rear of the train. It was also imperative that passenger trains maintain their schedules.

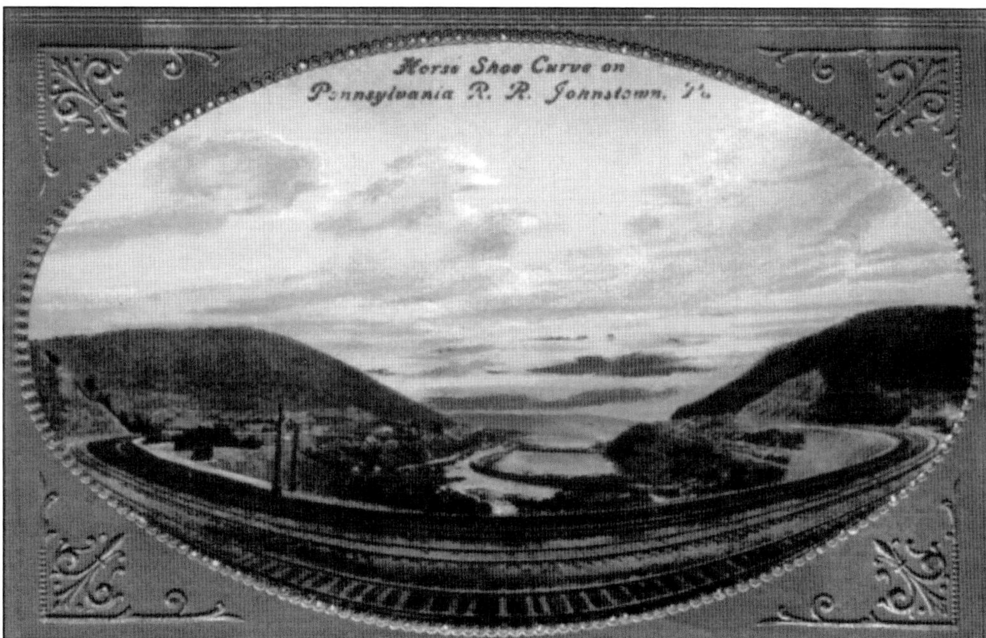

This early panoramic view of Horseshoe Curve replicates the early photography of William Herman Rau, who was commissioned by the PRR in the 1890s to photograph the system and whose images fortunately survive in museums today, including the Southern Alleghenies Museum of Art in Altoona. William Rau designed a camera to take the first panoramic view of Horseshoe Curve. This card is dated 1908.

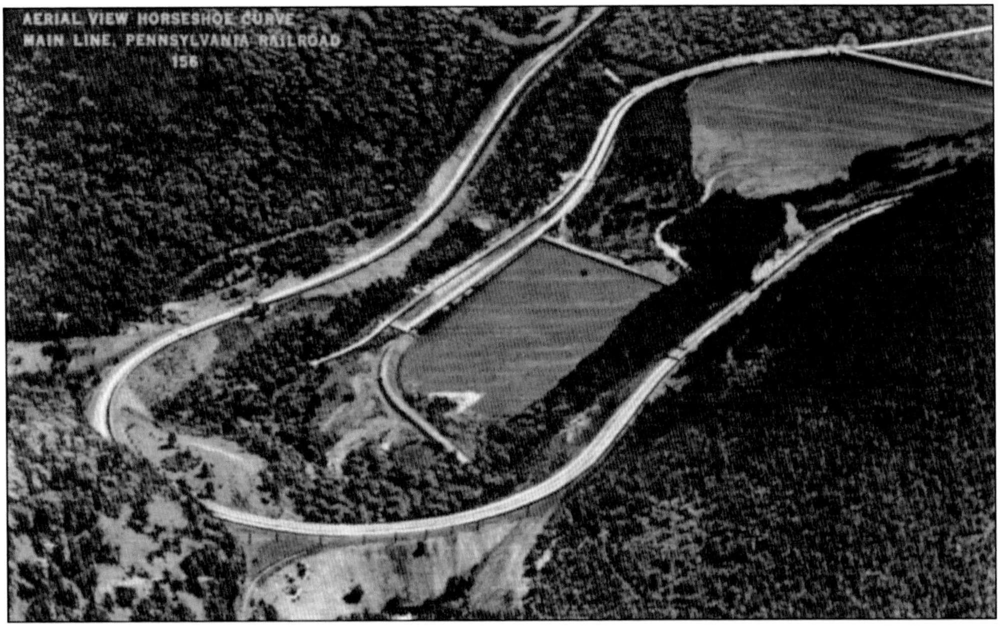

The geography of Horseshoe Curve is dramatic when viewed from the air. This cul-de-sac type valley enabled the PRR to gain elevation gradually, and the bowl of this valley provided space for three water reservoirs to supply the city of Altoona and the railroad. For its first 100 years the PRR used vast quantities of coal and water to power its locomotives and manufacturing shops. This linen style card dates from the 1950s.

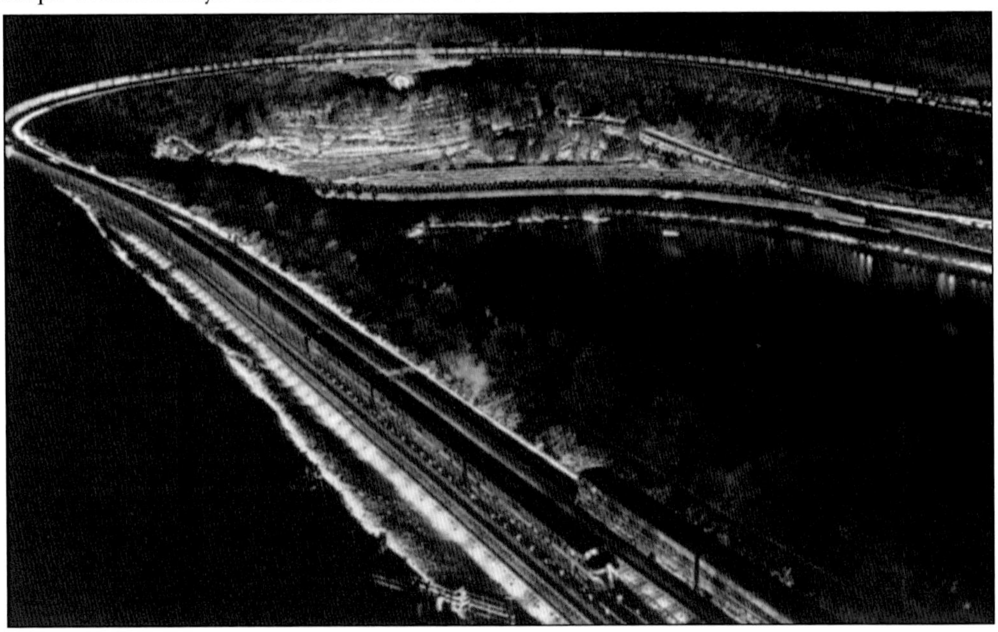

February 15, 1954, marked the 100th anniversary of Horseshoe Curve, but it was observed by this impressive night flash photograph on October 20, 1954. The PRR and Sylvania Electric Products joined to make this image, which required 6,000 flashbulbs on pie-plate reflectors. In the foreground, the westbound *Trailblazer* pauses for the photograph with red flares illuminating the Tuscan-red livery of the locomotives and passenger cars.

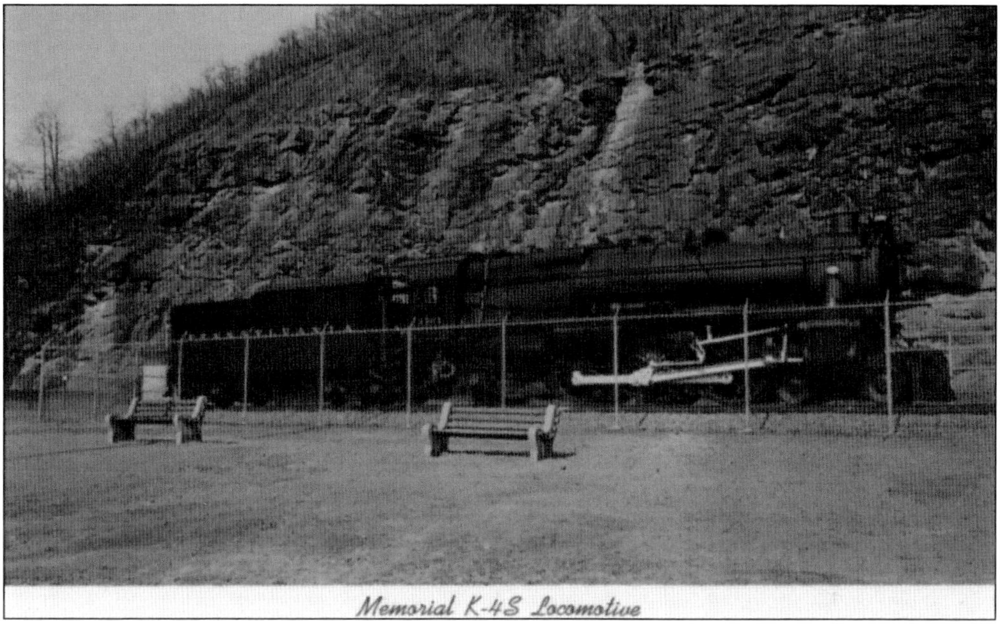

This class K-4s steam locomotive, one of 425 produced by the PRR to power the passenger fleet, was presented to the city of Altoona and placed at Horseshoe Curve as a lasting memorial to the age of steam and the contributions of railroad workers who helped manufacture, maintain, or operate these locomotives. It was dedicated on June 8, 1957, the last year for steam locomotives on the railroad.

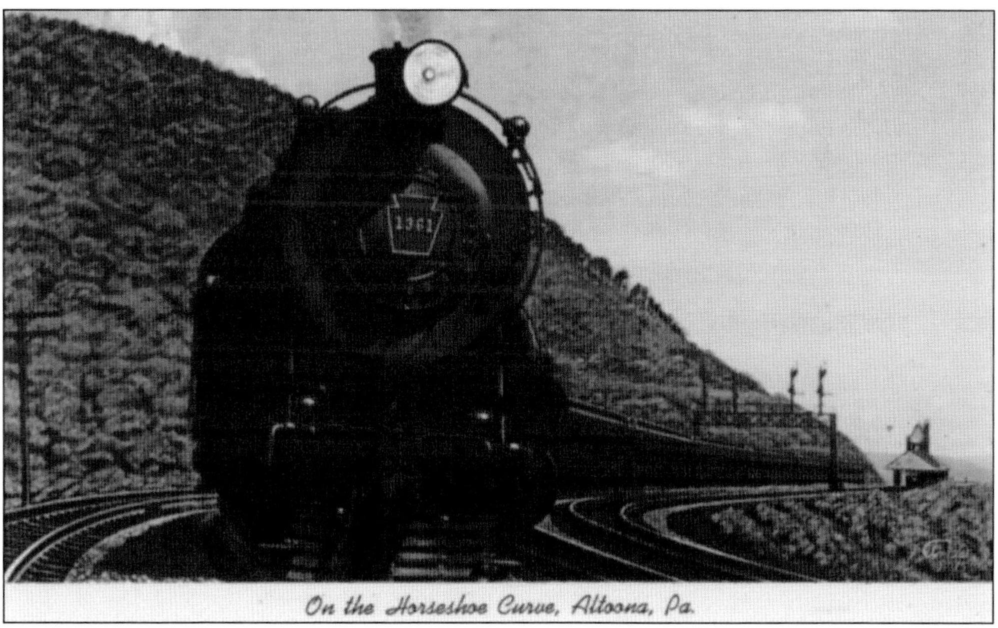

This artistic rendering is labeled "Rounding the curve is the World Famous K-4-s Pacific Steam Passenger Locomotive No. 1361, enroute to western cities . . ." This rendition by artist Don Antes of State College enshrines not only Horseshoe Curve but the famed passenger iron horse of the PRR, built and maintained in the Altoona Locomotive Shops. K-4s Locomotive No. 1361 survives and is owned by Railroader's Memorial Museum in Altoona.

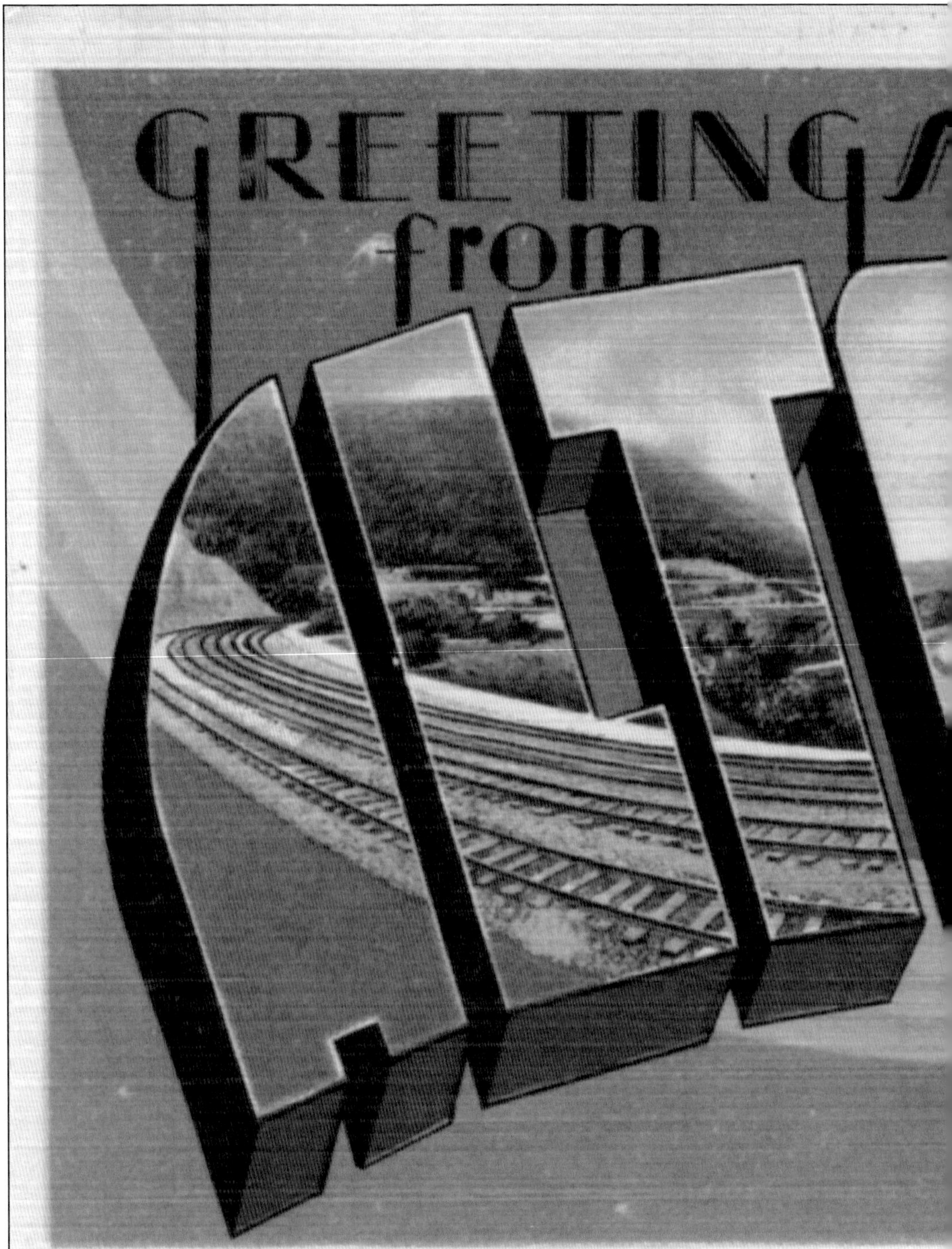

This linen-style card from the 1950s commands the viewer's attention by boldly proclaiming Altoona's association with Horseshoe Curve, the city's most notable landmark. Located 5 miles west of the city, Horseshoe Curve represents one of the most famous advances in civil engineering by being the first of its kind to enable railroads to conquer mountain ranges at

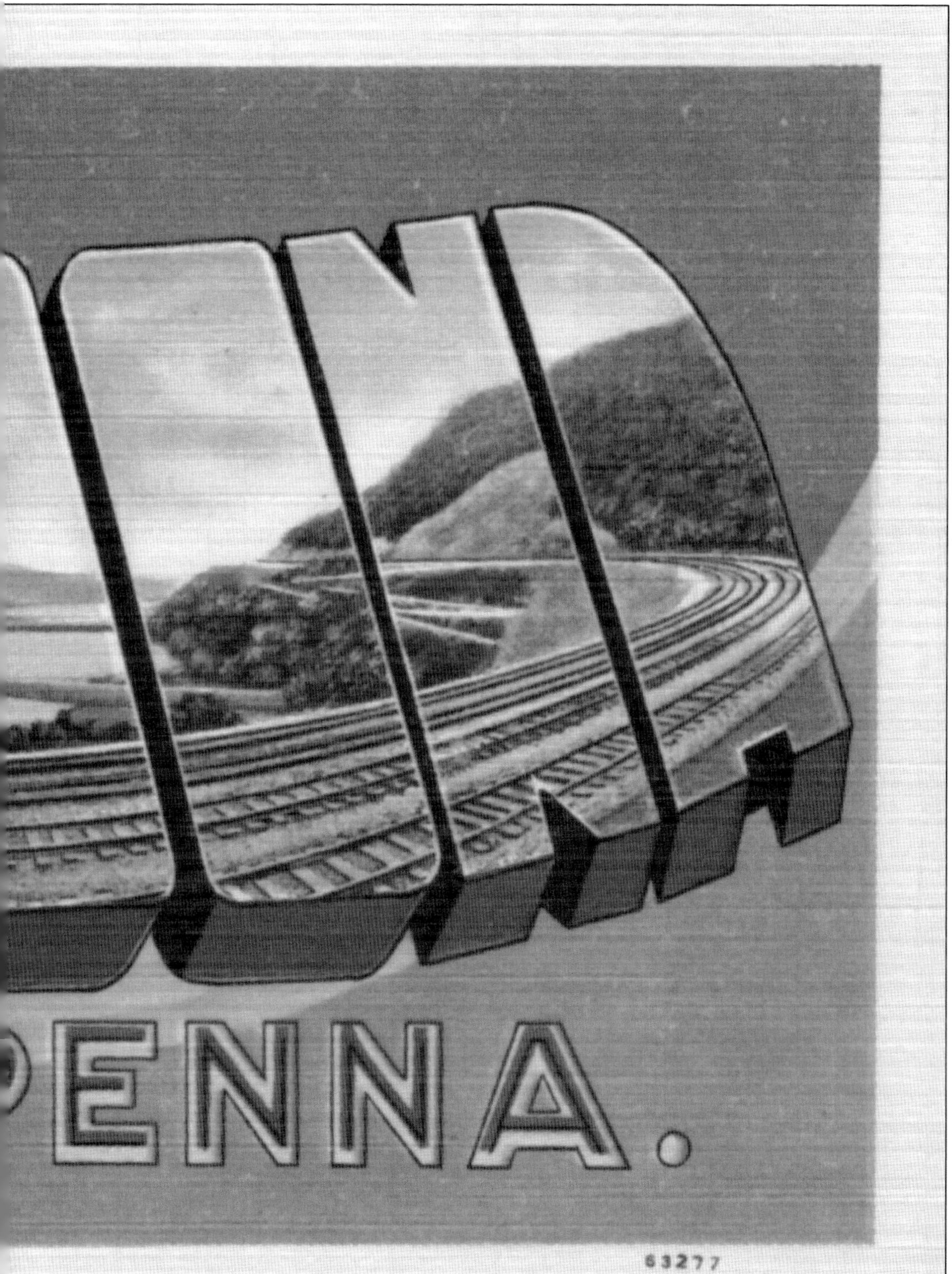

an acceptable gradient. Altoona's ties to the railroad industry that founded it continue 159 years after inception, adding credibility to its distinction. It has been designated a national landmark.

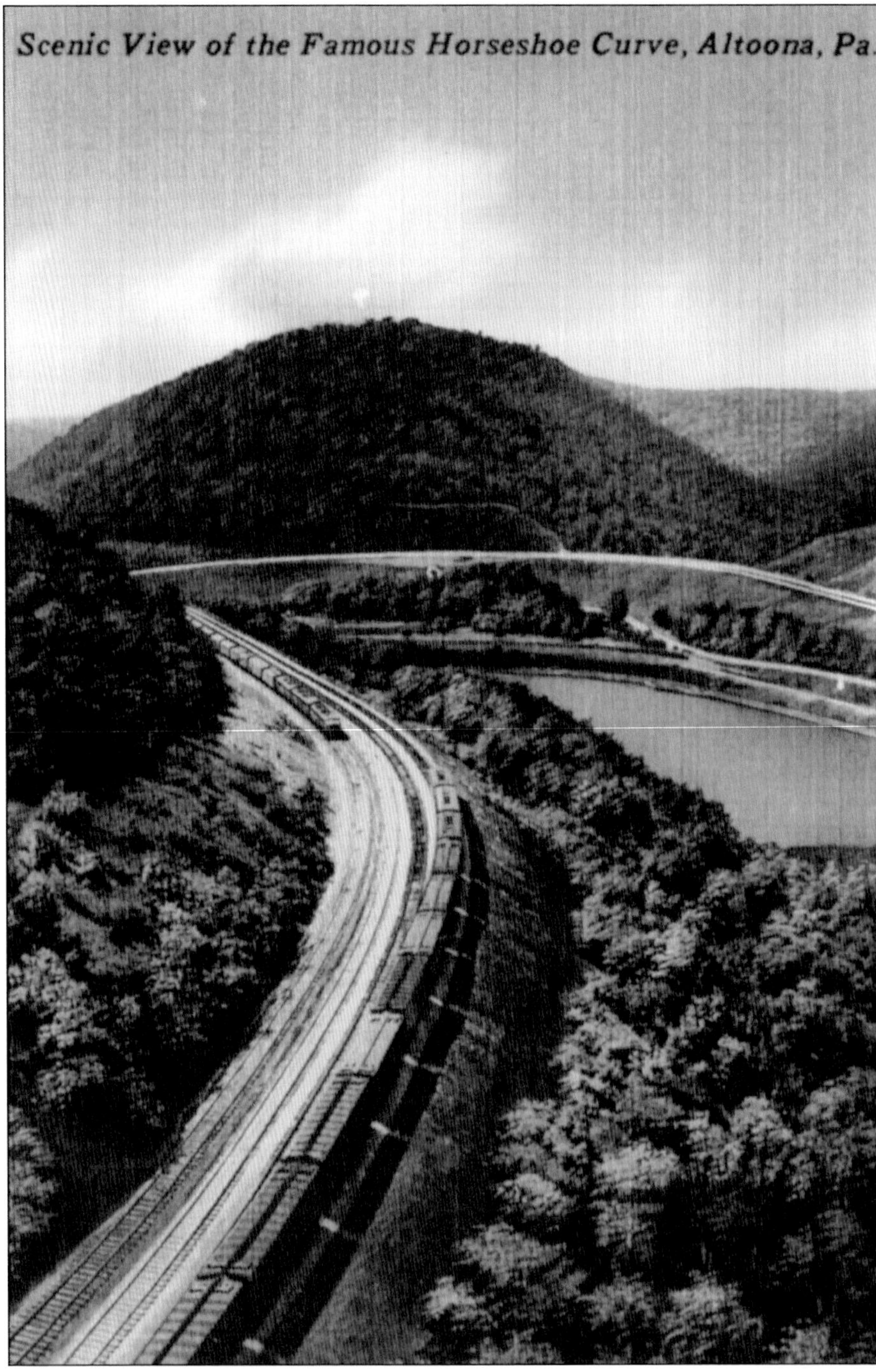

In this linen-style postcard from Altoona News Agency, the Horseshoe Curve is seen from high on the western ridge. The postcard states "The Horseshoe Curve is a noteworthy piece of railroad engineering on the PRR along the slopes of Allegrippus Gorge near the summit of the Allegheny Mountains. It may be seen on the left of the train, traveling westward just beyond Altoona, Penna., and with a graceful curve of 1845 ft. nearly 1600 ft above the sea, presents many magnificent scenic vistas to the traveler."

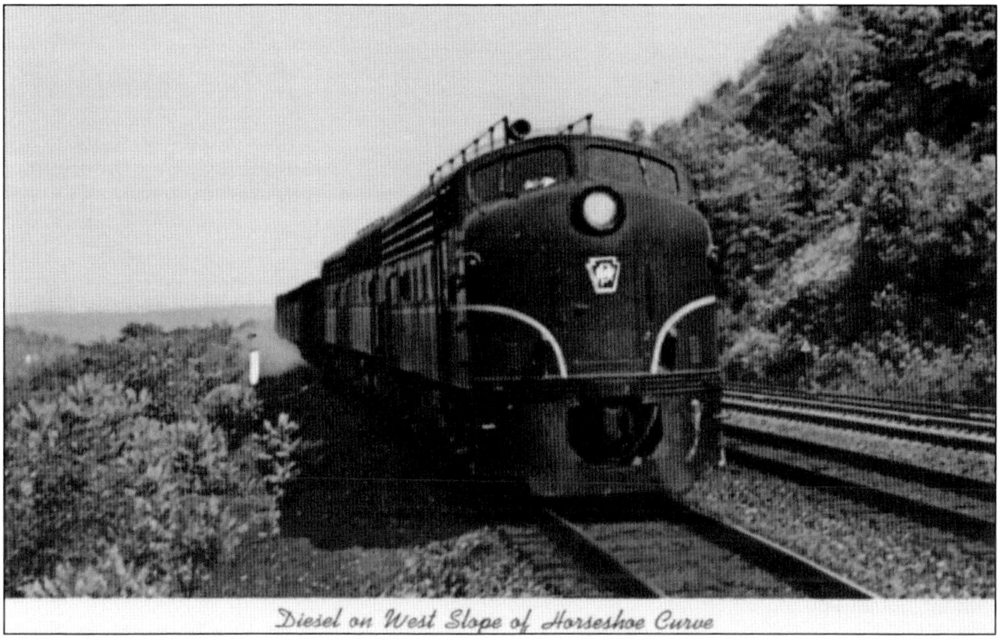

In this late 1950s scene, a trio of EMD F-7s approaches Horseshoe Curve eastbound with a coal train, nearing milepost 242. Coal has remained a major commodity for shipment through the 19th and 20th centuries, and into the 21st century. This train will enter the Altoona yard at South Tower and will move over the Juniata scales for weighing prior to being sent to Eastern destinations. (Photograph by Sheldon L. Burns.)

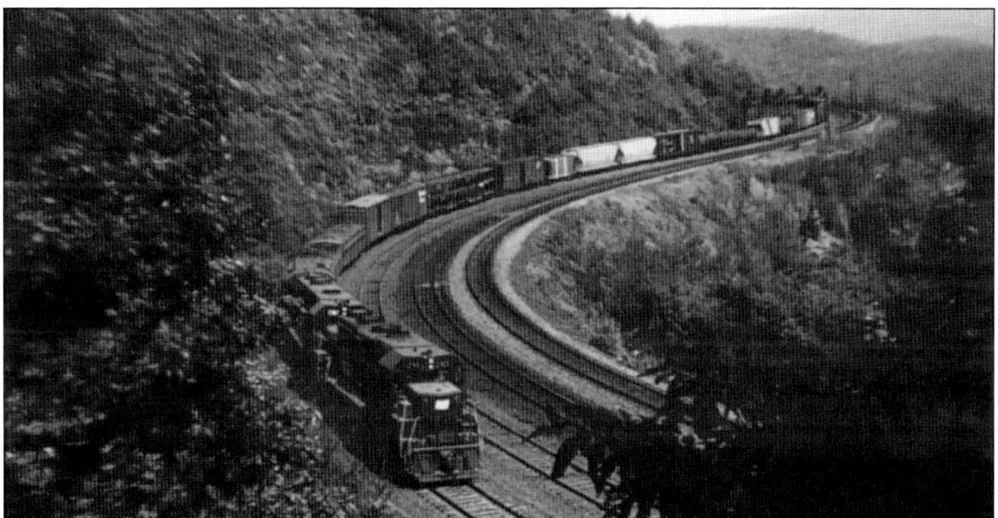

On February 1, 1968, the PRR merged with the New York Central Railroad, thus ending its 122-year reign. Known as Penn Central Transportation Company, this ill-fated merger resulted in bankruptcy on June 21, 1970, representing the largest industrial business failure in history at that time. Penn Central continued to operate with deferred maintenance until Congress created Conrail (Consolidated Rail Corporation) to rescue Penn Central and other bankrupt Eastern railroads. Here a Penn Central train is westbound on the four track Horseshoe Curve in September 1970. (Photograph by Carl H. Sturner; published by Audio Visual Designs.)

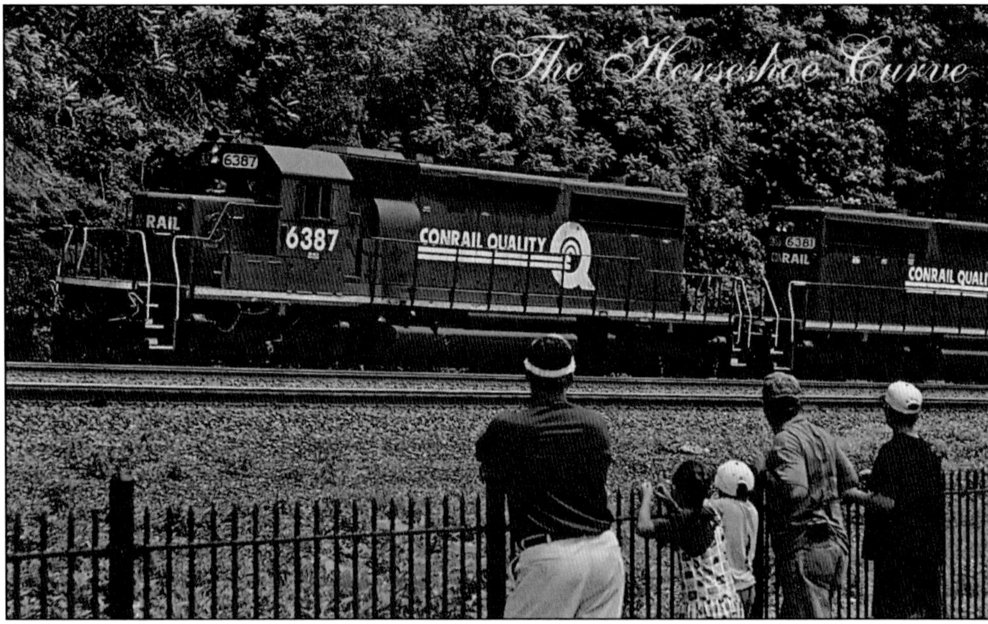

In the Conrail era a pair of SD-40-2 locomotives can be seen heading westbound on Horseshoe Curve in their fresh blue paint. With Conrail, work-rules changes, divestiture of passenger train services, and modernization created cost-saving efficiencies and stabilized employment in an industry previously known for job fluctuation. Under Conrail, Horseshoe Curve was reduced from four tracks to three.

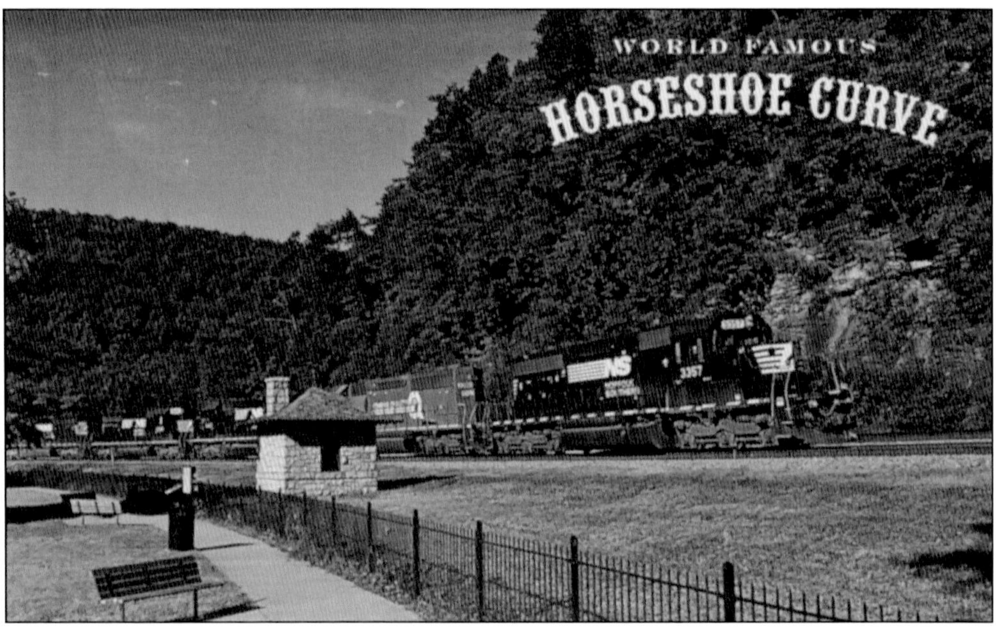

On June 16, 2006, a light power move consisting of five Norfolk Southern SD40-2s passes Horseshoe Curve Park at 8:30 a.m. Unlike its four stablemates, No. 3392 has not yet been repainted from the old Conrail blue. Norfolk Southern became the fourth owner of the railroad in the Altoona area, including the Pittsburgh Line and Horseshoe Curve, on June 1, 1999. And the torch has been passed once again.

Four

Lakemont Park

Although this sylvan spot was already popular with local residents for picnicking, the Altoona and Logan Valley Electric Railway (trolley line) is credited with formally creating Lakemont Park. Portions of the tract were previously used by the Elias Baker family holdings to extract ore for their iron furnaces, but these operations closed in 1884. On October 22, 1894, John Lloyd, president of the Altoona and Logan Valley Electric Railway, acquired 113 acres to formally create the trolley park, and subsequently 13 of those acres were used to create a lake for boating, fishing, and ice-skating. Patrons rode the trolleys to the park and the park flourished. However, on March 17, 1936, a rapid spring thaw and hard rain created severe flooding across Pennsylvania, and the park sustained substantial damage. Coupled with Depression-era economics, this forced the trolley company to divest itself of the park.

Lakemont Park was deeded to Blair County and remained a destination for picnickers. The Altoona and Logan Valley Electric Railway went out of business in July 1954, and the tracks were removed from the system. Blair County sold the park to the Altoona-based Boyer Candy Company, which created Boyertown Park in 1985. Unfortunately, this enterprise went bankrupt, but not before Boyer's "improvements" had removed most of the park's 200-year-old-plus hardwood trees. Primary lien holders in the bankruptcy kept the park viable, however, resurrecting the original Lakemont Park name, but the trees were gone.

Other improvements to the real estate kept the park alive, particularly the arrival of the Galactic Ice Rink and a new AA baseball stadium built by former Altoona resident Robert Lozinak. The ballpark is home to the Altoona Curve (a Pittsburgh Pirates affiliate), and both the baseball team and the ice rink are beloved by local residents. Unfortunately, with private ownership in a litigious society, the lake is now fenced and not casually accessible to visitors for fishing or (in winter months) for ice skating. Today, Lakemont Park is different but still very popular and transforms itself with elaborate light displays during the holiday season, as well as distinctive model train displays erected by the Alto Model Train Museum.

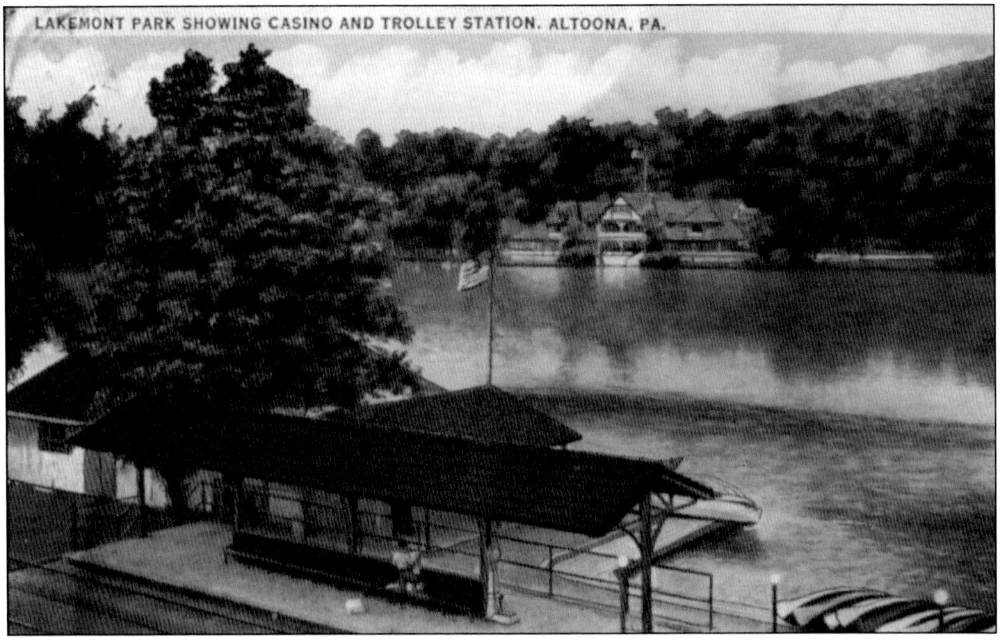

This view of Lakemont Park shows the casino and trolley station. Although the trolleys are long gone, the trolley station shelter still survives in the park as part of the miniature golf course. Paddleboats have replaced the row boats and canoes, and the open-air casino is now a fully enclosed upscale catering facility that has faithfully restored and enhanced the original architecture. The card is postmarked 1934.

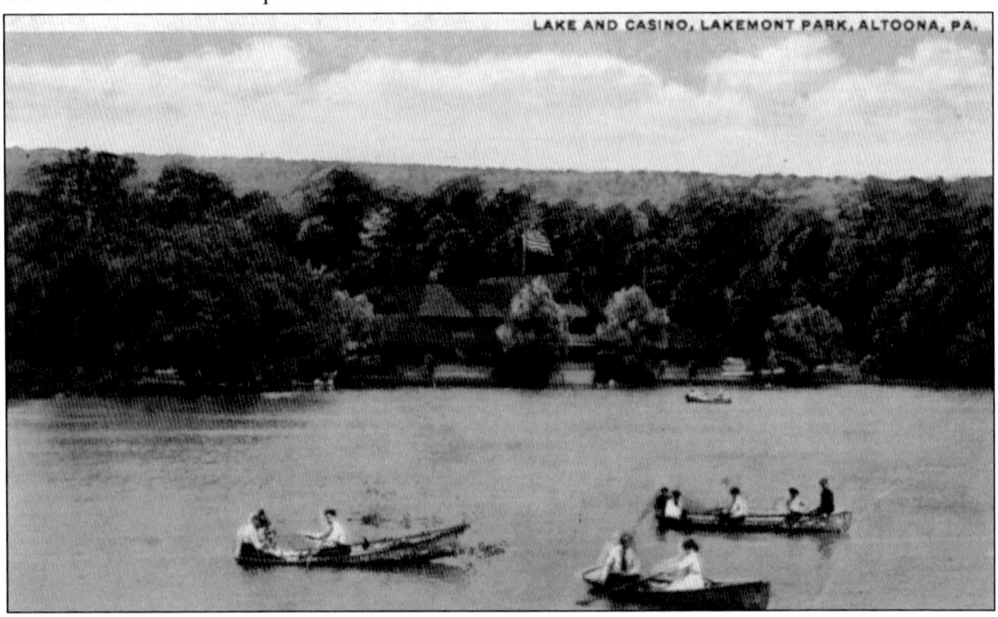

Boaters enjoy the lake with the open-air casino in the background. Note how the casino is surrounded by the stately trees comprised of some 60 varieties, which provided the most-sought-after shade in the summer months, as well as leaf samples for countless school children. The casino was used for band concerts, convocations, and dances but was never a gambling facility as the name might imply. This card was postmarked August 15, 1921.

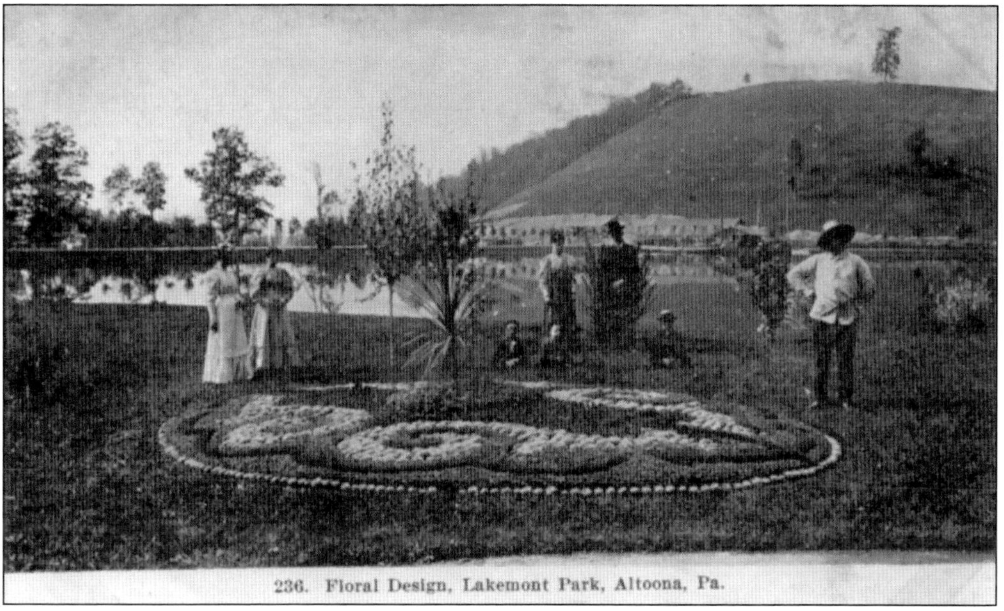

In this late 19th-century view, patrons admire a floral design of the park's name. Lakemont Park was noted for its floral plantings; a greenhouse was maintained for that purpose near the trolley station but was destroyed in the St. Patrick Day Flood of 1936 and never rebuilt. Many of the plantings and arrangements were by head gardener Wesley Motter and James Hewitt.

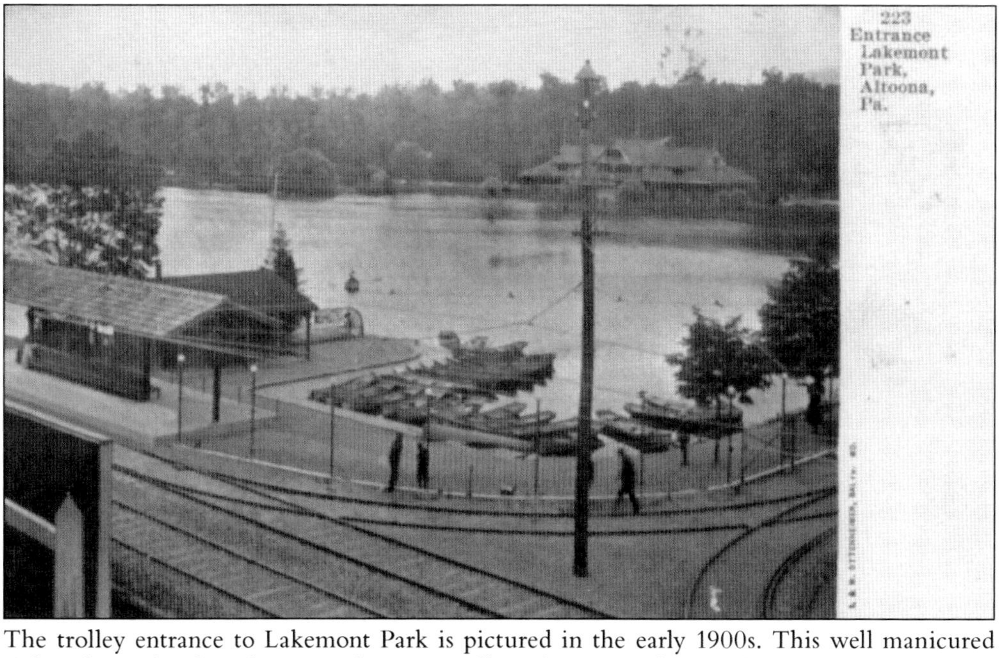

The trolley entrance to Lakemont Park is pictured in the early 1900s. This well manicured right-of-way for the Altoona and Logan Valley Electric Railway indicates prosperity in the park's early years. The boat dock, lake, and casino all contribute to inviting scenes for trolley patrons to beckon them back to this sylvan setting. Picnicking, amusement rides, and strolls in the park made this location very popular with local residents.

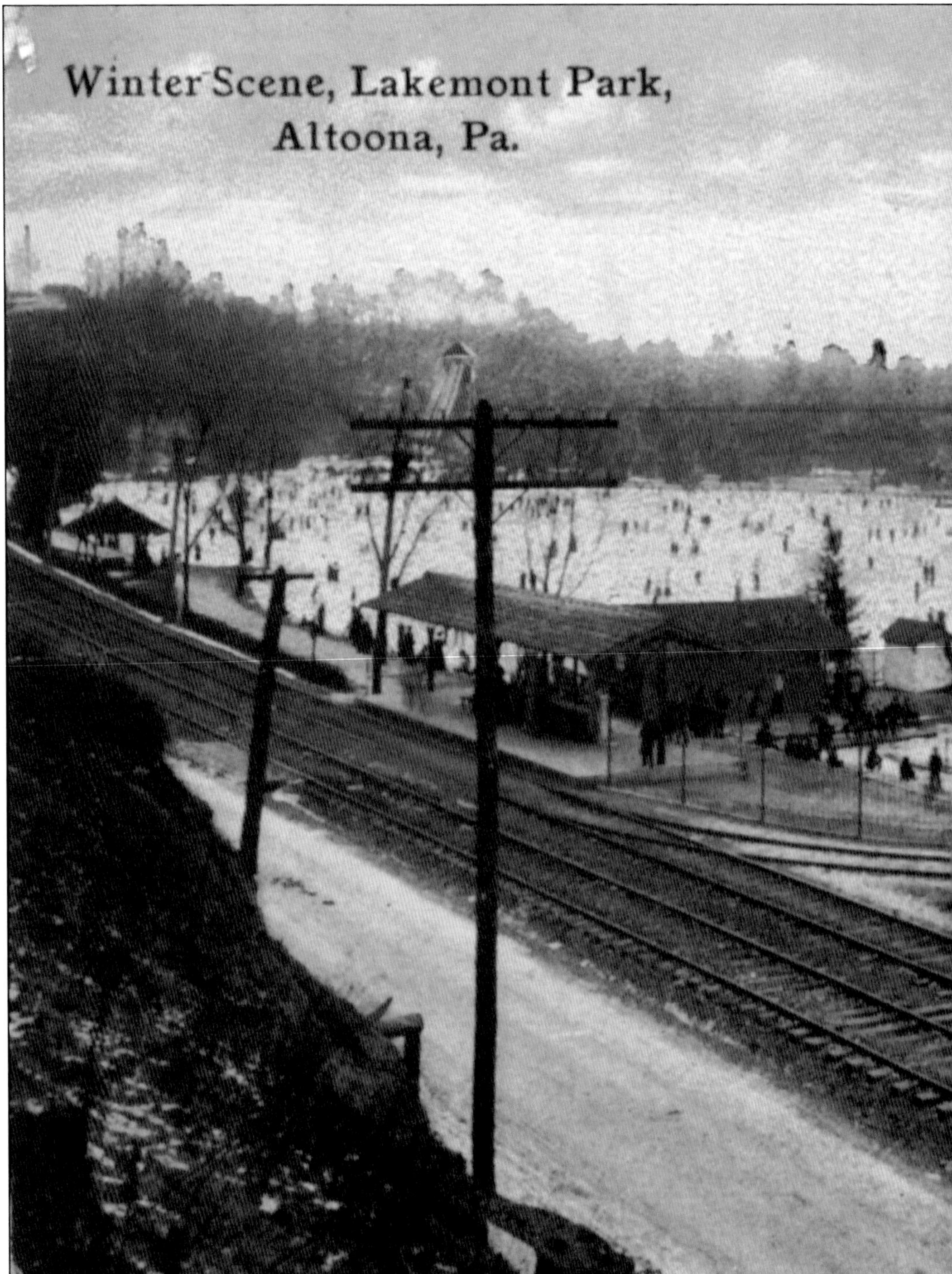

Lakemont Park in all seasons was the focal point for leisure time activities out-of-doors. The Altoona and Logan Valley Electric Railway hung a red ball on the trolley cars in winter to announce that the ice was thick enough to skate on. As this view demonstrates, the popularity of the lake in winter was significant, and almost everyone arrived by trolley.

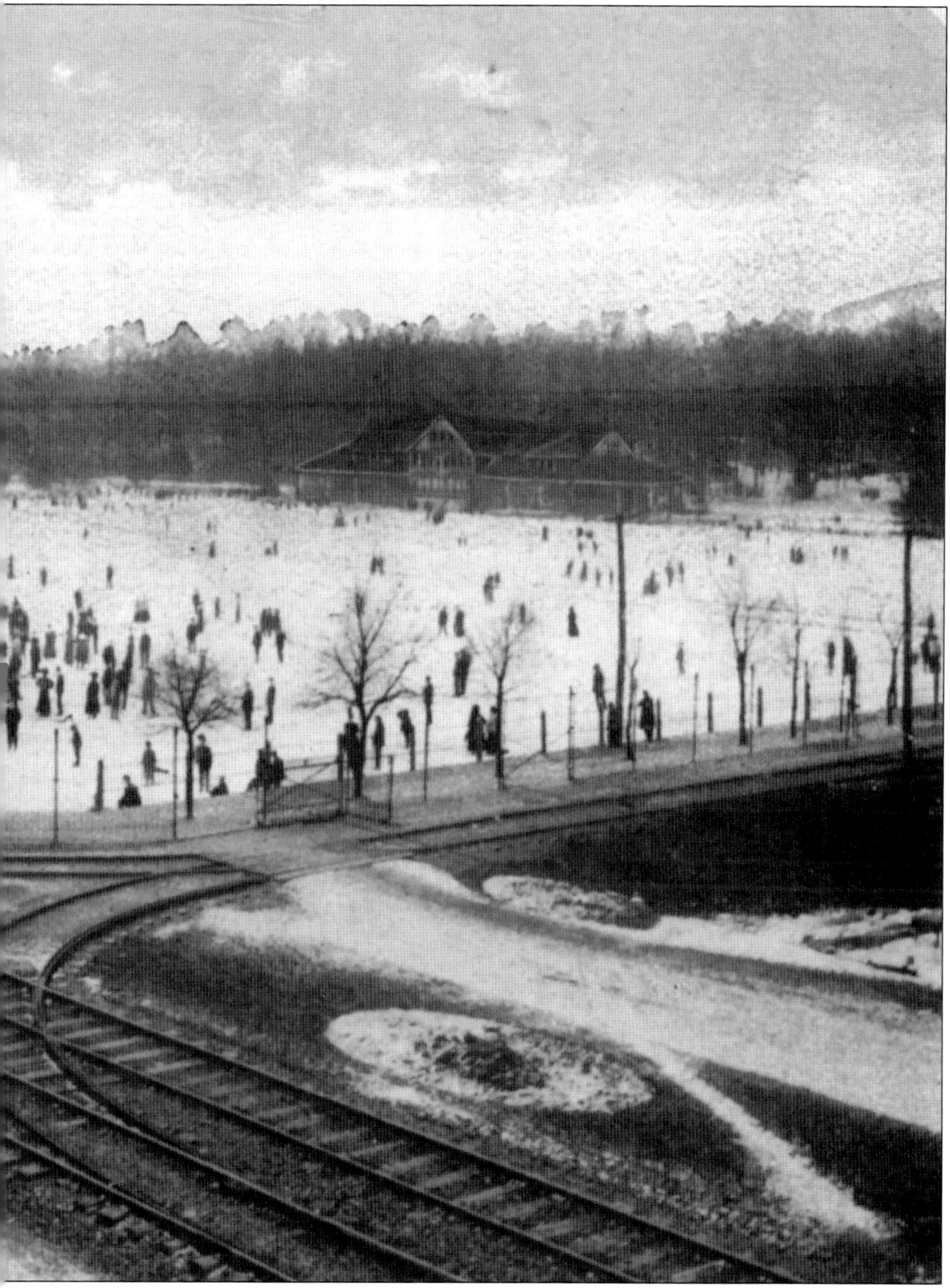

Though Lakemont Park's lake is now fenced to preclude liability issues, a century ago, skaters enjoyed this lake while warming themselves in the greenhouse nearby or by the fireplace in the casino (upper right).

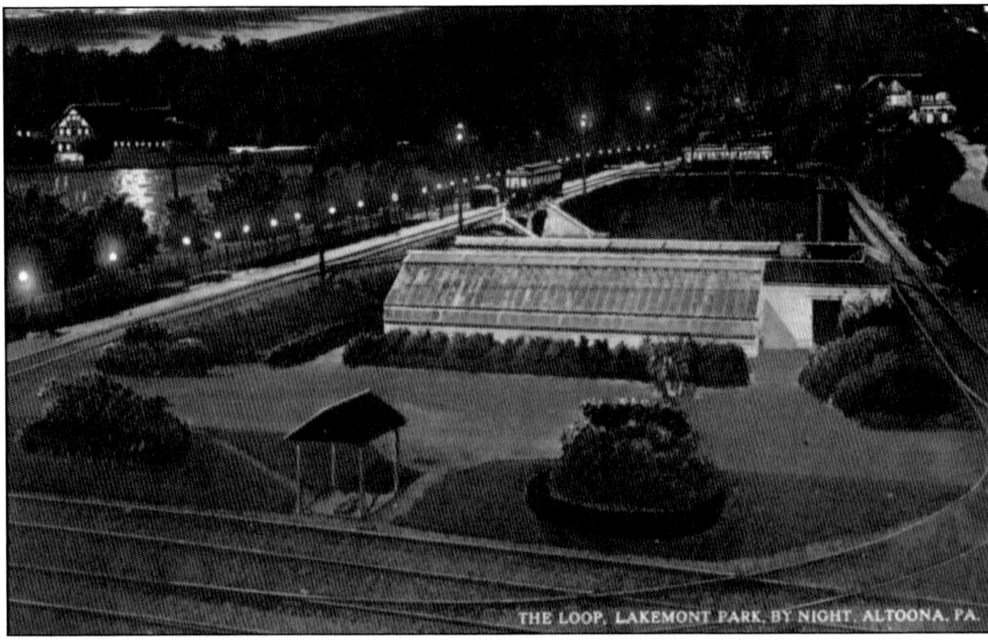

The trolley loop is seen by night at Lakemont Park. Note the greenhouse at this location, which supplied the floral plantings throughout the park. The boulevard lights along the lakeside illuminated the breast of the dam and the walking entrance to the park proper. The greenhouse served as shelter to frozen skaters in winter, as well as the winter home of the park's alligators.

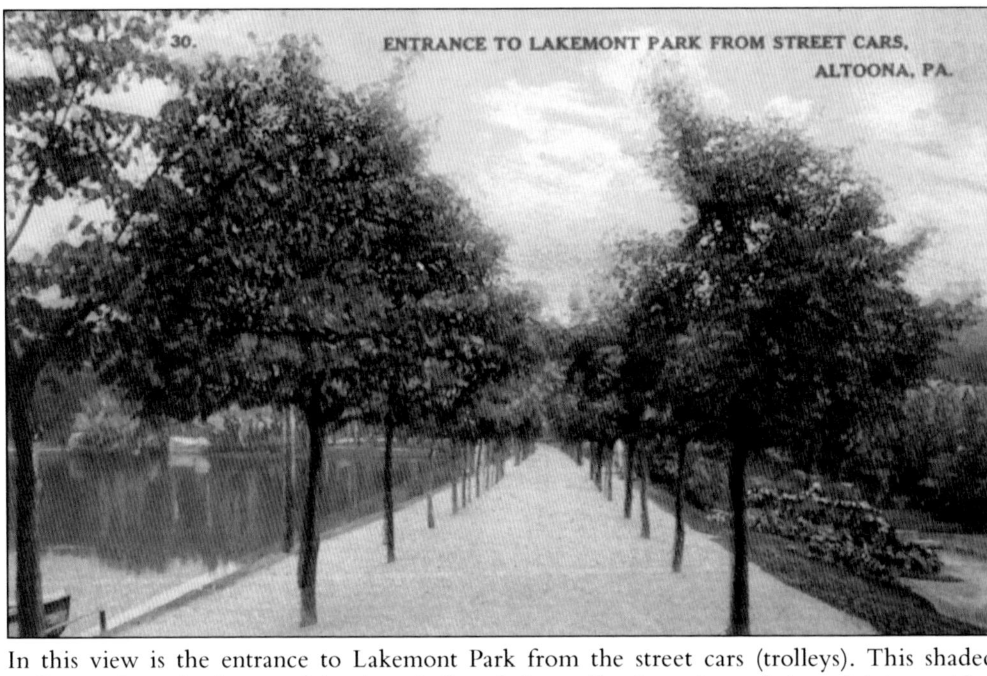

In this view is the entrance to Lakemont Park from the street cars (trolleys). This shaded walkway along the breast of the dam (left) and the trolley loop (out of view right) provided a pleasant promenade for park visitors. In later years, an iron fence with sliding gates would parallel the walkway on the right that provided ingress and egress for groups on the trolleys, particularly school picnics.

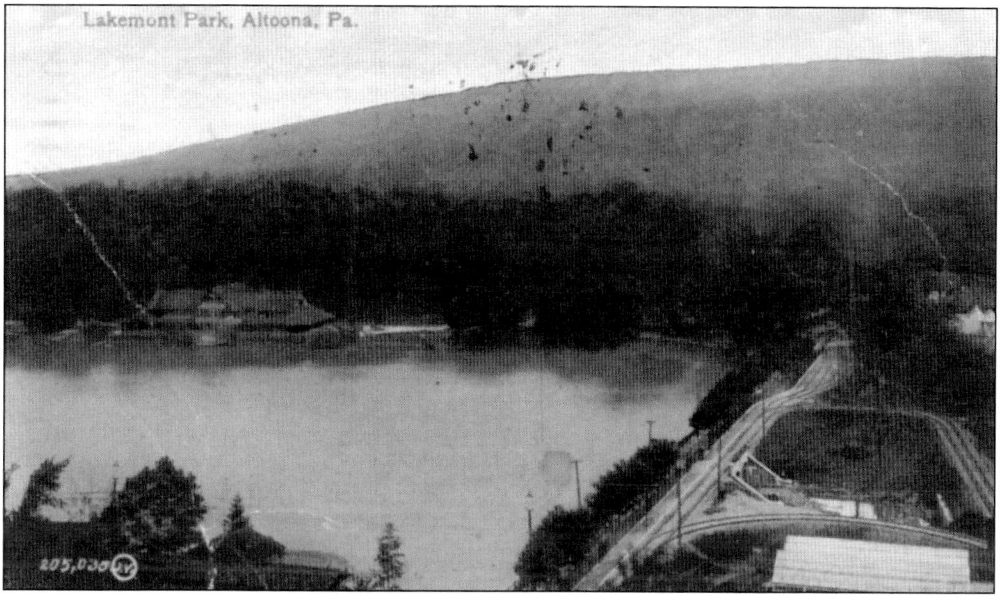

This elevated view of the trolley loop and lake clearly illustrates a double trolley loop with a stacking siding for the Altoona and Logan Valley Electric Railway with the floral greenhouse at lower right. The casino has been a focal point of the park since its early years and remains so today as an upscale banquet and catering facility that is fully modernized for year-round use. This card is postmarked December 26, 1919.

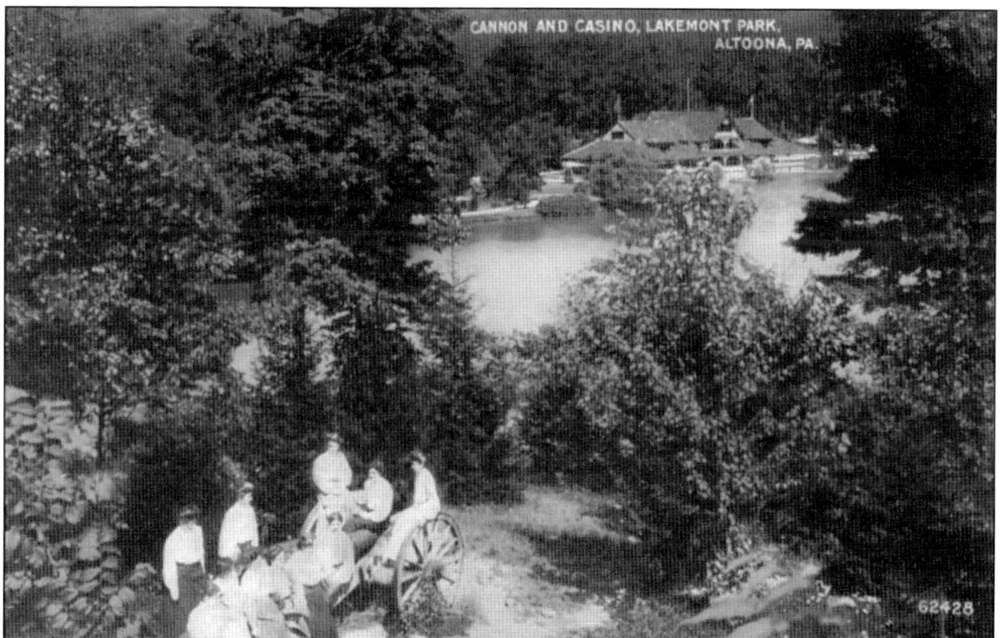

Here is a view of the lake and casino from elevation on Park Hill with visitors gathered around a memorial cannon from the Civil War. These cannon were popularly used by war reenactors using blank cartridges. Also popular in the late 19th century were events honoring Union war veterans, particularly at the Lt. S. C. Potts Post No. 62 GAR. Potts was killed during the battle at Fredericksburg in December 1862. This card is postmarked December 19, 1913.

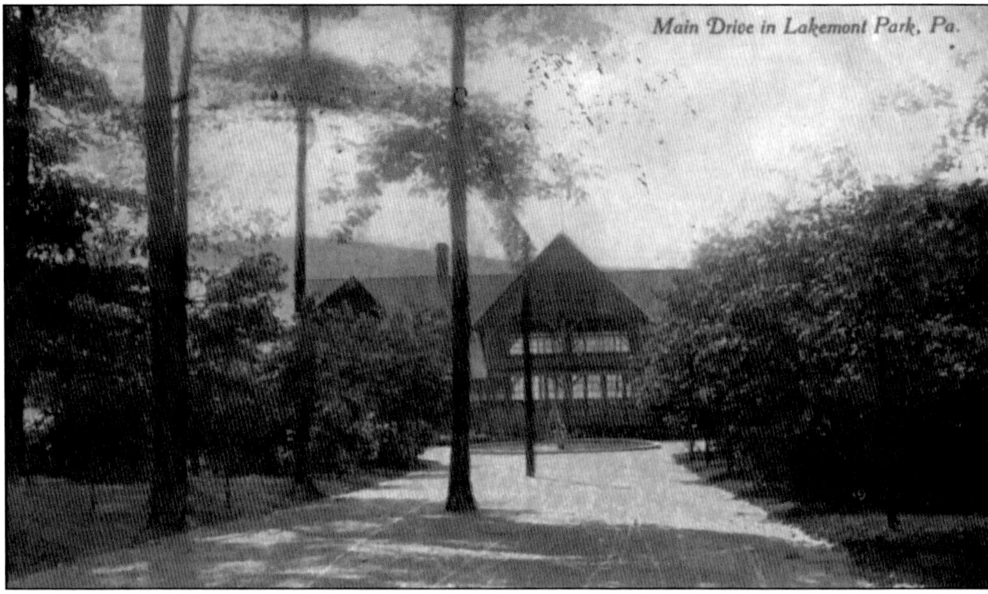

Shown is the central promenade drive to the casino. Originally known as the Pavilion, the casino was completed in 1889 or 1890 prior to the opening of the park and was used for theatre, dances, and social functions. Although open-air, ice skaters in winter were able to warm themselves next to a large indoor fireplace at one end of the main room. Nationally-known entertainer and Tyrone native Fred Waring made his first professional appearance here in 1916 with a four-piece band. This card is postmarked April 30, 1910.

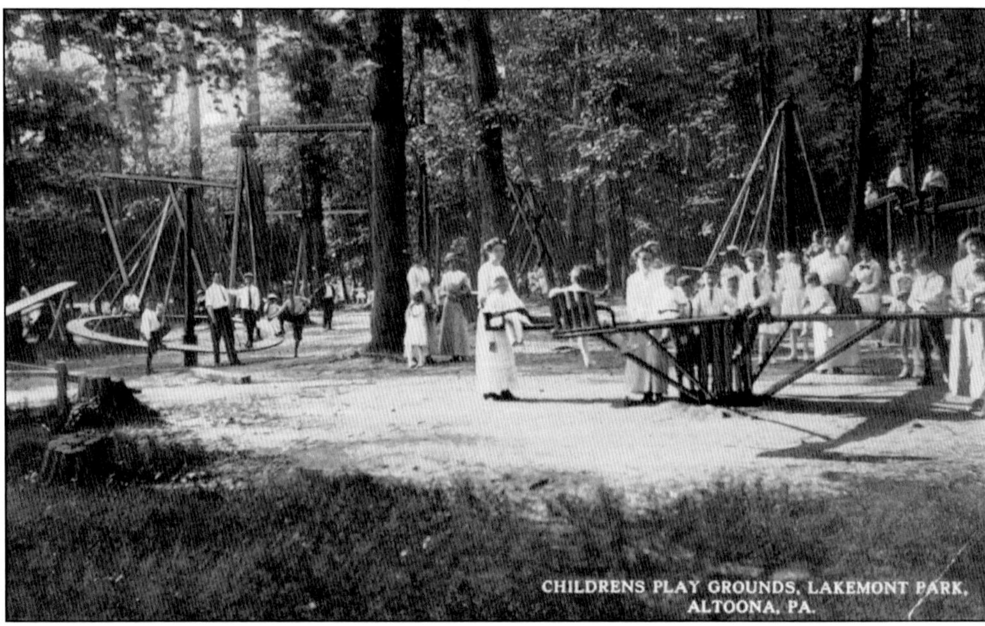

The children's playgrounds are seen in this *c.* 1900 view. As Lakemont Park developed in later years, the mechanical amusements were added, but the playground remained as a staple for picnickers into the 1980s, almost 100 years later. Some of the early playground equipment probably would not pass muster with child safety issues in the late 20th century, but they were enjoyed nonetheless. This card is postmarked September 28, 1917, during World War I.

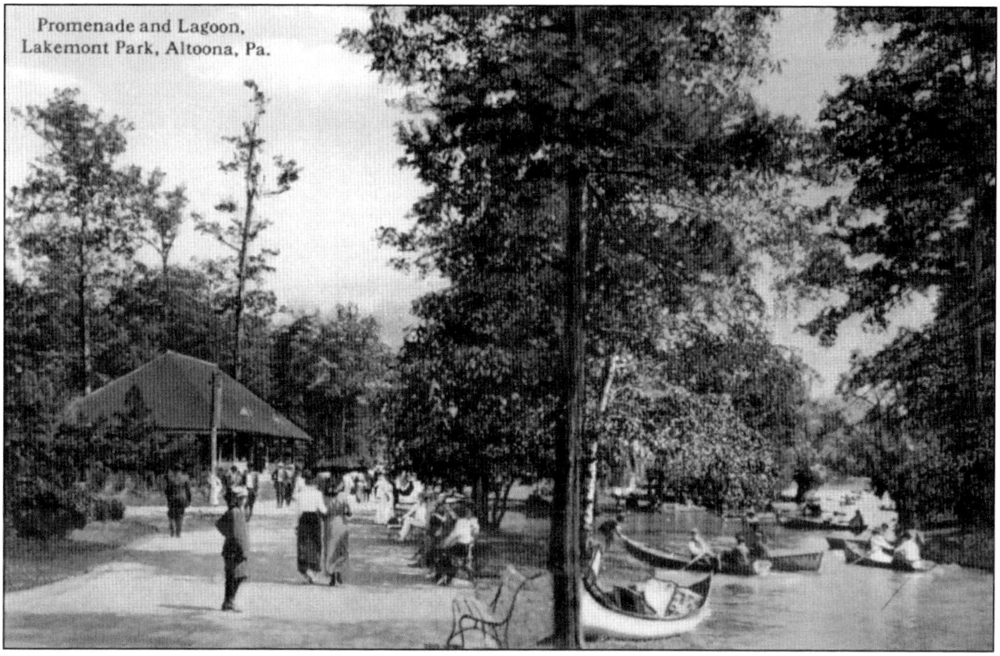

Here are the promenade and lagoon. Picnickers in the early 1900s dressed in their best for leisure-time activities; the shade came as a welcome respite from the summer heat and heavy garments of the day. Lakemont Park was also a favorite location for courtship.

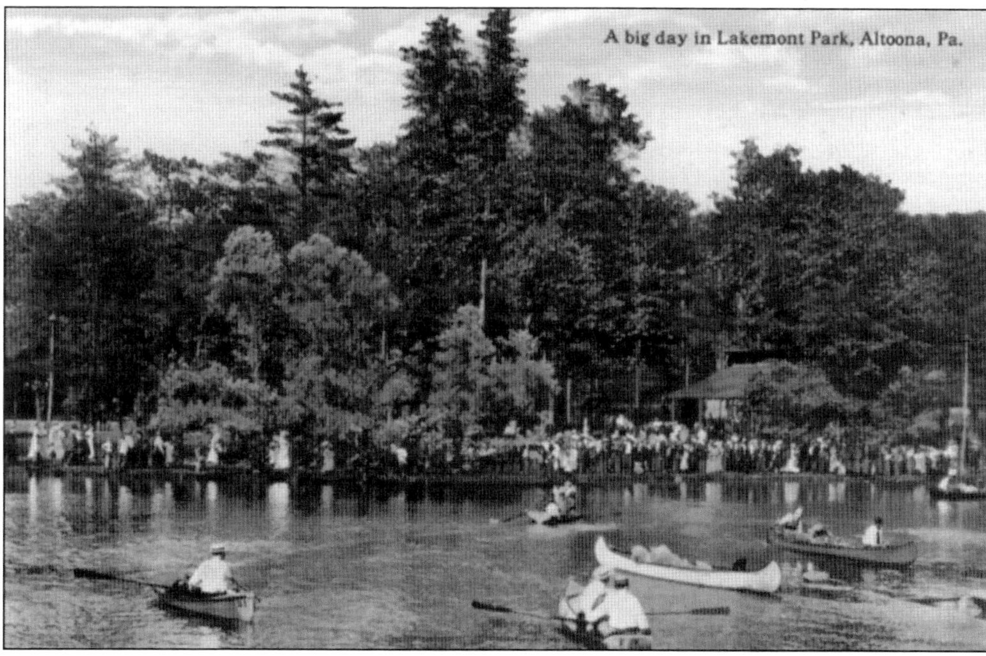

This was obviously a big day in Lakemont Park, probably a holiday such as Independence Day. Most visitors to the park would arrive and depart on the lines of the Altoona and Logan Valley Electric Railway. Lakemont Park was the only venue with a lake for fishing or boating within close proximity to the city, and other means of transportation like the horse and buggy or the very early automobile on poor roads made travel an arduous task.

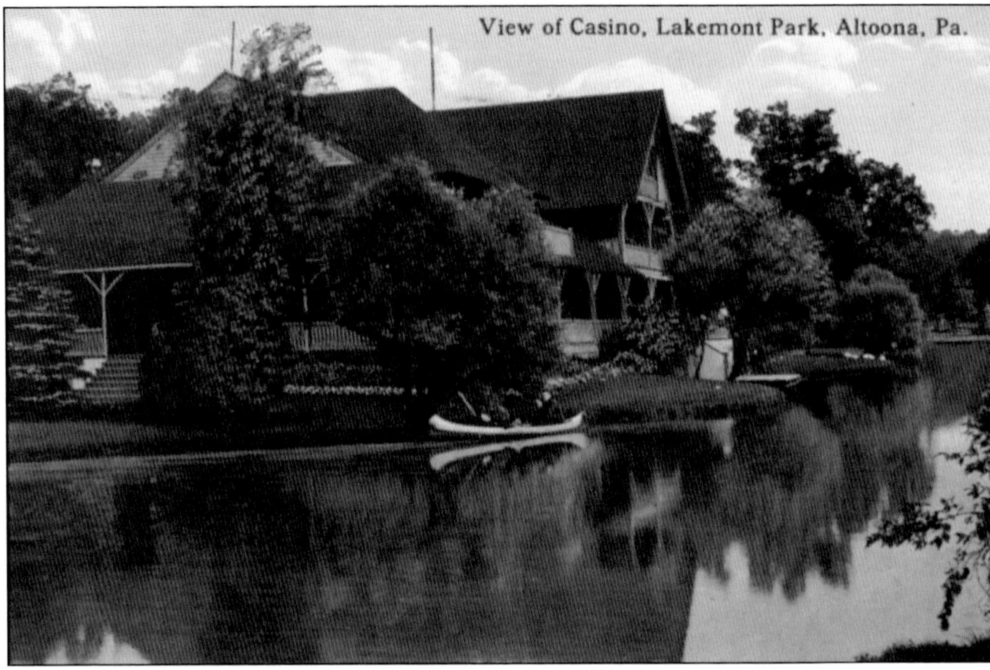

Here is a serene view of the casino on the mirror-glass lake. A popular event at the casino each summer for much of its history was an annual Central Pennsylvania Bible Conference, which evolved from a meeting on February 20, 1920, and formally began on July 1, 1920. The annual conferences lasted until 1979. This card is postmarked November 15, 1917.

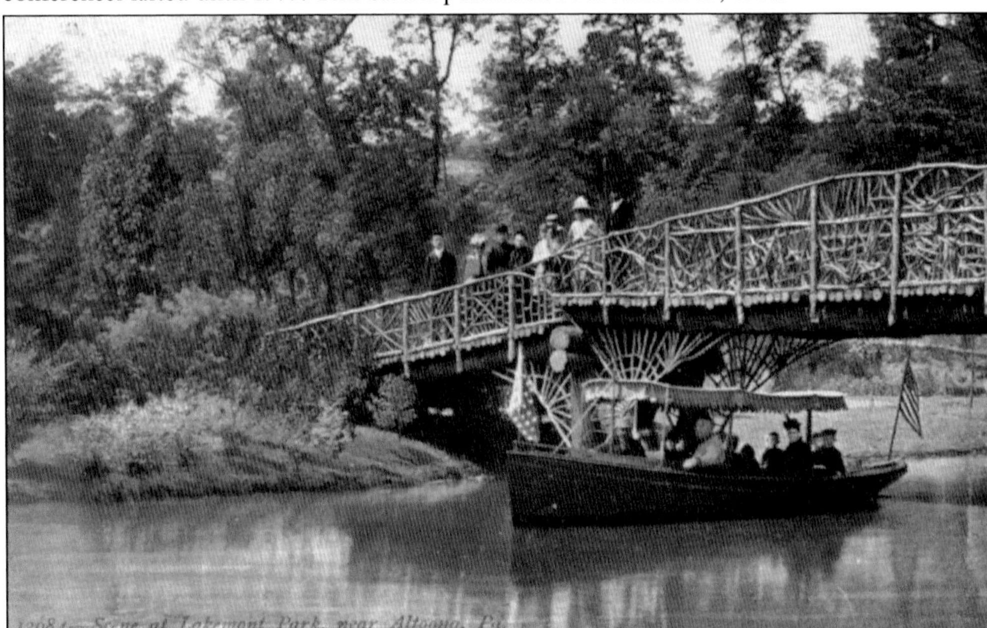

This picturesque crossing, known as the Rustic Bridge, enabled park visitors to pass to the island. A motor launch can be seen passing underneath. This was always a popular spot for visitors to feed the fish, mostly carp, which became accustomed to the popcorn meals under the bridge, a custom that continues to this day. This card is postmarked June 14, 1907.

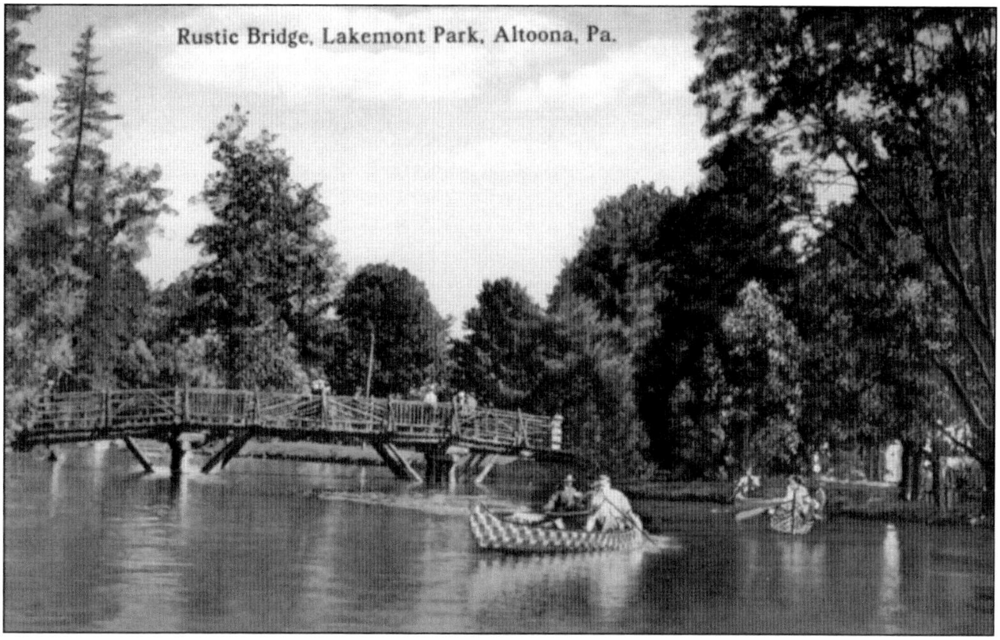

This is another view of boaters and the Rustic Bridge in Lakemont Park. Constructed of native tree limbs, the structure was later replaced with more durable materials, especially after the St. Patrick's Day Flood of 1936, which damaged many park facilities. The rustic bridge afforded access to the island, noted for pleasant paths beneath shade trees, where one could escape the summer heat.

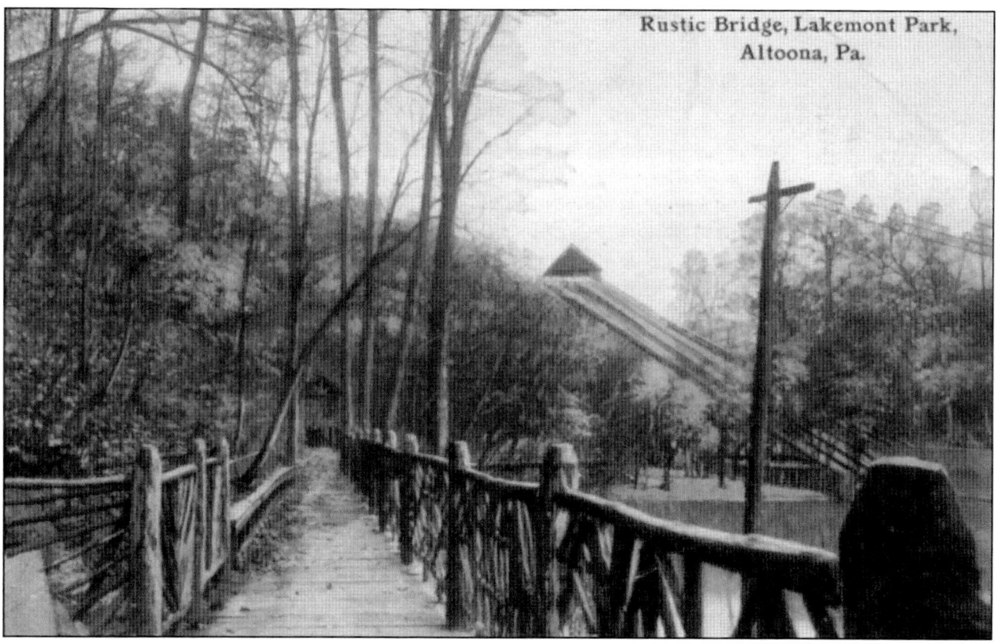

This is a view of the Shoot the Chute ride from the Rustic Bridge. After 1940, the island became the focal point of the park with the addition of Blue Island Pool. The Shoot the Chute Ride existed in the early years, prior to the St. Patrick's Day Flood of 1936. This card is postmarked December 18, 1911.

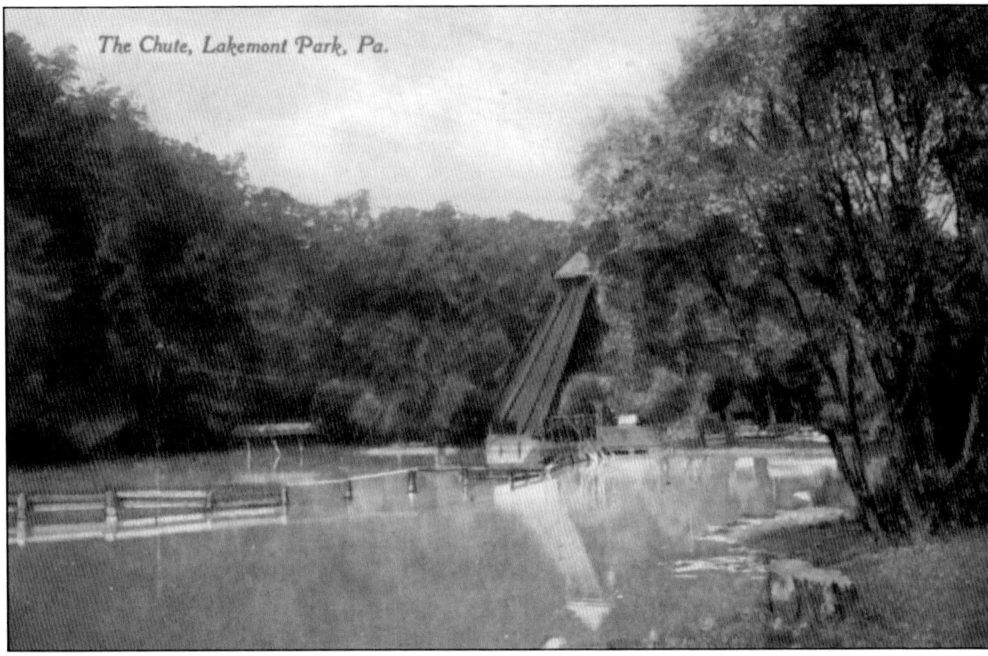

Here is another view of The Chute, also known as the Shoot the Chute, a toboggan boat on rails. It was pulled to the top of the chute, then released to plummet down into the lake, skipping over the water's surface.

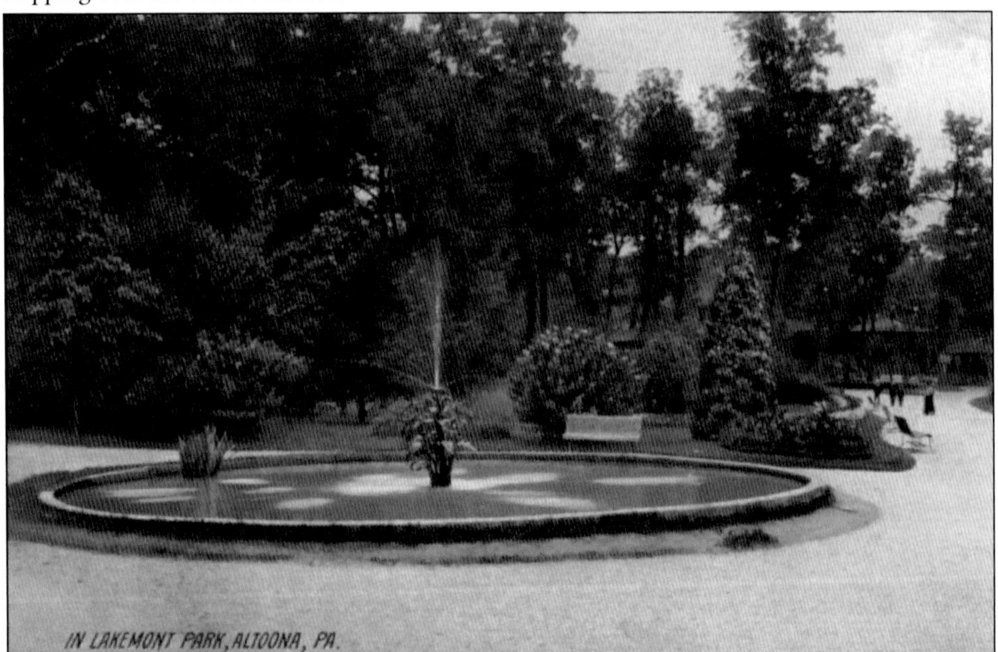

The central fountain was located on the main promenade in front of the casino and contributed to the serenity of the park in combination with the superb floral plantings and groundskeeping under Wesley Motter. A form of this fountain is still in place today. This card is postmarked March 14, 1910.

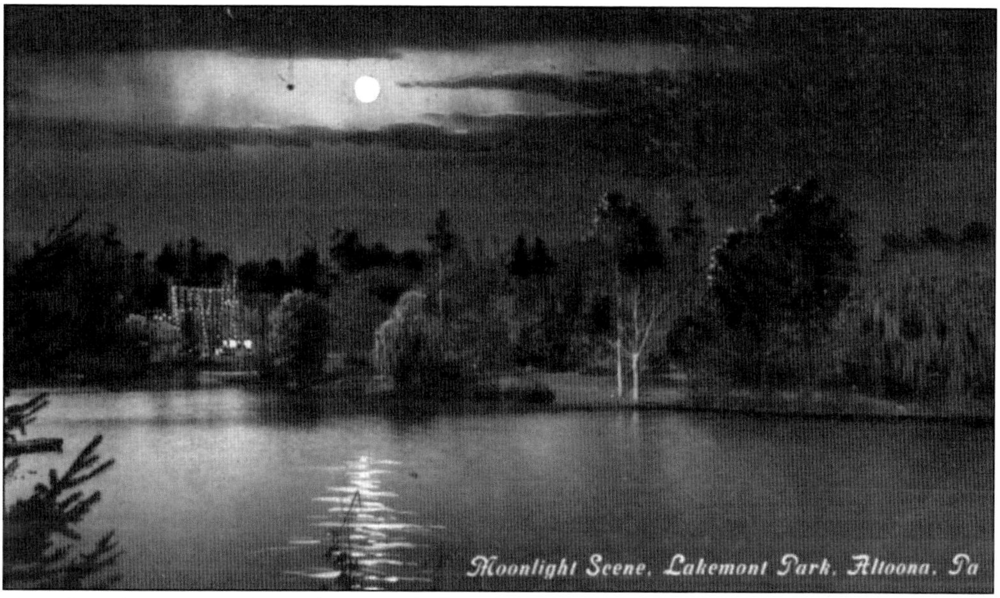

Here is Lakemont Park in the moonlight. This park and the city of Altoona have been intertwined for over a century. Many changes have taken place over the years, but the park is still a focal point for community life and events. The trolley line is gone, replaced by new highways, and much of the park is altered today, but it remains popular. This card is postmarked on the Railway Post Office of Train No. 6, February 23, 1913.

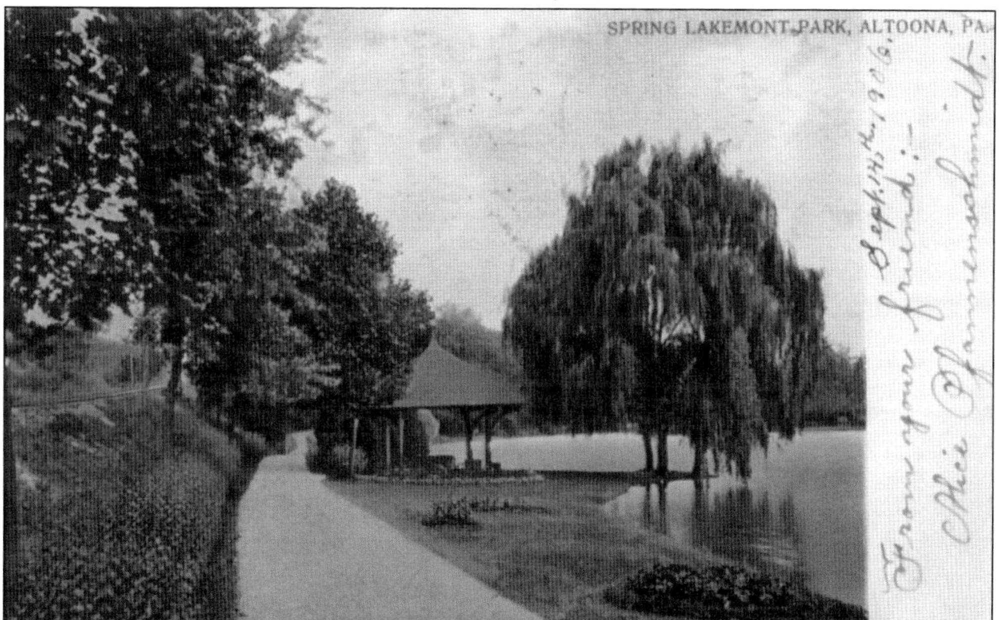

This is a scenic walkway around the spring at Lakemont Park. Located along the slope of Park Hill and the Altoona and Logan Valley Electric Railway trolley line, this scenic path allowed for strolling the park's more peaceful locations. Farther along the hillside was a cave-like opening where ore was extracted in the mid-19th century for the Elias Baker iron furnaces. This card is postmarked September 14, 1906.

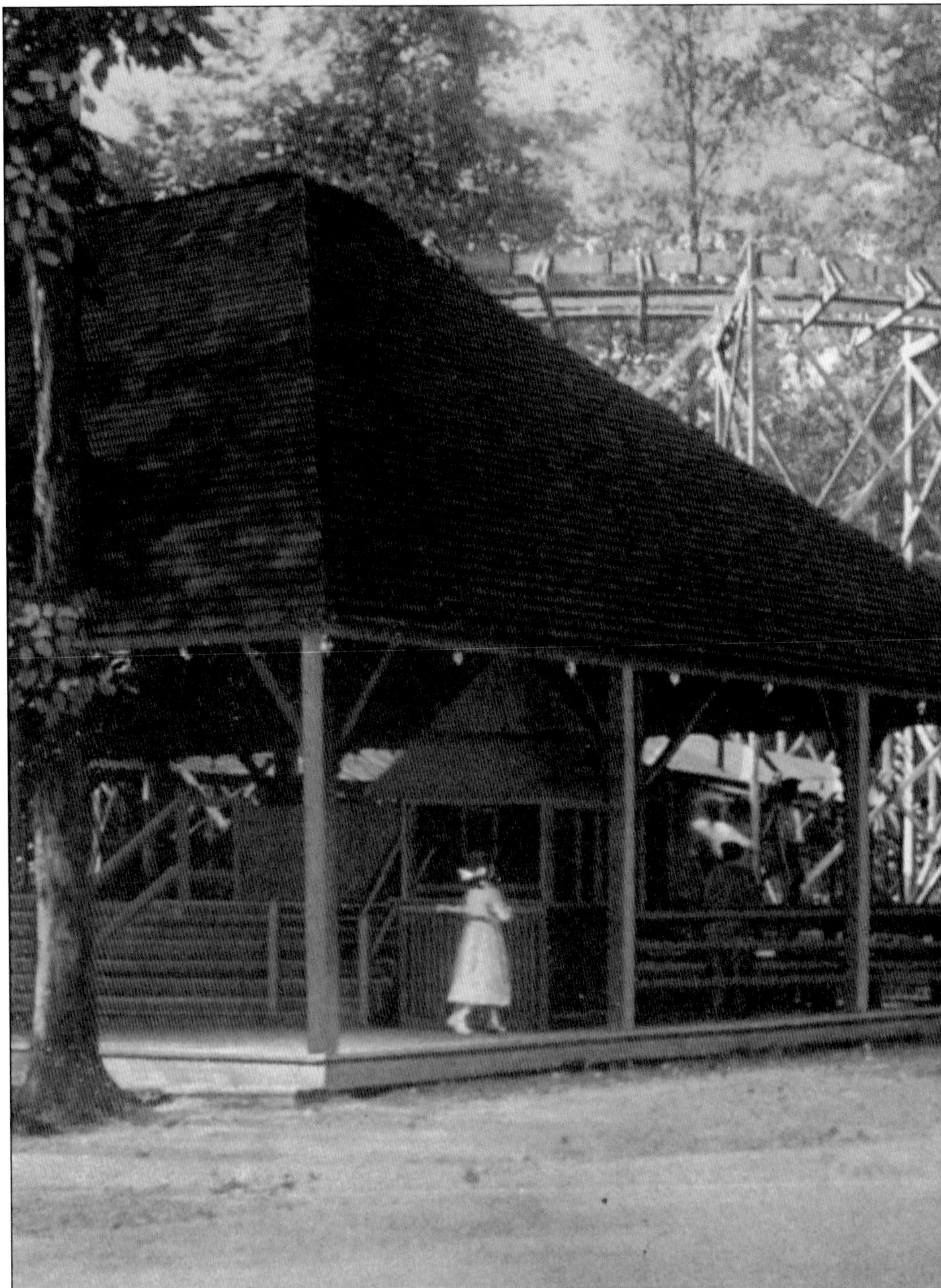

This is a view of the revered Leap The Dips rollercoaster. Built in 1902 and originally known as the Gravity Railroad, this side-friction figure-eight coaster is the oldest such surviving coaster in the U.S. The coaster was closed due to deterioration in 1985, but preservationists and

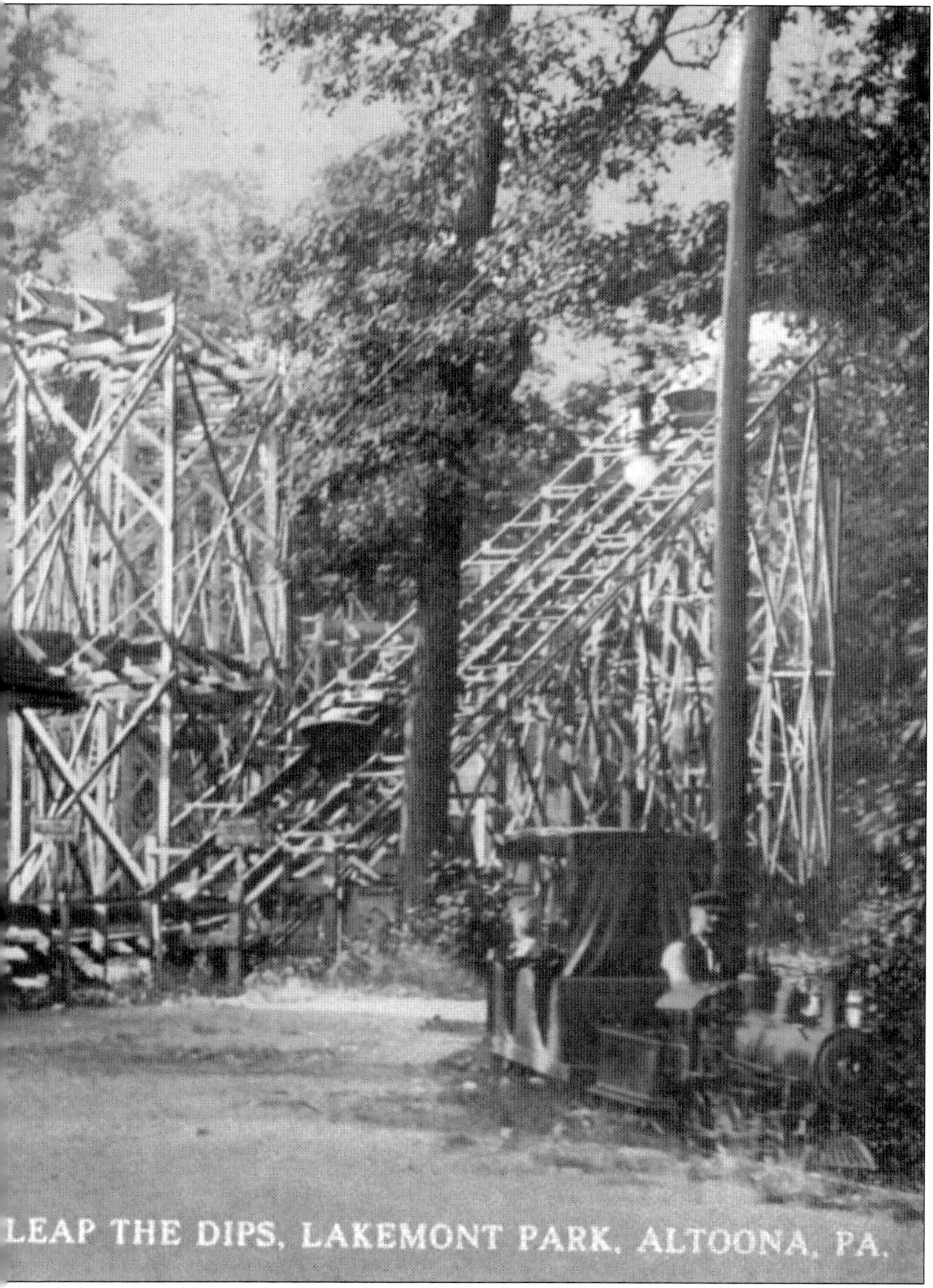

Altoona area citizens raised funds to restore the ride. National landmark status was awarded in 1996, and the coaster received a Pennsylvania state historical marker on November 28, 2000. It reopened on Memorial Day 1999.

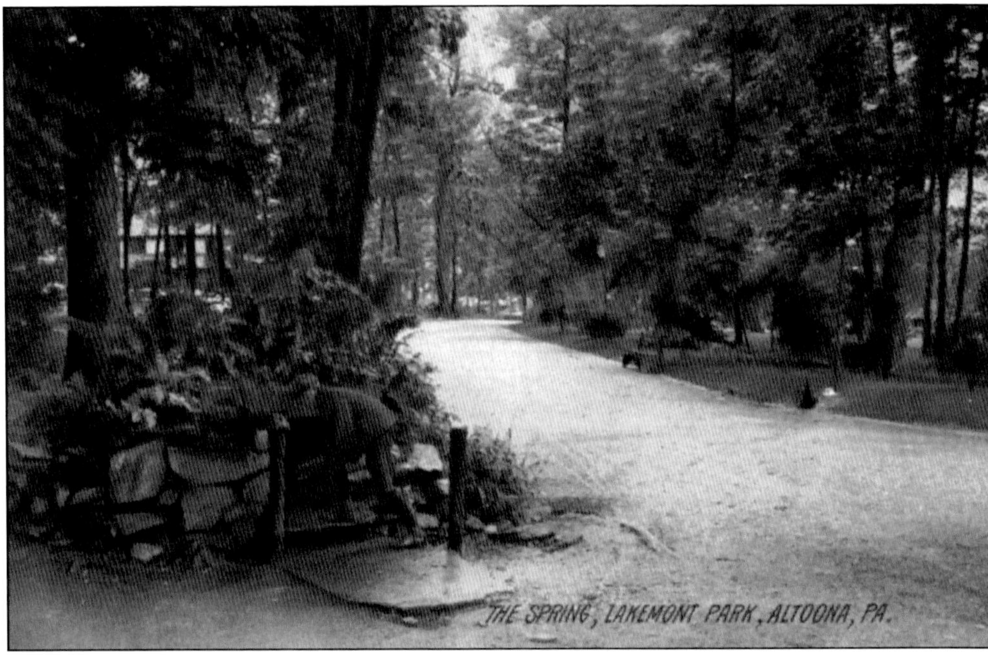

Also titled the Spring, this location was on the opposite side of the lake from the postcard on page 117. Since the park was heavily wooded and located at the base of Brush Mountain, springs were commonplace in the early years of the park. The trees were the park's greatest asset, but they became a casualty of the attempt to create Boyertown in 1985. This card is postmarked August 2, 1907.

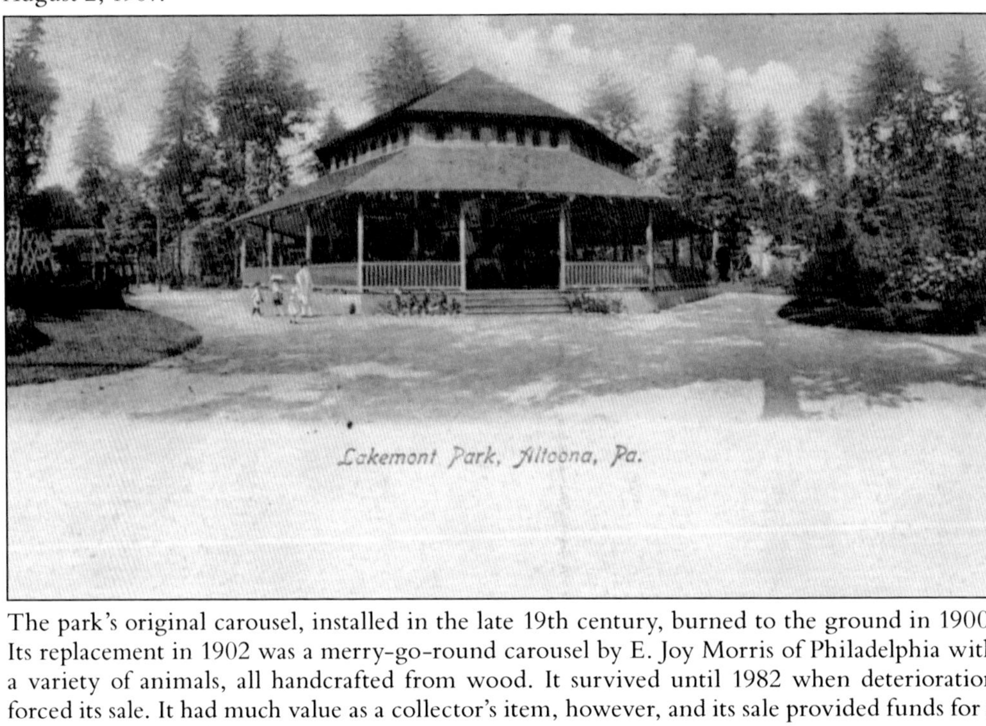

The park's original carousel, installed in the late 19th century, burned to the ground in 1900. Its replacement in 1902 was a merry-go-round carousel by E. Joy Morris of Philadelphia with a variety of animals, all handcrafted from wood. It survived until 1982 when deterioration forced its sale. It had much value as a collector's item, however, and its sale provided funds for a replacement and other park improvements.

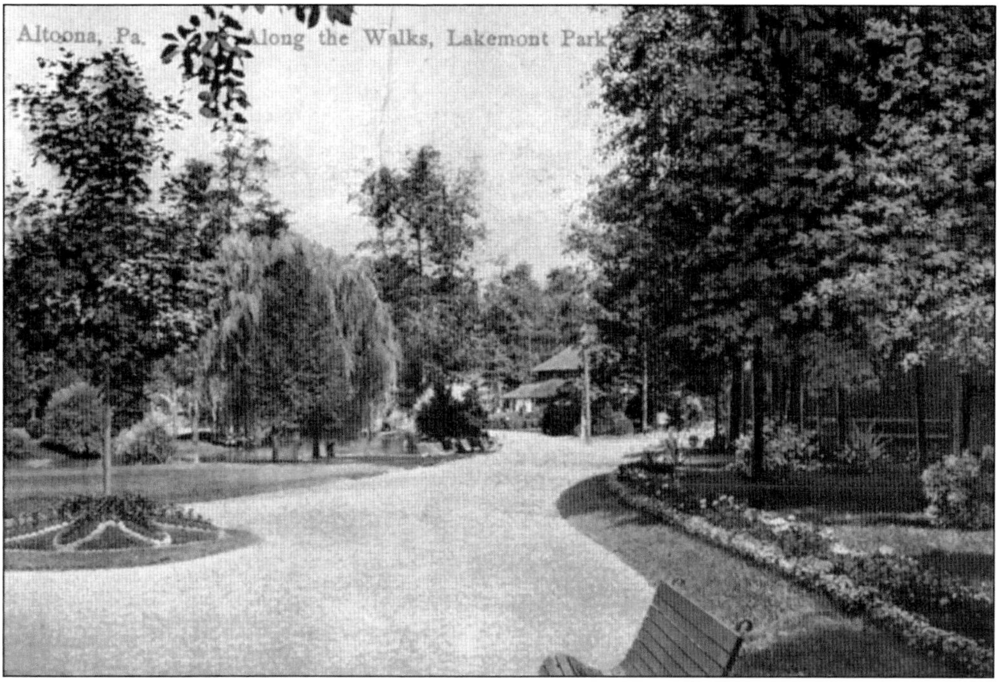

Here is another of Lakemont Park's promenades with exquisite floral plantings in the early 1900s. This scene was obviously captured when the park was closed; on Saturday and Sunday throngs would stroll the sylvan paths and enjoy picnics and amusements.

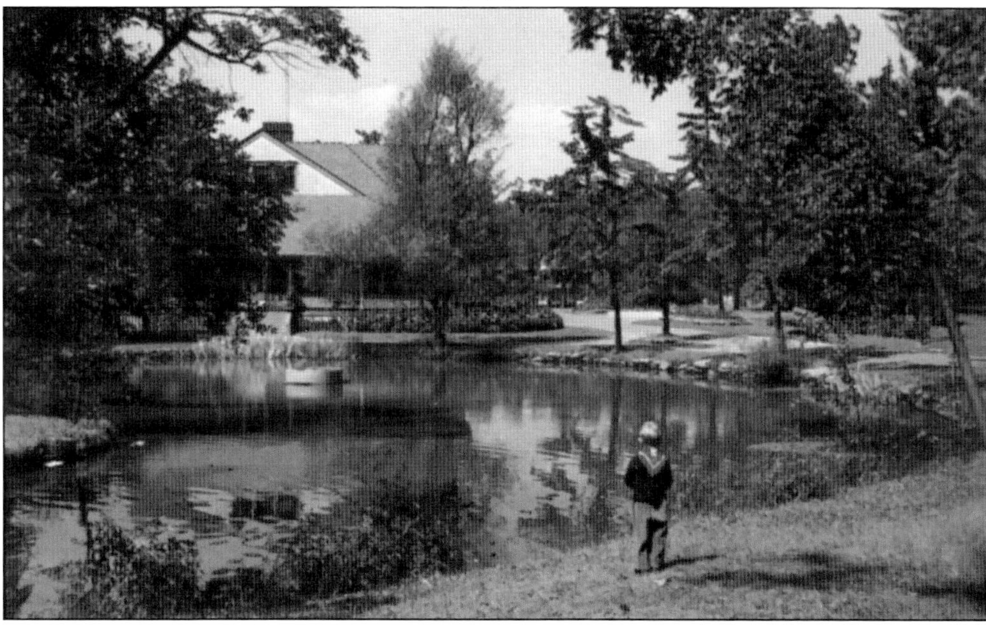

A young Boy Scout stands by the Lilly Pond on the south side of the casino in this 1950s view. Lilly Pond had a fountain, aquatic plants, frogs, and of course the ubiquitous waterfowl. Today, much of this end of the park has been developed commercially. Some natural elements remain, but much is fenced off. (Photograph by Jack Taylor for Wonday Film Service, Wilkinsburg, Pennsylvania.)

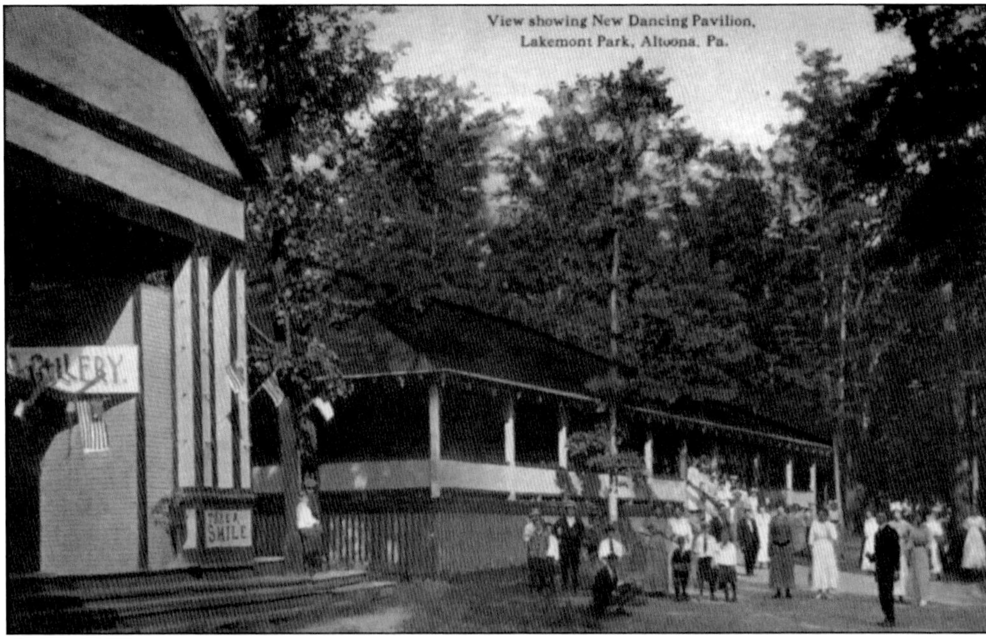

This is a view of the new dancing pavilion near the midway. Located near some of the amusements and playground, it was in the heart of all the activity but surrounded by the picnic grounds and wood-fired kitchens. The smell of wood smoke wafting through the stately trees mixed with aromas of meals being prepared to the sound of children and adults enjoying the wood lot acres of the park, creating memories for all. This card is postmarked December 1, 1913.

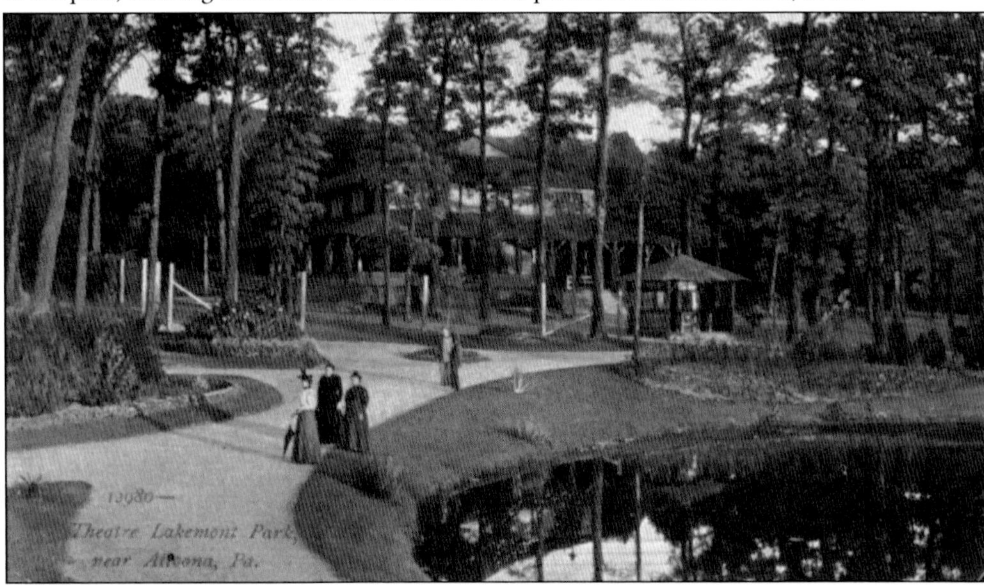

The Theatre in the Woods at Lakemont Park was the place to be from 1892 until its last performance on August 5, 1929. It was one of the first summer playhouses in the country. The theatre was host to vaudeville and summer stock productions, such as the Chicago Stock Company, as well as the Elite Burlesque Comedy Company. Notables performing here were Sarah Bernhardt, the Barrymores, and many others. The theatre later became Skateland from 1945 through the 1970s. This card is postmarked September 20, 1907.

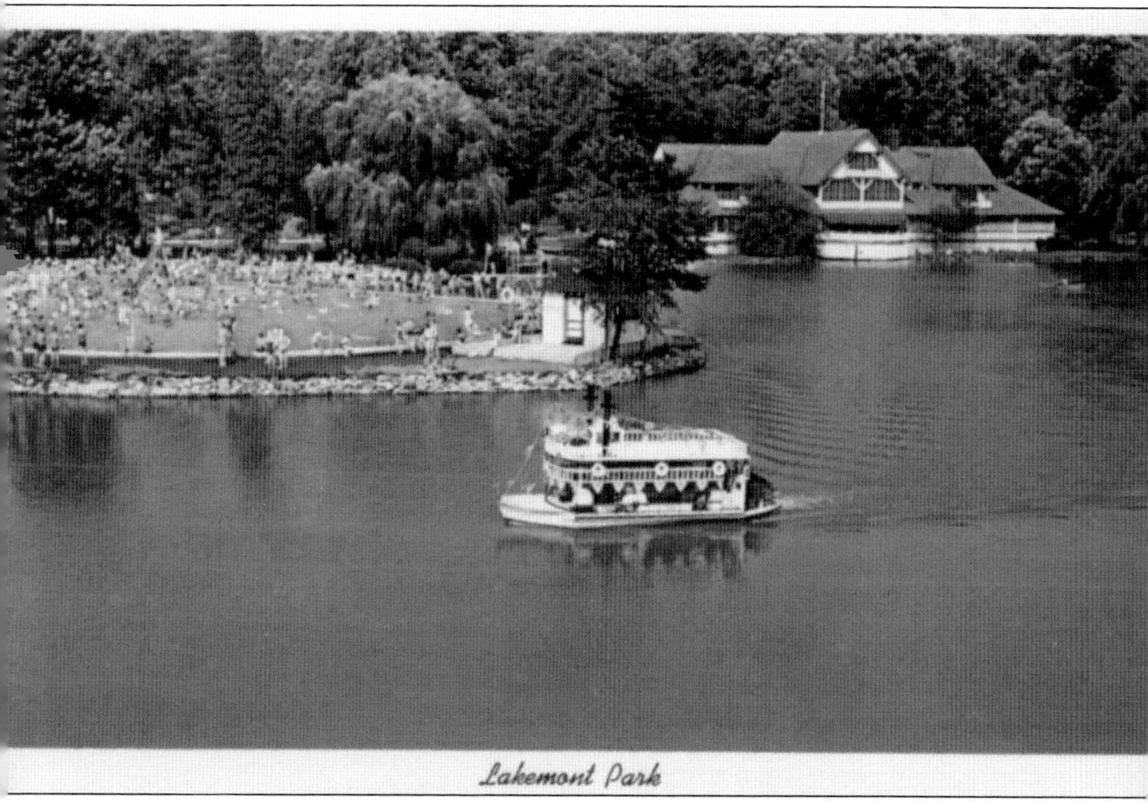

The Depression years of the 1930s forced Lakemont Park's owner, the Altoona and Logan Valley Electric Railway, to sell the park. Through the leadership of Frank Hunter, after two years of dormancy, the devastating St. Patrick's Day Flood of 1936, and an attempt at non-profit status, the park ownership passed to Blair County, qualifying the park for a WPA grant. Blue Island Pool was designed by Hunter and opened on Independence Day 1939. Blue Island Pool was visible from the trolley cars and motorists on Park Hill, beckoning as an oasis of blue-green water in contrast to the earth tones of the lake water. It was very popular with local residents of the greater Altoona area through 1985, when it was decommissioned during the attempted creation of the Boyertown theme park.

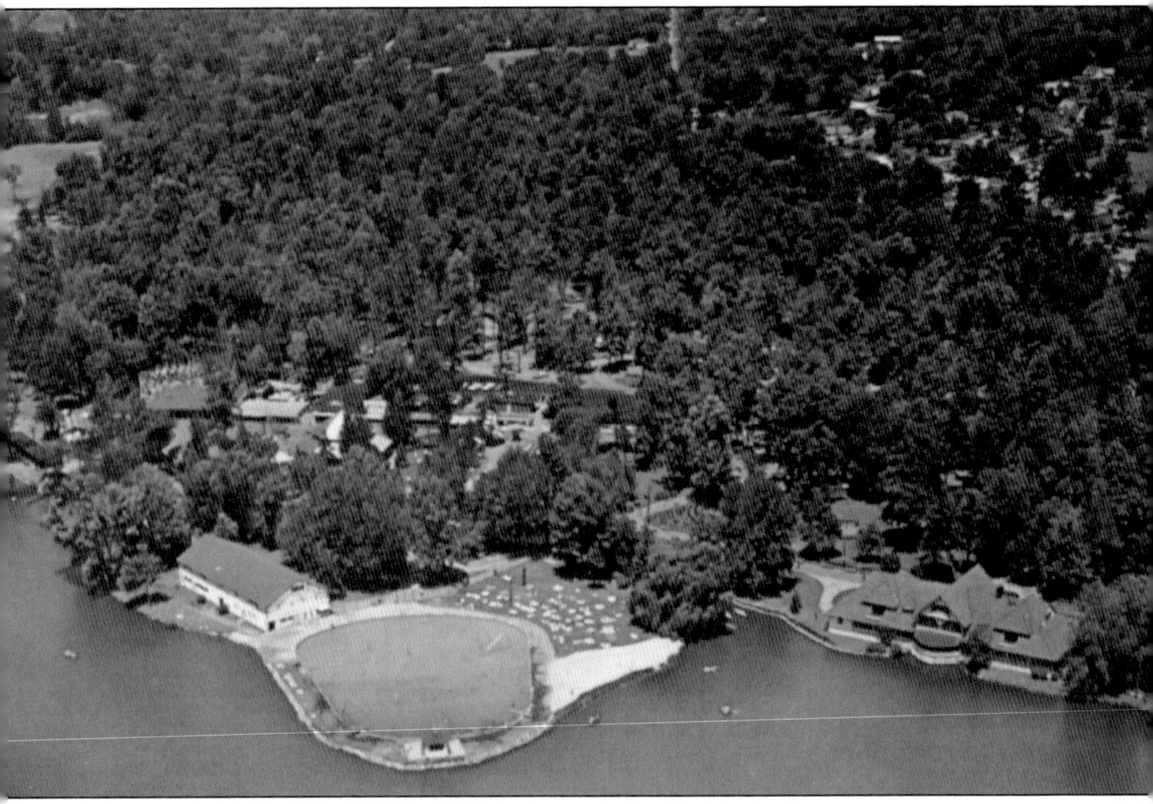

In this aerial view of Blue Island Pool, the large bath house and concession services are in the large building to the left. While the construction of the pool at this location was impressive, it was not without its problems due to expanding and contracting of the cement. Prior to the pool, the "island" was home to lush flower beds, willow trees along the lake's edge, and pleasant shaded paths. In this view, the amusement area of the park is directly to the rear, with the open-air casino to the right. The primary asset of the park was its plethora of mature shade trees. Today, Blue Island Pool has given way to a popular water park. Nonetheless, the days of Blue Island Pool are fondly recalled by those who experienced them. This card is postmarked August 10, 1966.

Five

Ivyside Park

Before World War II, another amusement park existed adjacent to Altoona. Located in the city's northeast corner, 38-acre Ivyside Park was near the Juniata Gap section before falling on hard times during the Depression and World War II. One of the park's most remarkable features was its swimming pool, roughly the size of a football field. Fed by a spring run descending from Wopsononock Mountain, its water was channeled first to a shallow warming pond before passing into the pool. The east end of the pool was noted for a magnificent rollercoaster and a swan boat ride known as the Tunnel of Love, which passed under the coaster. Despite all the mechanical amusements, swimming was the major draw for the park. The pool area was also known for its very large bath house. The park was served by the Altoona and Logan Valley Bus Company. The Wopsononock Railroad line ran through the property prior to Ivyside's status as a park.

Closed for the war years, the park was purchased in 1947 for $50,000, with money raised in the local community to help establish a new home for Pennsylvania State University's Altoona campus, known in its early years as the Altoona Undergraduate Center, which had begun in two older city elementary schools in 1939. Since then, the campus has steadily grown, but despite all the progress and growth, developers respected the mature and stately hardwood trees of the park's nucleus, and consequently, they remain to this day. Most initial classes at Ivyside Park campus were held in the old bathhouse, which led to the nickname of "Bathhouse U" for many years.

Remarkably, the keystone of the old park, the pool, is still there, but its outline contains a parking lot today. The warming pond is still in use and is the main focal point in the cluster of campus buildings, creating a beautiful reflecting pond, enhanced by a fountain, and home to fish and waterfowl. The campus has flourished and now offers four-year baccalaureate degrees. The amusement park is but a treasured memory. Only a few postcard images survive. A specialized history of the campus and the park, *Penn State Altoona*, is available through Arcadia Publishing's Campus History Series.

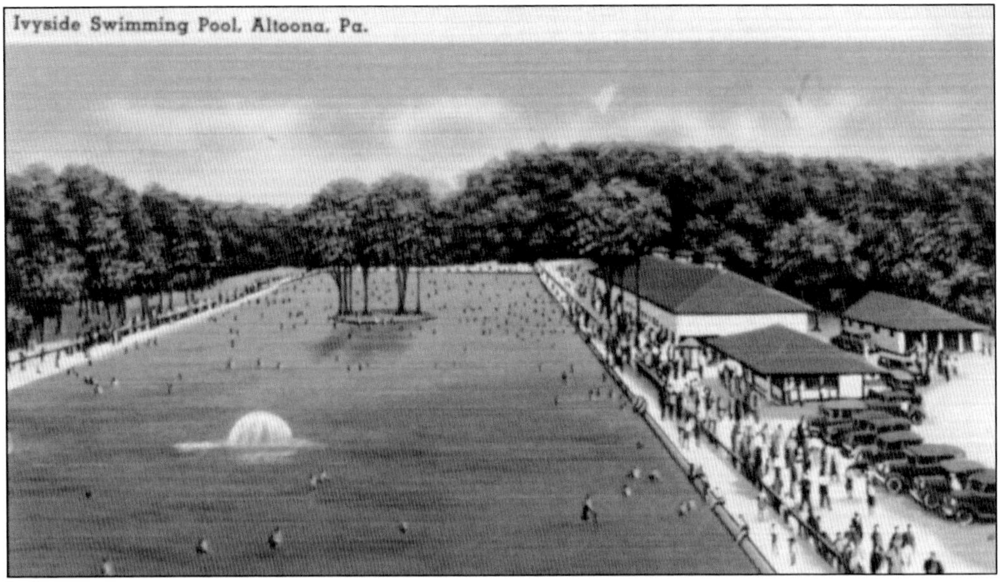

The Ivyside swimming pool is seen in this view. The vintage automobiles appear to date this to the 1920s or the 1930s in the Depression years. The island was popular with swimmers. The large bath house on the right became the first classroom space when Pennsylvania State University moved its Altoona branch campus here in 1947 when the school needed to expand to welcome returning veterans of World War II

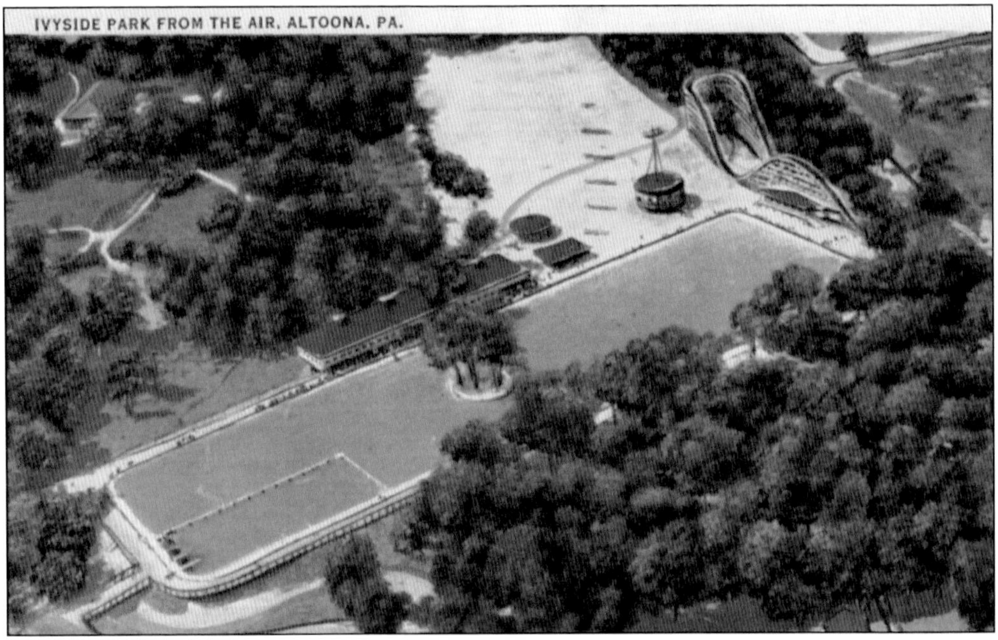

This is an aerial view of Ivyside Amusement Park and Pool. As the viewer can tell, the swimming pool was the dominant feature of the park's layout. The rollercoaster at right extends toward the trees toward the adjoining residential area. The park has been home to Penn State Altoona since 1947, which has continually grown through the acquisition of additional acreage and expansion of curriculum, which now includes four-year baccalaureate degree programs. This card is postmarked July 21, 1937.

Bibliography

Altoona Centennial Committee. *Altoona Centennial Booklet.* 1949.
Alwine, Leonard E. 90th Year Central Pennsylvania Bible Conference. July 2009.
Alwine, Leonard E. and David W. Seidel. *Altoona and Logan Valley Electric Railway.* Charleston, SC: Arcadia Publishing, 2005.
Bell Telephone Directory. Altoona, 1948.
Bulwark of Loyalty: A Retrospective of the 110th Anniversary of the Loyal War Governor's Conference of 1862 in Altoona, Pennsylvania.
Cathedral of the Blessed Sacrament (visitors guide). Undated.
Centenary Committee. *Our Lady of Mount Carmel: 100 Years a Parish.*
Gable, William F. *Gable's 30th Anniversary Booklet: A Brief History of Altoona and The People's Store.* 1914.
Juniata Centennial Committee. *Juniata Centennial Booklet (1893–1993).*
Lakemont Park Historical Museum Committee. *A History of Lakemont Park 1894–1989.* 1990.
Lamborn, Debbie and Patrick Baechle for the Altoona Renaissance Coalition for Historical Integrity in Time-Honored Urban Renewal, Inc. *Places of Distinction–An Illustrated Historic Tour of Altoona's Finest Architecture.* 1991.
Memorial Volume of the Dedication of the Cathedral of the Blessed Sacrament. Altoona, 1930.
Seidel, David W. *Horseshoe Curve.* Charleston, SC: Arcadia Publishing, 2008.
Staufer, Alvin F. *Pennsy Power.* 1962.
Wagner Loeb, Betty and the PRR Technical and Historical Society. *Altoona and the PRR–Between a Roar and a Whimper.* 1999.